Theology of Participation

A Conversation of Traditions

Daniel G. Oprean

Langham

MONOGRAPHS

© 2019 Daniel G. Oprean

Published 2019 by Langham Monographs
An imprint of Langham Publishing
www.langhampublishing.org

Langham Publishing and its imprints are a ministry of Langham Partnership

Langham Partnership
PO Box 296, Carlisle, Cumbria, CA3 9WZ, UK
www.langham.org

ISBNs:
978-1-78368-638-4 Print
978-1-78368-639-1 ePub
978-1-78368-640-7 Mobi
978-1-78368-641-4 PDF

Daniel G. Oprean has asserted his right under the Copyright, Designs and Patents Act, 1988 to be identified as the Author of this work.

All rights reserved. No part of this publication may be reproduced, stored in a retrieval system or transmitted, in any form or by any means, electronic, mechanical, photocopying, recording or otherwise, without the prior written permission of the publisher or the Copyright Licensing Agency.

Requests to reuse content from Langham Publishing are processed through PLSclear. Please visit www.plsclear.com to complete your request.

Scriptures taken from the Holy Bible, New International Version®, NIV®. Copyright © 1973, 1978, 1984, 2011 by Biblica, Inc.™ Used by permission of Zondervan.

British Library Cataloguing-in-Publication Data
A catalogue record for this book is available from the British Library

ISBN: 978-1-78368-638-4

Cover & Book Design: projectluz.com

Langham Partnership actively supports theological dialogue and an author's right to publish but does not necessarily endorse the views and opinions set forth here or in works referenced within this publication, nor can we guarantee technical and grammatical correctness. Langham Partnership does not accept any responsibility or liability to persons or property as a consequence of the reading, use or interpretation of its published content.

I dedicate this work first, to my beloved wife, Ana, and my two boys, Cristi and David. Second, to the Romanian Christian family that I have the honour to serve, to all my friends who never ceased to believe in me.

Contents

Preface xi

Chapter 1 1
Introduction

Part 1: The Dynamic of Spiritual Journey in Stăniloae's Theology 7

Chapter 2 9
Stăniloae's Spiritual Journey
    2.1. Spiritual and Intellectual Climate in Romanian Orthodoxy
    at the Beginning of the Twentieth Century 9
    2.2. Stăniloae's Biography and Spiritual Legacy 15
    2.3. Stăniloae's Way of Doing Theology 18
    2.4. Summary of Chapter 2 33

Chapter 3 35
Trinitarian Theology of Participation in Stăniloae's Thought about Baptism
    3.1. The Frame of Stăniloae's Theology of Participation 35
    3.2. The Heart of Stăniloae's Theology of Participation 45
    3.3. Baptism in the Context of the Theology of Participation
    in the Thought of Stăniloae 49
    3.4. Summary of Chapter 3 57

Chapter 4 59
Stăniloae's Theology of the Eucharist as a Reflection of Perichoresis
    4.1. The Triad of Baptism, Chrismation and the Eucharist 61
    4.2. Real Presence and Human Sacrifice of Submission 63
    4.3. Christ, the Priest and the Church 67
    4.4. Summary of Chapter 4 69

Chapter 5 73
Stăniloae's Theology of Spirituality as Actualization of the Trinitarian Christological-Pneumatological Convergence
    5.1. The Cruciformity of Christian Spirituality 73
    5.2. The *Telos*, the Foundation and the Way of
    Christian Spirituality 78
    5.3. The Stages of Christian Spirituality 81
    5.4. Summary of Chapter 5 96

**Part 2: The Dynamic of Spiritual Journey in
Paul Fiddes's Theology** **99**

Chapter 6 101
   Paul Fiddes's Spiritual Journey
      6.1. Place of Paul Fiddes within the Baptist World 101
      6.2. Fiddes's Spiritual and Intellectual Journey 102
      6.3. Paul Fiddes's Theology 108
      6.4. Summary of Chapter 6 126

Chapter 7 131
   Fiddes's Theology of Participation in His Thought about Baptism
      7.1. Trinitarian Participation as the Atmosphere for
          Human Participation 131
      7.2. Baptism and the Process of Christian Initiation 135
      7.3. Baptism in the Context of the Theology of Participation 138
      7.4. Summary of Chapter 7 142

Chapter 8 143
   Fiddes's Perichoretical Theology in His Thought about the Eucharist
      8.1. The Framework of Fiddes's Theology of the Eucharist
          in a Perichoretical Key 143
      8.2. The Heart and Dimensions of Fiddes's Theology
          of the Eucharist 145
      8.3. Fiddes's Eucharistic Theology in an Ecumenical Perspective 155
      8.4. Summary of Chapter 8 158

Chapter 9 159
   Fiddes's Covenantal Theology in His Thought about Spirituality
      9.1. The Concept of Covenant as a Framework for Fiddes's
          Theology of Spirituality 159
      9.2. The Story of Christ as the Centre for Fiddes's Theology of
          Spirituality 162
      9.3. The Poles and the Coordinates of the Embodiment of
          Christian Spirituality 165
      9.4. Summary of Chapter 9 169

Part 3: Conclusions **171**

Chapter 10 173
   The Dialogical Dimension of the Spiritual Journey:
   Results of the Conversation
      10.1. Theology of Participation and the Spiritual Journey 173

  10.2. Perichoretical Theology and Spiritual Journey 179
  10.3. Trinitarian Theology and the Spiritual Journey 187

Chapter 11 195
 The Transformative Dimension of the Spiritual Journey:
 Lessons from the Conversation
  11.1. Baptism as a Way of Living 195
  11.2. The Eucharist as a Perichoretical Reflection 212
  11.3. Spirituality as a Shared Pilgrimage 222

Chapter 12 237
 General Conclusion
  12.1. Summary of the Study 237
  12.2. Conclusions 238

Appendix A 241
 Bibliography of Paul S. Fiddes

Appendix B 245
 Select Works of Dumitru Stăniloae

Bibliography 247

Preface

This book is a revised version of my doctoral thesis submitted to Wales University, UK, in 2013. This work explores the way in which the existent theological resources could be used for enhancement of the theological conversation between Baptists and Orthodox in Romania. As such it aims to contribute to the mutual understanding of the two, Orthodox and Baptist, and towards a proper understanding of how many things they have in common, as well as how important acknowledgment of the differences could be in order to understand the limits of what could be translated from one to the other. The research starts with an introduction that states first, the context of Romanian Baptists. Second, it states the need of Romanian Baptists for a non-reductionist understanding of baptism, the Eucharist and spirituality as important elements for a holistically understood process of the spiritual journey. Third, the introduction states the way that this holistical understanding could be fostered by ecclesiology, via a conversation between an Orthodox theologian, Dumitru Stăniloae and a Baptist theologian, Paul Fiddes. After the introduction in part one the research aims to explore the context of Dumitru Stăniloae and the development of his theology and spiritual practices. In part two the research aims to explore Paul Fiddes's context and the development of his theology. In part three, the conclusion, the research aims to underline the dialogical and transformative dimensions of the spiritual journey.

CHAPTER 1

Introduction

I grew up in a Baptist family and have always been a member of a Baptist church in Romania. I was baptized when I was eighteen years old in the church where I grew up. I soon became one of the preachers in that community and later a Bible study teacher. I did this for thirteen years. During that time I was studying in my first university and was involved in the underground student ministry movement, which was focused on evangelism and discipleship. So, from the beginning of my Christian life I thought and believed, as many Baptists in Romania, that baptism was an external expression of a previous inward conversion experience. I believed that evangelism was the way to convert unbelievers to Christ and that discipleship was a way to follow Christ in spiritual growth.

Yet very soon I realized that the reality in many Baptist churches was that, for many people baptism is an end in itself, and the conversion experience replaces discipleship with the end result of a perpetual immaturity coming from a lack of interest in spiritual development. Arguably, this has led in the last few decades to a more and more present phenomenon of nominalism among such members of Baptist churches. The lack of interest in spiritual development and growth in knowledge is many times covered over cosmetically in legalistic attitudes inside the same community and by an aversion towards members of the Orthodox Church. Without any differentiation between sincere believers of the Orthodox Church and merely nominal members of Orthodox churches, a general consideration of all Orthodox as unbelievers leads to a declared necessity for Orthodox believers to be converted under the slogan that "if religion will not change you, then you have to change your religion." Such a slogan betrays a lack of understanding that when we speak of Orthodox and Baptist churches we speak of different expressions of manifestation in the same Christian family and the same Christian religion. As I have served in many Baptist churches in Romania, I have been able to observe that this is a widespread mentality in regard to the members of the Orthodox tradition. That mindset needs to be corrected.

One of the possible explanations for such an attitude of Baptists against the Orthodox could be the fact that from the beginning of their existence in Romania, Baptist communities have faced the denial of their identity as Christian communities. They have faced hard times of persecution that contributed equally to the reaction of encapsulation and to a hermeneutic of suspicion towards the other traditions that were many times contributors to the persecution being it from the political regimes before communism[1] or the communist regime.

Yet, even though the extreme attitudes against each other are more or less absent today, the Baptist communities still have the scars of the hard times of their recent history that make them remain in isolationism and suspicion. Moreover, with all the salutary exceptions of some ministers and churches, a really formal dialogue between Baptists and Orthodox has still been an unfulfilled reality, at least for the first fifteen years after 1989. Now, even if a really formal theological dialogue between these two different groups was almost impossible during the Communist regime, there was still an ongoing bilateral underground theological exchange that was at most times unacknowledged. That is seen in the streams and influences from the hierarchical view of the church in the Orthodox tradition via the Reformed (Calvinistic) tradition, which became part of the baptistic[2] practices, even though not

---

1. Alexa Popovici, *Istoria Baptiștilor din Romania, 1856-1989* (Oradea: Faclia, 2006), 632. Popovici speaks of eight waves of persecution between 1920 and 1944, one of the eight was between 1941 and 1944, consisting in the eradication of the Baptist denomination, many Baptists being deported and all continuing to function illegally, 636–644.

2. In using the term "baptistic" we are following Parushev's explanation of the term: By "baptistic" [it] is meant those of the Free Church and believers' baptism tradition. This term is used as an umbrella term for a variety of believing communities ("gathering" churches) practicing believers' baptism, and demanding radical moral living, such as [Anabaptists,] Baptists or Pentecostals. It can also include a number of other groups in the regions, such as Adventists and [Mennonite] Brethren. (There is an overlap with the use of the term "Evangelical" in the Central and Eastern contexts—sometimes in denominational names). It excludes churches in which members think in terms of ethnicity or geographical

always based on a meaningful theological reflection. I realized in time that there was something wrong with limiting your vision for ministry on ideas or ideologies that are foreign to your own context.

When the Revolution of 1989 came as gift from God, we soon entered a time as a country in the process of change and transition from oppression to democracy, and Romanian society found itself in reconstruction. That process still continues. In the new Romanian society in transition, Baptist communities soon faced an identity crisis, even though it was dissimulated by big evangelistic strategies coming mainly from fundamentalist Baptists from the United States, and we were in the position to experience a significant infusion of new members in our churches.[3]

Big church buildings started to replace the smaller ones and big hopes were connected with that change. But the identity crisis continued and its signs were visible in the way theological education continued to be done,

---

and political boundaries and in which people typically baptise their children into these ethno-geo-religio-identities. That is, "baptistic" excludes traditionally state sponsored ecclesial bodies.

See, Parush V. Parushev, "Doing Theology in a Baptist Way," in *Doing Theology in a Baptist Way: The Plenary Papers Collection of the Symposium*, ed. Teun van der Leer, (Amsterdam: Vrije Universiteit, 2009), 3. Parushev also offers a bibliography for the origination of the terms "baptist," "baptistic," James W. McClendon, Jr, "*The Believers Church in Theological Perspective*," in *The Wisdom of the Cross: Essays in Honor of John Howard Yoder*, eds. Stanley Hauerwas, Chris K. Huebner, Harry J. Heubner, and Mark Thiessen Nation (Grand Rapids, MI: Eerdmans, 1999), 309–326, and Lina Andronovienė and Parush Parushev, "Church, State, and Culture: On the Complexities of Post-soviet Evangelical Social Involvement," *Theological Reflections: Euro-Asian Journal of Theology* 3 (2004): 194–212. Cf. McClendon's earlier account of the theological heritage of baptistic (or "baptist") communities in *Systematic Theology*, vol. 1, *Ethics*, revised edition published posthumously (Nashville, TN: Abingdon, 2002), 17–34. For a collection of writings produced from a baptistic perspective since the beginning of the fifteen century, see Curtis W. Freeman, James William McClendon, Jr, and Rosalee Velloso de Silva, eds., *Baptist Roots: A Reader in the Theology of a Christian People* (Valley Forge, PA: Judson Press, 1999).

3. Ivana Noble signals what seems to have been an invasion of foreign missionaries in former communist countries, with evangelistic strategies that mediated simplistic forms of conversion, instead of "conversion as transformation and sojourn from inauthenticity towards authenticity." See Ivana Noble, "Memory and Remembering in the Post-Communist Context," *Political Theology* 9, no. 4 (2008): 467. She also argues against any "proper meaning of conversion" that will transform it in conformation to a set of rules rather than transformation to live a new life, a transformation that will enable a meaningful journey from unauthenticity towards authenticity, in the inter-relatedness of all aspects of conversion, Ivana Noble, "Conversion and Postmodernism," in *Bekehrung und Identität: Ökumene als Spannung zwischen Fremdem und Vertrautem*, ed. Dagmar Heller (Frankfurt am Main: Lembeck, 2003), 45–68.

being mainly focused on the preservation of "what we have received" from our Baptist antecessors. Yet, over the years it became clear that if we are to think seriously about the Christian mission in Romania in contemporary times, our thoughts need to include the sincere sojourners from the Orthodox churches.

It is also imperative that instead of continuing to be isolated and encapsulated, Baptist communities should be in the process of reconstructing the ways in which they relate to the other churches from the Christian family, and to the society around them, through meaningful and constructive conversation.[4] It is equally true that during the times of persecution extensive theological formation within the Baptist communities was impossible, yet things have changed in the last twenty years.

A new generation of ministers, much better educated and with access to more theological resources than ever in the history of Baptists in Romania, has flourished. From among them, some have become in recent years the theologians who are respected for their capacity to converse with Orthodox theologians. Nowadays it is no longer a surprise that in the Baptist Union in Romania we have theologians able not only to understand the Orthodox tradition but also able to contribute at the academic level in many common projects with Orthodox theologians.[5]

We should add to the three examples given above, the appearance in the last period in the theological arena of the Romanian academy, a series of

---

4. In this context Ivana Noble is right when describing the situation after the fall of communism, she says that "In tandem with the democratic changes in the society, the churches had to develop a different mode of presenting their life as free and equal participants in society." Nobel "Memory and Remembering, " 465.

5. I want to give three examples that reflect this reality. First, see Danut Mănăstireanu, *Locul Scripturii in tradiția ortodoxă* (Cluj-Napoca: Alma Mater, 2006). It is a notable fact that the preface of this book, was written by a leading contemporary New Testament scholar of the Orthodox Church, who after reading the book affirms, about the author, that "it is a refined knower of the spirituality and tradition of the Orthodox Church," 14. The second example is that of Emil Bartoș, *Deification in Eastern Orthodox Theology: An Evaluation and Critique of the Theology of Dumitru Stăniloae* (Carlisle, Cumbria: Paternoster, 1999). In the preface of this book the Bishop of Diokleia, Kallistos Ware says about the author "it is a worthy monument to a great Christian thinker," (Bartoș, *Deification*, x). The final example is Silviu Eugen Rogobete, *O ontologie a iubirii: Subiect și Realitate Personală în gândirea părintelui Dumitru Stăniloae* (Iasi: Polirom, 2001). In the preface of this book the Metropolitan of Banat, Nicolae Corneanu says about the author that "is one of our valuable youngsters . . . who became a theologian . . . an intellectual extremely profound," 5.

doctoral research on the theology of Stăniloae.⁶ From many such meaningful initiatives has started to come the understanding not only for the need of interdisciplinary dialogue of theology, but also for an enhanced conversation between Orthodox and Baptist traditions. If we want to be of help for the spiritual change of Romania, providing theological reflection that will be ecumenical not exclusivistic is essential.

In the actual project we acknowledge the fact that the previous studies done on Stăniloae by Baptists show that Stăniloae was a theologian of his time, who meaningfully addressed contemporary theological issues, and looked for the revitalization of the spiritual life of the Romanian Orthodox Church, a model that could be important for Baptist theologians of contemporary Romanian society. Yet, we also acknowledge that these studies neither show the way in which Stăniloae's theological work could or should be relevant for Baptist communities in Romania, nor the way of exploring different avenues of the necessary ongoing conversation. This is the way in which this research could be a platform to help the Baptist communities to enable authentic Christian witness and mission in Romania. In this context the research aims to contribute to the reflection of the riches that could be discovered in a meaningful conversation between Baptists and Orthodox in Romania.

It is our firm conviction that as communities living in a country in which the majority of the population is Orthodox, baptistic theology should reflect an engagement with the theology of the Orthodox Church, rather than only be an echo of the imported theologies of foreign missionaries that are soon transformed in ideology. Therefore, it is the hypothesis of this research that there is a need for theological formulations that will help these communities to overcome their extreme isolation and encapsulation, and

---

6. Paul Negruț, "The Development of the Concept of Authority within the Romanian Orthodox Church during the twentieth Century," (unpublished PhD diss., London, Brunel University, 1995); Silviu Rogobete, "Subject and Supreme Personal Reality in the Theological Thought of Fr. Dumitru Stăniloae. An Ontology of Love," (unpublished PhD diss., London, Brunel University, 1997); Bartoș, *Deification*; Eugen Matei, "The Practice of Community in Social Trinitarianism: A theological evaluation with reference to Dumitru Stăniloae and Jürgen Moltmann," (unpublished PhD diss., Fuller Theological Seminary, Pasadena, CA, 2004); Dănuț Mănăstireanu, "A Perichoretical Model of the Church: Trinitarian Ecclesiology of Dumitru Stăniloae," (unpublished PhD diss., Brunel University, 2005); Marius Daniel Mariș, "Biblical Theology of Creation as Basis for the Christian Dialogue between Evangelicals and the Orthodox Church in Post-Communist Romania," (unpublished PhD diss., Bucharest University, 2006).

that there are theological and ecclesial resources for this process, both in the Orthodox Church as well as in the contemporary European evangelical arena. Moreover, the actual research aims to contribute to the mutual understanding of the two, Orthodox and Baptist, and towards a proper understanding of how many things the two have in common, as well as how important the acknowledgment of the differences could be in order to understand the limits of what could be translated from one to the other.

Methodologically, the research will start with part 1 in which I aim to explore the dynamic of spiritual journey in Stăniloae's theology. Accordingly, chapter 2 will aim to explore Stăniloae's spiritual journey. As such the chapter will start with a description of the spiritual and intellectual climate in Romanian Orthodoxy at the beginning of the twentieth century. Chapter 2 will continue with an exploration of Stăniloae's biography, spiritual legacy and theology. In chapter 3 the research will focus on the way Stăniloae's theology of participation informs and roots his view of baptism as the first step in the spiritual journey of a Christian. In chapter 4, the research will focus on the way Stăniloae's theology of the Eucharist reflects the concept of *perichoresis* and chapter 5 will focus on the way in Stăniloae's theology of spirituality, the christological-pneumatological convergence is actualized.

In part 2 I aim to explore the dynamic of spiritual journey in Paul Fiddes's theology. Accordingly, in chapter 6, I will start with Fiddes's spiritual journey, aiming to understand his place in the contemporary Baptist world as well as to understand some dominant influences for his spiritual and intellectual journey. In this context I will then try to explore the way his theology developed. In chapter 7, I will then explore the way Fiddes's theology of participation informs his thought about baptism. In chapter 8, I will explore the way Fiddes's perichoretical theology informs his thought about the Eucharist and in chapter 9 the way his covenantal theology informs his thought about spirituality

In part 3, the conclusions, I aim to underline, based on the conversation between Stăniloae and Fiddes, the dialogical and the transformative dimensions of the spiritual journey. Therefore, in chapter 10 I will focus on the way the theology of participation, the perichoretical and Trinitarian theology are connected with the spiritual journey. In chapter 11, I will focus on the subjects of baptism as a way of living, the Eucharist as a perichoretical reflection, and spirituality as a shared pilgrimage.

Part 1

The Dynamic of Spiritual Journey in Stăniloae's Theology

The aim of part 1 of the book, is to explore the dynamics of spiritual journey in Stăniloae's theology. In order to show the importance of Stăniloae as a theologian for the conversation between Baptists and Orthodox in contemporary Romania, and in order to understand Stăniloae's uniqueness for Romanian Christianity we will explore first the spiritual and intellectual climate in Romanian Orthodoxy at the beginning of the twentieth century. Second, in order to understand why Stăniloae is a possible entrance door for the enhancement of the conversation between Baptists and Orthodox in Romania we will explore his life through three lenses, his biography, spiritual legacy, and theology. As such we will focus on the person of Stăniloae as a theologian and we will provide at this point a general scan of his theology. In the subsequent chapters 3, 4 and 5 we will focus on the way his theology of participation frames his view of baptism, how his Trinitarian *perichoresis* is mirrored both in his theology of the Eucharist and how christological-pneumatology roots his view of spirituality, all of which are part of Stăniloae's holistic understanding of the Christian spiritual journey.

CHAPTER 2

Stăniloae's Spiritual Journey

2.1. Spiritual and Intellectual Climate in Romanian Orthodoxy at the Beginning of the Twentieth Century

For centuries, the population of the Romanian territories was under foreign domination. While the Transylvanian population and territory were under the domination of the Habsburg Empire since the eleventh century, the Walachian and Moldavian populations and territories were under the domination of the Byzantine Empire until 1417 and for the next three centuries under Turkish domination.[1] Yet in spite of these dominations that were political, administrative, and ideological, the majority of the population in the territories remains predominantly Orthodox, even with some positive influences from East and West.[2] Explaining the uniqueness of the Romanian ethos that developed under these influences Dumitru Stăniloae says about the being of the Romanian people:

> ... his being structured as a border being between East and West. He cannot become unilaterally Western or multilaterally Eastern ... Yet the spirit of synthesis of our people is not explained through his persistence from immemorial times in the middle space between East and West, but also through

---

1. Alexandru Popescu, *Petre Țuțea: Between Sacrifice and Suicide* (Aldershot: Ashgate, 2004), 271.
2. Charles Miller, *The Gift of the World: An Introduction to the Theology of Dumitru Stăniloae* (Edinburgh: T & T Clark, 2000), 8.

the penetration of the Latin character and of Orthodox Christianity.[3]

The development of Romanian nationalism, expressed in the "cultural regeneration" of the eighteenth century, and the establishment of the United Principalities of Moldavia and Walachia in 1859,[4] culminated with the formation of the Romanian unitary State in 1918, which included Moldavia, Walachia and Transylvania.[5] Yet, even as a new state, Romania experienced a short period of political stability until 1920,[6] it entered soon a period of twenty years of turmoil before the Second World War, characterized by "a passionate and profound confrontation of ideas,"[7] a confrontation that involved political as well as religious thinkers. Miller says in regard to Stăniloae in that period:

> Amid the polarities of traditionalism and modernism, nationalism and internationalism, orthodoxy and "western materialism," we find Stăniloae deepening his appreciation for the Romanian Orthodox cultural and theological tradition. A lasting influence was exercised upon Stăniloae by the militantly Orthodox journalist and poet Nichifor Crainic (1898-1972) who championed attempts to define a specifically Romanian mentality and return natural culture to traditional Christian roots.[8]

In fact the tradition of Romanian nationalism started with the greatest poet of Romanian history Mihai Eminescu (1850–1889), he was named by Alexandru Popescu, "the leading political theorist of the nation-State,"[9] having as followers the philosopher Petre Țuțea (1902–1991) and the theologian Dumitru Stăniloae (1903–1993).[10]

---

3. Dumitru Stăniloae, *Reflexii despre spiritualitatea poporului român* (Craiova: Scrisul Românesc, 1992), 8, 14.
4. Popescu, *Petre Țuțea*, 271.
5. Popescu, 272.
6. Popescu, 273.
7. Miller, *Gift of the World*, 15.
8. Miller, 15.
9. Popescu, *Petre Țuțea*, 30
10. Popescu, 31

The period between the two world wars, was also a period of spiritual struggle. For some important Romanian philosophers of those times, the spiritual struggle took the form of a critique of "the political theory divorced from God" that "would lead to the exaltation of power as the only truth."[11] Petre Țuțea, together with "two distinguished Romanian philosophers, Sorin Pavel (1903—1957) and Nicolae Tatu (1910—2000), produced The National Revolution Manifesto."[12] According to Alexandru Popescu in the Manifesto, "the Orthodox identity of the Romanian people was proposed as the basis for a national policy."[13] It also "presents the country as being in a sorry spiritual state," and "identifies the real 'enemy' as those who undermine the Church."[14]

However, the nationalism of this period also took secular forms that tried to promote a secular Romanian ethos, having as one of its representatives "the philosopher-poet Lucian Blaga (1895–1961)."[15] Also, there was an attractive nationalistic Christian ideology, attractive for many intellectuals of the period who were embodied in the extreme nationalistic organization called the Legionary Movement, whose ideologue was one of the famous philosophers of those times, Nae Ionesco.[16]

For Dumitru Stăniloae, this spiritual struggle took the road of what Charles Miller named as "Orthodox Via Media."[17] Miller is right when affirming that Stăniloae's balanced character was formed in the religious ethos of Romanian Orthodoxy of his native Vlădeni in Transylvania. Miller describes it as, "In its restraint, the discomfort with extremes, in its modest expressiveness; in its light-heartedness as well as its reasoned sensitivity to the mystery of God, the religious ethos of Romanian Orthodoxy is preeminently one of spiritual balance."[18] In his search for balance, we find in Stăniloae, says Miller, "a religious sensibility in tune with the notion of via media . . . understood as a fundamental spiritual disposition whose

---

11. Popescu, 16
12. Popescu, 16.
13. Popescu, 16.
14. Popescu, 17.
15. Miller, *Gift of the World*, 16.
16. Popescu, *Petre Țuțea*, 20.
17. Miller, *Gift of the World*, 10.
18. Miller, 12.

instinctive preference is for the observances of balance and due proportions," a disposition that embarked Stăniloae on "a long, at times painful, theological journey."[19]

Due to his spiritual sensibility, Stăniloae found himself from the beginning of his theological studies in Cernăuți, in 1922, dissatisfied with the way Orthodox theology was being taught.[20] Radu Bordeianu describes accurately the status of Orthodox theology in those times, "Orthodox theology suffered an unhealthy influence during its 'Western captivity:' Its neoscholastic theology was overly intellectualistic, an academic exercise divorced from spirituality."[21]

This state of affairs had a long history with a decline that could be detected in Orthodox theology after the patristic period, culminating during the time of the Ottoman Empire, with the East turning "rather uncritically to the West," and adopting Western neo-scholasticism.[22] Bordeianu speaks of several reactions to this situation over the centuries. He starts with the philokalic movement of the eighteenth century, with the promotion of the Hesychast literature that represented "a spiritual approach to theology in contrast with the rationalism of neoscholasticism."[23] Then there was the Slavophile movement of the nineteenth century, with the departure from the Catholic and Protestant West, and the movement in the twentieth century to depart from neo-scholastic theology, represented by, Nicholas Afanassief, Alexander Schmemann, John Meyendorff, Vladimir Lossky, and Georges Florovsky.[24] However, Bordeianu considers that "Stăniloae was the first Orthodox theologian to successfully break away from manual theology."[25]

For Stăniloae, this break consists not in its rejection per se, rather he was looking to replace it with a theology that would be a profound actualization

---

19. Miller, 12.

20. Mircea Păcurariu, "Pr. Prof. Acad. Dumitru Stăniloae. Câteva coordonate biografice," in *Persoană și Comuniune: Prinos de cinstire Părintelui Profesor Academician Dumitru Stăniloae la înplinirea vârstei de 90 de ani*, ed. Antonie Plămădeală (Sibiu: Editura Arhiepiscopiei ortodoxe, 1993), 3.

21. Radu Bordeianu, *Dumitru Stăniloae: An Ecumenical Ecclesiology* (London: T & T Clark, 2011), 13.

22. Bordeianu, *Dumitru Stăniloae*, 14.

23. Bordeianu, 18.

24. Bordeianu, 19.

25. Bordeianu, 27.

of the patristic heritage. This started earlier in his theological activity with the discovery of St Gregory Palamas (1296–1359). Palamas's thought helped Stăniloae to find balance for the concepts that he learned from theologians of other traditions. For example, Bordeianu signals the fact that after discovering in Karl Barth's theology "the transcendence of God before man,"[26] he balanced that view with the Palamite view of uncreated energies, a theology that facilitates an understanding of "God's real involvement with humankind and the world without compromising his essential unknowability and transcendence."[27]

Also, through Palamas's thought, Stăniloae found a starting point for what he aimed for, a spiritual theology. Palamas is considered one of the theologians instrumental for the full development of Hesychasm,[28] and considered "the theologian of Hesychasm."[29]

> The synthesis of hesychast mystics owed to St Gregory Palamas closes theologically all the efforts, starting with the Alexandrian theologians to Simeon the New Theologian to express in a framework of a biblical and patristic theology, the most authentic Christian experience, proper to the Apostles on the Tabor, to the first martyr, Stephen, to Ap. Paul on the Damascus Road and to all monk – saints or to simple believers along the entire Christian history.[30]

In Romania, the Hesychast tradition was present even from the time when the Romanian Principalities were not united. The presence of "a very ancient monastic tradition of prayer" was in existence in Walachia by the time St Nikodimos of Tismana (1320–1406) came in these territories.[31] Nikodimos was instrumental for the revitalization of this Hesychast

---

26. Bordeianu, 23.
27. Bordeianu, 23.
28. Popescu, *Petre Țuțea*, 279.
29. Serafim Joantă, "Din istoria isihasmului până în secolul al XV-lea," in *Persoană și Comuniune: Prinos de cinstire Părintelui Profesor Academician Dumitru Stăniloae la inplinirea vârstei de 90 de ani*, ed. Antonie Plămădeală (Sibiu: Editura Arhiepiscopiei ortodoxe, 1993), 559.
30. Joantă, "Din istoria," 561.
31. Popescu, *Petre Țuțea*, 280.

spirituality, which continued and spread in monasteries and caves, from Walachia, to Transylvania, and in Moldavia.³²

Some of the representatives of Romanian Hesychasm among monks, were Daniel the Hesychast (in the fifteenth century), Elder Basil of Poiana Mărului (in the eighteenth century), Paisy Velichkovsky (1722–1794) – who translated into Slavonic the Hesychast writings from Greek, a collection that was named Philokalia.³³ Considered "the first to achieve that synthesis of Byzantine and Russian spirituality that is so characteristic of Romanian Orthodoxy,"³⁴ Paisy was followed by disciples such as St Calinic of Cernica, and in the twentieth century by Arsenie Boca (1910–1989) in Transylvania and Ilie Cleopa (1912–1998) in Moldavia.³⁵

The novelty introduced by the Paisyan view of Hesychast spirituality, followed by his disciples, was that of opening the practice of Hesychasm outside the monastery to lay believers, something that was a kind of recapture for Nicolas Cabasilas "adapted Hesychast spirituality for laity."³⁶ This Paisyan innovation was embodied and revitalized in the "Burning Bush movement" a movement that reunited monks, intellectuals and scholars of Romania at the end of the Second World War.³⁷ Dumitru Stăniloae, as one who was part of this movement, translated and published the second edition of Philokalia,³⁸ to be available for the larger public. Mircea Păcurariu speaks about the diversity of the Burning Bush group:

> Part of the group were the Archimandrites Benedict Ghiță and Sofian Boghin, the physician Alexandru Mironescu, professor Constantin Joja, the poet Vasile Voiculescu, the poet and journalist Sandu Tudor, the writer and journalist Ion Marin Sadoveanu, the young assistant Andrei Scrima and others. They met periodically at the Antim Monastery or in one of their houses, and they were trying to keep alive the Orthodox and

---

32. Popescu, 281.
33. Popescu, 281.
34. Popescu, 282.
35. Popescu, 282.
36. Joantă, "Din istoria," 561.
37. Popescu, *Petre Țuțea*, 282–283.
38. Popescu, 283.

authentic Romanian conscience in the new condition of the political and social life of our country.³⁹

Also, in one of his last interviews, on 1 April 1992, Dumitru Stăniloae, points out this new way of seeing Hesychasm. He considered that the prayer of the heart is "a gift and a result of a spiritual exercise."⁴⁰ As such it is a gift not to be used only in solitude but it is communitarian.⁴¹ Therefore it is not to be limited as a monastic practice, but also as a day-to-day practice.⁴² During the Antonescian dictatorship and the beginning of the Communist regime, Hesychasm flourished in political prisons.⁴³ Later on under the Communist dictatorship of Gheorghe Gheorghiu-Dej, the members of the Burning Bush movement were arrested in 1958 and imprisoned. For them as for others before them, Hesychast prayer was a means for survival "that sustained them through the Soviet experiment of re-education."⁴⁴

2.2. Stăniloae's Biography and Spiritual Legacy

Regarding Stăniloae's biography (1903–1993), the first notable thing from a theological point of view is that he was a contemporary witness to twentieth-century Romanian history with its greatest events (1918, the Second World War, the Communist regime, the revolution in 1989). As a contemporary of this history the issues concerning the society and the church, are reflected in his theology. So, Stăniloae was a theologian of his time, doing theology in a relevant way. "He is a spiritual father . . . A man of profound modesty and piety . . . A witness of his epoch he passes the history of this century with the trust and serenity of a witness of faith. He is a monument of contemporary experience of Christ."⁴⁵

The second notable thing is that he tried not to be enslaved by previous systems of thought. He was always a theologian pushing the boundaries.

---

39. Păcurariu, "Pr. Prof. Acad. Dumitru Stăniloae," 9.
40. Sorin Dumitrescu, *7 dimineți cu părintele Stăniloae* (București: Anastasia, 1992), 82.
41. Dumitrescu, *7 dimineți cu părintele Stăniloae*, 83.
42. Dumitrescu, 84.
43. Popescu, *Petre Țuțea*, 284.
44. Popescu, 284–285.
45. Ion Bria, *Spațiul nemuririi sau eternizarea umanului în Dumnezeu* [The space of immortality or the eternization of humaness in God] (Iași: Trinitas, 1994), 7.

He had no hesitation to address critically, yet in a constructive way, the philosophy, theology and spirituality of his times.[46]

Third, Stăniloae tried never to evade in an academic tower of thought, or in the academic mediocrity so often practiced by churches (of any denomination) especially in times of crisis. Proud to be Romanian and Orthodox, Stăniloae was in himself and through his theology, representing Romanian Orthodox thought and spiritual ethos at the superlative, in a unique way of seeing the complementarity of different areas of thought such as philosophy, history, science and theology. His interdisciplinary dialogical approach to theology was not only a feature of his theological thought, but also of his character and spirituality. He not only addressed each epoch of the history he participated in afresh and relevant theologically, but he also suffered for his theological convictions and spirituality during the communist regime.[47] The reality described above is the reason one cannot separate Stăniloae's biography from his theology and his theology from his spirituality.[48]

How all these complex dimensions of his life and theology are embodied today can be seen in what could be called Stăniloae's spiritual legacy, the first dimension of which can be seen in the school of thought he represents for his disciples. "There is a 'Stăniloae's generation,' a school, a current, an influence, an attraction. It was his generous presence that gathered around himself with love and true interest and he was considered a master."[49]

Another important feature of Stăniloae's legacy is his life of discipleship. In a time when Romanian Orthodox Christianity was characterized by a

---

46. Bria, *Spațiul nemuririi*, 8.

47. Silviu Eugen Rogobete, *O Ontologie a Iubirii: Subiect și realitate personală în gândirea părintelui Dumitru Stăniloae* (Iași: Polirom, 2001), 26. Rogobete refers to the time spent in prison by Stăniloae during the Communist regime in the period 1958–1963, the time when he practiced the prayer of Jesus. This spiritual experience in difficult times of imprisonment rooted Stăniloae's view of spirituality, that will be analyzed in chapter 6. The truth of the *the practice of hesychasm* is proved by Stăniloae's own confession in a discussion with Olivier Clement, in the preface to Dumitru Stăniloae, *Rugăciunea lui Iisus și experiența Duhului Sfânt* (Sibiu: Deisis, 2003), 18. Also see, Dumitru Stăniloae, *Priere de Jesus et experience du Saint-Esprit* (Paris: Desclee dr Brouwer, 1981).

48. Ivana Noble, "Doctrine of Creation within the Theological Project of Dumitru Stăniloae," *Communio Viatorum* 49, no. 2 (2007): 206. Also, Rogobete, "Subject and Supreme," 28. Also, Rogobete, *O Ontologie a Iubirii*, 27.

49. Fr. Antonie Plămădeală, "Generația Stăniloae" [Stăniloae's Generation], in *Persoană și Comuniune: Prinos de cinstire Părintelui Profesor Academician Dumitru Stăniloae la împlinirea vârstei de 90 de ani*, ed. Antonie Plămădeală (Sibiu: Editura Arhiepiscopiei ortodoxe, 1993), xi.

crisis of models and spiritual direction, he was in himself a way to be followed towards revival. In the words of one of his disciples: "What Council Vatican II realized at the pastoral and structural level for the Roman Catholic Church, the same Father Stăniloae realized for Orthodoxy at the level of theological reflection."[50]

Third, part of Stăniloae's legacy is his enormous volume of work, twenty books; 1,300 articles; thirty translations.[51] Considered an "Eastern Karl Barth,"[52] Stăniloae embodied in his writings the unique experiences of his philosophical and theological encounters.[53] This dialogical formation is expressed in his writings where the dialogue with philosophy and different Christian traditions is a constant feature. Reading the Bible, the fathers and also contemporary Catholic and Protestant theology extensively, as well as Eastern Orthodox theology, Stăniloae had no problems using their arguments and ideas when they were appropriate for his arguments.[54] In this regard Mănăstireanu affirms that "Stăniloae's theology in general . . . was firstly *patristic* . . . thoroughly *Trinitarian* . . . profoundly *Romanian* . . . *dialogical*, characterized by *an ecumenical spirit*."[55] Even though Stăniloae is often critical and polemical he proves, in most cases at least, that he does not suffer from what I call "illiteracy of other traditions." The way the

---

50. Bria, *Spațiul nemuririi*, 43.

51. Emil Constantinescu, "Pr. Prof. Dr. Dumitru Stăniloae: profil de teolog și filosof creștin ortodox," in *Persoană și Comuniune: Prinos de cinstire Părintelui Profesor Academician Dumitru Stăniloae la înplinirea vârstei de 90 de ani*, ed. Antonie Plămădeală (Sibiu: Editura Arhiepiscopiei ortodoxe, 1993), 93.

52. Virgil Ierunca, "Teologia Dogmatică Ortodoxă' a Părintelui Dumitru Stăniloae," in *Persoană și Comuniune: Prinos de cinstire Părintelui Profesor Academician Dumitru Stăniloae la înplinirea vârstei de 90 de ani*, ed. Antonie Plămădeală (Sibiu: Editura Arhiepiscopiei ortodoxe, 1993), 103.

53. Bria, (*Spațiul nemuririi*, 8) says that, "We can distinguish now the three great omnipresent influences in his work: Greek and Byzantine patristic having as model, for the point of view of theological systematisation, Maximus the Confessor and Gregory Palamas, and from the point of view of ethical and spiritual expressions, Simeon the New Theologian; Western philosophy, especially Christian existentialism (Martin Heidegger, Charles Peguy, Karl Jaspers, Gabriel Marcel), and the cultural forms in which Orthodoxy is embodied in Romania."

54. For a list of Staniloae's arguments in this context, see Appendix B.

55. Dănuț Mănăstireanu, *A Perichoretic Model of the Church: The Trinitarian Ecclesiology of Dumitru Stăniloae* (Saarbrucken: Lambert Academic, 2012), 238–239, (henceforth referred to as *PM*).

characteristics of his character and spirituality contributed to the way he was doing theology will be explored in the next section.

2.3. Stăniloae's Way of Doing Theology

To explore deeply into the complex personality and thought of Dumitru Stăniloae, one can observe that he was a theologian of complementarities. First, Stăniloae starts from the revelation of God in history, combining creatively the two forms of God's revelation, namely, natural and supernatural revelation. He states "The Orthodox Church makes no separation between natural and supernatural revelation. Natural revelation is known and understood fully in the light of supernatural revelation, or we might say that natural revelation is given and maintained by God continuously through his own divine act which is above nature."[56] Stăniloae continues to develop the concept of the inseparability of the two forms of revelation by the avenue of combining scriptural arguments with patristic teachings. He appeals to proofs from the biblical texts such as Job, Romans, and Psalms,[57] and from the patristic fathers such as Saint Maximos the Confessor, Saint Athanasios, Saint Simeon the New Theologian and Kabasilas.[58] From this combination Stăniloae develops the concept of the interdependence of the natural and supernatural revelations.

The framework in which Stăniloae considers that this interdependency can be seen best is the history of salvation. In this space of revelation of God in history, Stăniloae asserts, we can see the unity of God's plan for the salvation of humanity. Taking in consideration the message of both the Old Testament and New Testament, and in the unity of their message, Stăniloae sees the harmony of God's way of revelation through both natural and supernatural acts, in the formation and maturation of Israel as the people of God.[59] For Stăniloae this process of revelation is profoundly Trinitarian. It is the Father who reveals himself through the work of the Holy Spirit culminating

---

56. Dumitru Stăniloae, *The Experience of God* (Brookline: MA: Holy Cross Orthodox Press, 1994), (henceforth referred to as *EG*).

57. Dumitru Stăniloae, *Teologie Dogmatică Ortodoxă*, 1 (Bucuresti: EIBMBOR, 1996), 26–27 (henceforth referred to as *TDO*).

58. Stăniloae, *EG*, 20–30. Mănăstireanu, *PM*, 238–239.

59. Stăniloae, *EG*, 24–25.

in the person and work of Christ.[60] The spiritual movement that Stăniloae sees is the dynamic of descent and ascent, which constitutes the whole of the salvation process. The descent dimension is seen in the supernatural acts of God in history, and the ascent dimension is seen in the response of human beings in what Stăniloae calls, "the ascending spiritual progression."[61]

"Clearly, the history of salvation does not consist of supernatural acts alone, because these do not occur continuously; just as God's supernatural revelation is not given continuously. These acts are found, however, within the order of an ascending spiritual progression and, in this sense, they have a history, which is the history of salvation."[62] This is an important insight into the participatory dimension of human salvation. Stăniloae is very clear about this reality of salvation asserting that the entire movement is not one way, from God to humanity, but also that the history of salvation that is "guided, enlightened, and strengthened in good by divine revelation . . . is made up also of our responses."[63]

Moreover, this concept of salvation is in harmony with the constitutive elements of God's revelation in the history of salvation. For Stăniloae, the starting point for this participatory reality of salvation is Christ, being also the culmination or the final stage of supernatural revelation, and consecutively, "the period after Christ . . . is the ultimate stage in the history of salvation . . . Thus, Christ represents the climax of supernatural revelation and the full confirmation and clarification of the meaning of our existence through the fulfillment of this existence within himself, the one in whom our ultimate union with God, and thus our perfection also, is achieved."[64] Stăniloae continues to explain the way this becomes reality in the life of believers. He considers that a believer becomes part of this movement if he accepts being drawn closer to God by the Word, through the Holy Spirit. The Word, Christ, made the first move, namely, to take "our own image into himself in order to restore it . . . exalting that humanity of ours which he assumed." He states this complementary work of the Word and the Holy

---

60. Stăniloae, 25.
61. Stăniloae, 25.
62. Stăniloae, 26.
63. Stăniloae, *TDO*, 1, 27.
64. Stăniloae, *EG*, 28.

Spirit as, "This cooperation of the Word of God and of the Holy Spirit can be observed first of all, in revelation down to the time of its conclusion in Christ, and after that in the Church, in Scripture, and the Tradition."[65]

For Stăniloae the model for this complementary work is the life of the Trinity. As in the revelation of the Father is expressed through the Word in the Holy Spirit, the same happens in the final stage of revelation that is Christ. The Christ event was prepared and revealed by the Spirit, and he himself as the Word incarnate prepared the coming of the Spirit, who will prepare the creation for the second coming of the incarnate Word.[66] This circularity of movements of one divine person towards the other is for Stăniloae a reality that is to be replicated in the believer as part of the church. Stăniloae quotes Evdokimov in order to endorse this reality, "after Pentecost it is the relation to Christ which is brought about through and in the Holy Spirit . . . Pentecost restores to the word the interiorized presence of Christ and reveals him now not before, but within his disciples."[67]

Stăniloae finishes his assertion on the complementary work of the Word and of the Spirit, in a survey of the development of this reality from the Old Testament to the New Testament, by concluding that Christ is the model of the "total return of the Holy Spirit to human nature."[68] This leads to the second theological complementarity in the thought of Dumitru Stăniloae, that of Scripture and tradition in the life of the church. For him, "The Church is the dialogue of God with the faithful through Christ . . . the Church is Christ united in the Holy Spirit with those who believe and over whom has been spread and through whom is spreading Christ's own act of drawing the faithful."[69]

---

65. Stăniloae, 29. Also, John Calvin, *Institutes of the Christian Religion*, ed. John T. McNeill, trans. Ford Lewis Battles (Philadelphia, PA: Westminster, 1960), 95. Stăniloae's argument is very close with that of John Calvin who also argued that the intimate relationship between Word and Spirit is of vital importance. In his view the Word and Spirit not only "belong inseparable together" but also "the Word may abide in our minds when the Spirit, who causes us to contemplate God's face, shines." (Calvin, *Insititues*, 95.)

66. Stăniloae, *TDO*, 1, 33.

67. Paul Evdokimov, *L'Esprit Saint dans le tradition orthodoxe* (Paris: Éditions du Cerf, 1969), 89.

68. Stăniloae, *EG*, 33.

69. Stăniloae, 38.

To the question of how the church is an instrument of such a revelation in Christ and of Christ, Stăniloae answers: through Scripture and tradition. For Stăniloae, the church's capacity to interpret and understand the Scripture is rooted in Christ's presence through the Holy Spirit in the life of the church.[70] Yet this happens not in isolation of individuals but exactly in the *koinonia* of the believers mediated by Christ that mirrors the *koinonia* of the life of the Trinity. The centrality of Christ is vital, for he is the source and the means for the work of the Holy Spirit in the communion of believers.[71] Scripture, for Stăniloae is a space of explanation not only of the way in which God came to us in Christ through the Holy Spirit but also of the way in which through the Holy Spirit we can ascent to God, in Christ. Therefore Scripture is "a book that is always contemporary. . . . Thus, Scripture is one form through which the words of Christ are preserved, not only in the words spoken by him in the past, but also in the words which he is continually addressing to us."[72]

The medium in which the contemporaneity and actuality of Christ, in Scripture, is made reality in the life of the church, is the work of the Holy Spirit. In the Spirit's work the words of Scripture become the entrance door into "relation with the authentic person of Christ," a dynamic encounter with Christ, in and beyond Scripture, through the internal work of the Holy Spirit, an encounter that became possible not through simply meeting the words of the Scripture but through the process of transcending the words towards the meaning they signify.[73] For capturing this meaning, Stăniloae continues, the church needs the other form of preserving the revelation of Christ in Scripture, namely, tradition. The role of tradition is twofold, "Tradition keeps this dynamism of the Scripture contemporary without changing it, for tradition represents an application and a continuous

---

70. Stăniloae, 39.

71. Stăniloae, *TDO*, 1, 43.

72. Stăniloae, *EG*, 41–42. Stăniloae here is in agreement with what Romanian Baptists would affirm about Scripture. See in this regard Octavian Baban, "The Bible in the Life of the Orthodox Church," in *Baptists and the Orthodox Church: On the Way to Understanding*, ed. Ian Randall (Prague: International Baptist Seminary, 2005), 15–29. He says: "The Baptist call for a revitalized reading of the Bible is founded on the conviction that while the Scriptures shape our views of God they also invite us to engage the Word as faithful communities who struggle to live by it," (Baban, "Bible in the Life," 29).

73. Stăniloae, *EG*, 44.

deepening of the content of Scripture. At the same time as it preserves the authentic dynamism of Scripture, tradition, in its quality as true interpreter of Scripture, brings that dynamism to bear upon real life."[74]

In order to show the importance of such a complementarity, between Scripture and tradition, Stăniloae gives the example of the apostle Paul whose oral teachings were the needed hermeneutical key, or the lens, through which the community of the church could interpret the Christ event. Stăniloae considers the "apostolic teachings or explanation of faith" as a necessary "permanent model,"[75] for tradition is the means for interpreting and integrating the content of Scripture's message about Christ.[76] This is so, continues

---

74. Stăniloae, 45. See also Timothy Ware, *The Orthodox Church* (London: Penguin Books, 1993), 196, Ware defines Christian tradition as "the faith and practice which Jesus Christ imparted to the Apostles, and which since the Apostle's time has been handed down from generation to generation in the Church." See also, Jaroslav Pelikan, *Tradiția creștină: O istorie a dezvoltării doctrinei, 1: Nașterea tradiției universale (100-600)* (Iași: Polirom, 2004), 33, he says that "tradition is the living faith of the death; traditionalism is the death faith of the living." See also Mănăstireanu, *Locul Scripturii in tradiția ortodoxă* (Cluj-Napoca: Alma Mater, 2006). Commenting on the concept of tradition as icon in the thought of Jaroslav Pelikan in *The Vindication of Tradition* (New Haven, CT: Yale University Press, 1984), Mănăstireanu considers that "a viable model of the relation between Scripture and Tradition would imply that this inseparable pair be regarded as an icon of revelation," (Mănăstireanu, *Locul Scripturii*, 75). Mănăstireanu also considers that Stăniloae's "perichoretical model" of the relation between Scripture, tradition and the church, "has a value because it avoids the contradiction between its constitutive elements," (Mănăstireanu, *Locul Scripturii*, 91), even though Mănăstireanu sees its weakness in Stăniloae's "insistence on the preeminence of the Church over Scripture and Tradition," an insistence that "breaks the fragile equilibrium of the relation between Scripture and Tradition, in the favour of the latter, that leads on one hand in practice to a neglect of Scripture in the life of the Church, and on the other hand, to a diminishing of Scripture's authority in the validation and invalidation of specific traditions," (Mănăstireanu, *Locul Scripturii*, 92). Relevant in the context of the present project is the opinion expressed by a leading Romanian Baptist theologian, the president of the Baptist Union in Romania: Otniel Ioan Bunaciu, "The Meaning of Tradition," in *Baptists and the Orthodox Church: On the Way to Understanding*, ed. Ian Randall (Prague: International Baptist Seminary, 2005), 30–45. Bunaciu considers that "It is Stăniloae's approach that allows us, nevertheless, to link dynamically and permanently Tradition and revelation. This might be a possible way forward in ecumenical discussions," (Bunaciu, "Menaing of Tradition," 42). However, Bunaciu signals a concern that remains from a baptistic point of view with its emphasis on the fact that "Scripture remains, for the Church, the central witness of the Revelation of God in Christ," (Bunaciu, 44).

75. Stăniloae, *TDO*, 1, 43–44.

76. John Breck, *Scripture in Tradition: The Bible and Its Interpretation in the Orthodox Church* (Crestwood, NY: St. Vladimir's Seminary Press, 2001), 10. Breck affirms what is central for Orthodox biblical theology, to which Stăniloae is faithful, "Tradition provides the hermeneutic perspective by which any biblical writing is to be properly interpreted."

Stăniloae, exactly because the tradition "is both the invocation of the Spirit of Christ (*epiclesis* . . .) and the reception of the Spirit."[77]

In this context, for Stăniloae, the reality of sanctification in the life of the church, through the Spirit, is inseparable from the work of Christ in the church. If the essence of the sacramental life of the church, says Stăniloae, is in the invocation and the descent of the Holy Spirit, in the framework of the life of the believers prepared in the process of discipleship, it is based on "the saving works of Christ" and on his example. This is why for Stăniloae authentic Christian life is:

> [A]n imitation of Christ made possible by his own power, a progress towards his holiness which comes about through their sanctification, and has in view their liberation from the automatism of nature and from the passionate attachment to the pleasures offered by nature – for it is this liberation which is the condition for true communion with the person of Christ whose love is infinite and with all human persons.[78]

Moreover, for Stăniloae tradition cannot be conceived apart from the church and its life. This inseparability is seen in the fact that, if tradition is the invocation and receiving of the Holy Spirit, the church is the recipient of this reality. Of course it is the believer who receives the work of the Holy Spirit but it is not the believer in his individuality but the believer in community. For Stăniloae this is again the mirroring of the life of the Trinity, where the divine persons are persons in communion. Moreover, in Stăniloae's thought "the Church is a subject that bears tradition . . . and tradition is an attribute of the Church."[79] For Stăniloae the unity between Scripture, tradition and church is pneumatological, it is made by the presence and work of the Holy Spirit, in their synthesis. He asserts, "Scripture arose within the bosom of the Church and for her benefit, as a way of fixing one part of the apostolic tradition or of revelation in written form in order to nourish the Church from and maintain her in Christ who is authentically transmitted

---

77. Stăniloae, *TDO*, 1, 44.
78. Stăniloae, *EG*, 48–49.
79. Stăniloae, 53–54.

through the tradition as a whole."[80] The church as the body of Christ is, for Stăniloae, a reality brought into existence by the Holy Spirit in order to be the embodiment of the revelation of Christ. There the church is the reality of the continuation of the working power of revelation in the world. The circularity[81] of this movement between Scripture, tradition and the church is given by the movement of the Holy Spirit in the unity he creates between them: "The Church moves inside the revelation or inside Scripture and tradition; Scripture discloses its content inside the Church and inside tradition; tradition is alive within the Church. Revelation itself is effective within the Church and the Church is alive within revelation."[82]

The third complementarity in Stăniloae's theological thought is that of negative and positive ways of knowing God, namely apophatic and cataphatic. He says, "In our opinion these two kinds of knowledge are neither contradictory nor mutually exclusive, rather they complete each other. Strictly speaking, apophatic knowledge is completed by rational knowledge of two kinds, that which proceeds by way of affirmation and that which proceeds by the way of negation."[83]

There are two things Stăniloae warns against. First is the danger of living only through the rational way of knowing God. Even if, argues Stăniloae, the rational way of knowing God can be the starting point and is necessary at any stage of Christian life, not to complete it with experiential knowledge would be to live an incomplete life. However, in order for this completion to take place there is a necessary connection of the entire life to the content of the revelation of God's character. This is to happen by the way of purification of life, as the apostle Paul says in 1 Corinthians 2, the reality of God's presence is a spiritual one and can be apprehended by spiritual persons. Mirroring the saying of the apostle Paul, Stăniloae asserts:

> The presence of God as person – a presence that presses upon us and from which shines forth his infinity – is not the conclusion

---

80. Stăniloae, 55.

81. Mănăstireanu, *Locul Scripturii*, 90. He considers that Stăniloae "borrows from the doctrine of the Trinity, the concept of perichoresis and is using it to create a dynamic model of the relation between Scripture, Tradition and Church."

82. Stăniloae, *EG*, 58.

83. Stăniloae, 96.

of a rational judgment, as in the case of knowledge that is intellectual, cataphatic, or negative; rather it is perceived by one in a state of revived spiritual sensibility and this cannot come about so long as man is dominated by bodily pleasures or passions of any kind.[84]

Moreover, Stăniloae considers that the deepness of our knowledge of God is influenced and is dependent on our purification in life, showing the fact that it is experiential knowledge.[85] This is consistent with Stăniloae's idea, explored above, of the lifelong process of sanctification in believers' lives, on which an extended analysis will be provided in chapter 6 of the book.

The second thing Stăniloae warns against is the danger of transforming knowledge into an idol. The true knowledge of God is one, Stăniloae seems to say, that keeps the person conscious of how much we do not know from God, recognizing therefore, the limitations of our present ideas about God. This true humbling knowledge is in contrast with the idolater's knowledge that keeps God blocked in a certain, momentous understanding of him thus, placing "limits in God." "Every understanding that touches upon God must have a certain fragility and transparency; it cannot be something fixed once for all, but must itself urge us to call this understanding into question and stimulate us to seek one further along in the same direction."[86] But this dynamic, critical movement from what we know to what we need to discover continuously beyond our present knowledge is possible, Stăniloae seems to be arguing, only if we develop in our life what could be called the habit of going beyond, even going beyond the words of Scripture, as Paul says: "the letter kills, but the Spirit gives life" (2 Cor 3:6).

Stăniloae continues by arguing that the knowledge of God is intrinsic to everyday life. It is knowledge in the experience of life that is the space where the complementarity between the affirmative and negative knowledge of God is encapsulated, and therefore expressed. The knowledge of God in the experience of life is different than that of knowing theoretical concepts about him. It is knowledge of him in "his special care in regard to me,"[87]

---

84. Stăniloae, 100.
85. Stăniloae, *TDO*, 1, 85–86.
86. Stăniloae, *EG*, 105.
87. Stăniloae, 118.

that is framed by a personal relationship with him. This newness of knowing God in an intimate relationship becomes possible in Stăniloae's thought because of his unique way of understanding the triune divine being. For Stăniloae any separation between immanent and economic Trinity is inconceivable.[88] However, to prevent any idea of a possibility for a full knowledge of God in himself, that is an impossibility. Stăniloae distinguishes, following Gregory Palamas, between the being and the operations of God, arguing that "through each of these operations, it is God, who is one in being, who is at work."[89] The power of this refusal, to project any separation in God, is consistently seen first in his refusal to project any separation in knowing God, analyzed above.

Second, the consistency of his concept of the unity of God is seen in his conception of the double constitution of the church, as a christological-pneumatological reality. The model behind this idea is that of the "person in communion," rather than that of the "person is communion." He says "the indissoluble union between Christ and the Holy Spirit who truly constitutes the Church and sustains the life of the Christian within the Church has its profound roots in that indissoluble union which according to Orthodox teaching exists between them within the sphere of their inner Trinitarian relations."[90] The inner Trinitarian relations are for Stăniloae to be found in the manifestation of the economic Trinity. The key terms for Stăniloae are procession and irradiation. The Holy Spirit proceeds from the Father towards the Son and irradiates from the Son and through the Son towards the Father. "The Spirit proceeding from the Father comes to rest in the Son who is begotten of the Father, and like an arch, unites Father and Son in one embrace. Thus a unity among the three Persons is manifested which is distinct from their unity of essence."[91]

---

88. Karl Rahner, *The Trinity* (New York: Crossroad, 1997), 21–22. Stăniloae is in agreement with Karl Rahner who speaks of the axiomatic unity of the "economic" and "immanent Trinity." Rahner says: "The 'economic' Trinity is the 'immanent' Trinity and the 'immanent' Trinity is the 'economic' Trinity."

89. Stăniloae, *EG*, 125.

90. Stăniloae, *Theology and the Church* (Crestwood, NY: St. Vladimir's Seminary Press, 1980), 15.

91. Stăniloae, *Theology and the Church*, 23.

Speaking about the Christ event, Stăniloae considers that the Spirit is "the milieu in which Christ is seen."[92] We can neither know Christ nor experience the Spirit in separation of one from the other. Therefore, Christ is pneumatologically constituted and the manifestation of the Spirit is christologically framed. The believer cannot possess Christ without the Spirit and cannot possess the Spirit without Christ. Moreover, this relational circularity of the three persons of the Trinity is, for Stăniloae, to be seen at any moment of the Christ event. In the incarnation, a fully pneumatological reality, the Son uniting humanity with him is also uniting the ones who are united with him, with the love of the Father, in the response of love, of himself toward the Father in the irradiation of the Spirit towards the Father. For Stăniloae, "This is the climactic moment of the condition of salvation: the union of all with Christ in the Spirit, and through the Spirit, in the consciousness of the Father's love for them and in their own love for the Father."[93]

Stăniloae supports these assertions biblically, grounding them in the Pauline theology of spirituality,[94] and then he shows that the indissoluble relation between the Son and the Spirit is a matter of concern and agreement, in many regards, between Eastern Orthodox theology and Protestant theology.[95] He also extensively quotes the Protestant theologian T. F. Torrance who considers that the Spirit "through the crucified and resurrected Christ and in him, sustain the creative and redemptive work of the Holy Trinity, from beginning to end and brings it to its perfection."[96] Stăniloae understands this integrative view of the work of the Trinity in salvation, as a necessary and vital corrective for what he considers to be, "the permanent errors of Romanism and Protestantism: the former confusing the Spirit of God and the spirit of the Church . . . substituting *ecclesiaque* for the *filioque* . . . the latter confusing the Spirit of God with the human spirit and substituting for the *filioque* a *homineque*."[97]

---

92. Stăniloae, 24–26.
93. Stăniloae, 32.
94. R. P. Meye, "Spirituality," in *Dictionary of Paul and his Letters*, eds. G. F. Hawthorne, R. P. Martin and D. G. Reid (Downers Grove, IL: InterVarsity Press, 1993), 906–916.
95. Stăniloae, *Theology and the Church*, 33.
96. T. F. Torrance, "Spiritus Creator," *Verbum Caro* 23, no. 89 (1969): 82–83.
97. Stăniloae, *Theology and the Church*, 41.

Stăniloae considers the church as the fifth act in the salvation work of God, after the incarnation, crucifixion, resurrection and the ascent of Christ.[98] Also, for him any separation between Christ and the Holy Spirit is inconceivable. He considers that the Holy Spirit does not replace Christ after his ascension; rather the Holy Spirit is the Spirit of Christ.[99] Therefore, for Stăniloae, it is Christ who enters the life of the believer through the Holy Spirit and the model for that is the total pneumatization of Christ's body as seen in the resurrection.[100] The mutuality of the work of Christ and the Holy Spirit as expression of their Trinitarian relationship is expressed as follows, "From His perfect pneumatized body irradiates the fullness of the Spirit . . . He enters through the Spirit in the lives of the ones that believe in Him . . . from this point of view there can be said that through the descent of the Holy Spirit the Church takes concrete existence, for now Christ descends for the first time in the hearts."[101]

Even though he starts with Christ as foundation of the church and the Holy Spirit as the medium in which the church lives,[102] Stăniloae does not show the way in which the christological-pneumatological constitution of the church is to root consistently the way in which the church is structured. However, he reflects his interaction with Protestant theology, namely, John Calvin, when he considers the church's participation in the three offices of Christ, as king, prophet and teacher.

> Through the continuation of His threefold office in the Church, Christ maintains, with the Church and with every member of her, a progressive dialogue in which neither He nor the Church, nor any of her members are in a passive state. This is the meaning of kingly priesthood of the believers called to proclaim

---

98. Stăniloae, *TDO*, 2 (Bucuresti: EIBMBOR, 1997), 129.
99. Stăniloae, *TDO*, 2, 130.
100. Stăniloae, 130–131.
101. Stăniloae, 132, 134.
102. Tim Grass, "Orthodoxy and the Doctrine of the Church," in *Baptists and the Orthodox Church: On the Way to Understanding*, ed. Ian Randall (Prague: International Baptist Seminary, 2005), 5–14. He says: "While Christ founded the Church, it is the Holy Spirit, whose descent at Pentecost gave it life." (Grass, "Orthodoxy," 6).

the goodness of Christ and to avoid the carnal passions (1Pt 1:8-11; 1Jn 2:20).[103]

Stăniloae argues consistently the primacy of Christ's continuous teaching in the church, and the participatory dimension of it, as Christ has the church in the fellowship of this ministry, "encouraging internally her members through the Holy Spirit to teach each other."[104] Yet, even if one would expect that from here Stăniloae would "attribute to believers as a whole" a priestly role,[105] they will be surprised with Mănăstireanu "to observe that Stăniloae devotes only two paragraphs" to the subject of the general priesthood of believers.[106] Instead of seeing the general priesthood of the church as a normal embodiment of the vertical incarnation of Christ as a teacher in the life of the church in harmony with horizontal participation of the members of the church in teaching each other, he considers the representative role of the special priesthood of priests as symbols of Christ the mediator.[107]

We agree with Mănăstireanu, who quotes the orthodox theologian John N. Karmiris,[108] when he explains that one of the reasons for the limited role of the general priesthood and for the vital, representative role of the special priesthood in Stăniloae's view could be rooted in "a conviction that Protestantism has given the laity excessive rights and privileges."[109] We have also to note that, as Mănăstireanu says, Stăniloae's view of the two forms of priesthood, with the pre-eminence of the special priesthood, leads him to consider the limitation of laity to private teaching, the role for public teaching

---

103. Stăniloae, *TDO*, 2, 152. Also, Mănăstireanu, *PM*, 273. He agrees with Louth who says that even if Stăniloae considers the theme of the threefold office of Christ as being patristic, he does not give any reference. See Andrew Louth, "Review Essay: The Orthodox Dogmatic Theology of Dumitru Stăniloae," *Modern Theology* 13, no. 2 (1997): 253–267. He says that "it was only with Calvin's *Institutes* that the notion of Christ's threefold office assumed the structural significance with which he invests it," 259.

104. Stăniloae *TDO*, 2, 152.

105. Miller, *Gift of the World*, 96.

106. Mănăstireanu, *PM*, 275. He also considers that "the little attention given by Stăniloae to the priesthood of all believers is symptomatic for the reduced attention generally given to this topic in Orthodox ecclesiology."

107. Stăniloae, *TDO*, 2, 155–156.

108. John N. Karmiris, *The Status and Ministry of the Laity in the Orthodox Church* (Brookline, MA: Holy Cross, 1994), 1.

109. Mănăstireanu, *PM*, 282.

being the prerogative of the special priesthood.[110] However, Stăniloae is in harmony with the patristic tradition when he speaks of the priest and his duty to teach and the efforts necessary for this, namely a permanent purification and spiritual education.[111] Even though for Baptists in Romania Stăniloae's view of ministry would be considered problematic, it is worth noticing that it is developed in conversation with other traditions as pertinently explained by Mănăstireanu, "Stăniloae is animated by his constant drive towards balance when he seeks to work out the Christological/pneumatological basis for the theology of ministry over against what he perceives to be an exaggerated Christological approach to it in Catholic theology, and as exaggerated pneumatological approach in Protestant circles."[112]

In harmony with his desire for such a balanced view is Stăniloae's argument for the unity of the church that "is not institutional . . . but ontological-pneumatological in Christ and in His Holy Spirit."[113] He agrees with other Orthodox and Western theologians when they consider that "the separations of Christians in different Churches are only at the surface, they do not affect their deep unity."[114] Arguing the fact that "the unity of the Church is a dogmatic one"[115] he states the difference between traditions, "In a way the Church contains all the denominations separated from her, because they could not separate themselves totally from the Tradition present in her. In another way the Church in the fullness of the word is only the Orthodox Church."[116]

When Stăniloae speaks about the salvation of Christians from different denominations, especially ones who were born in these denominations, he

---

110. Mănăstireanu, 284. Also see, Stăniloae, *TDO*, 2, 162. For a different view than that of Stăniloae in the Orthodox tradition, see John Zizioulas, *Being as Communion: Studies in Personhood and the Church* (Crestwood, NY: St. Vladimir's Seminary Press, 1993), 214–225. Zizioulas asserts "the relational character of ministry" next to its "sacramental character, " (Zizioulas, *Being as Communion*, 214, 225). He argues that "there are no un-ordained persons in the Church," as baptism and confirmation are „essentially an ordination," (Zizioulas, 215–216). A possible development of this idea of baptism as confirmation will be argued in chapter 7 of the present project.

111. Stăniloae, *TDO*, 2, 160–163.

112. Mănăstireanu, *PM*, 284.

113. Stăniloae, *TDO*, 2, 172.

114. Stăniloae, 173.

115. Stăniloae, 175.

116. Stăniloae, 176.

argues that they could be incomplete participants in Christ[117] on earth and in eternity based on the text from John 14:2, where Christ says that in his Father's house are many rooms![118] When Stăniloae argues the church's holiness, he proves consistent with his desired christological-pneumatological complementarity. He starts by saying that Christ is the source of the holiness of the church,[119] and he asserts that no human being is holy in himself, but rather by participation in Christ's' holiness,[120] participation possible through a permanent cleansing from sin and in maintaining a pure life. He says, "The Church is the laboratory where the Spirit of Christ makes us holy or more complete images of Christ, in whom is concentrated as in a person the holiness and love of the Holy Trinity."[121] How this participation in Christ's holiness through cleansing happens in the lives of believers starting at baptism, expressed in the Eucharist and embodied in day-to-day spirituality will be extensively analyzed in chapters 3, 4 and 5 of this study. At this point we also underline Stăniloae's idea of the Christian life as a process in which the reality expressed at baptism needs to be actualized in daily life, holiness being "not only a gift but also a mission, a duty for the believers of the Church."[122] The inevitable tension between what we are potentially in Christ and the limits demonstrated in our life on the earth is to lead us to repentance as a way of living, through the practice of confession of sins (1 John 1:9).[123]

---

117. The article summarized by John Briggs from the report of World Council of Churches, September 2002 is interesting in this context, John Briggs, "Evangelicals and Orthodox," *Journal of European Baptist Studies* 12, no.1 (September 2011): 5–19. Briggs summarizes: "The Church recognizes in the other members of the WCC elements of the true church, even if it does not regard them as true churches in the full sense of the word," (Briggs, "Evangelicals and Orthodox," 15).

118. Stăniloae, *TDO*, 2, 177. Also, Sorin Dumitrescu, *7 dimineți cu părintele Stăniloae* (București: Anastasia, 1992), 221. See also Emil Bartoș, "Salvation in the Orthodox Church," in *Baptists and the Orthodox Church: On the Way to Understanding*, ed. Ian Randall (Prague: International Baptist Seminary, 2005), 60.

119. See also Sergius Bulgakov, *The Orthodox Church* (Crestwood, NY: St. Vladimir's Seminary Press, 1988), 95. He says that "the sanctity of the Church is that of Christ Himself" (Bulgakov, *Orthodox Church*, 95).

120. Stăniloae, *TDO*, 2, 177.

121. Stăniloae, 181.

122. Stăniloae, 181.

123. Stăniloae, 185. A more in-depth analysis of the features of Stăniloae's view on baptism will be done in chapter 4, at this point our desire being only to show the way

From the unity and holiness of the church, Stăniloae continues with the catholicity of the church, a subject on which he prefers the term *sobornicity* that in his opinion is more appropriate in defining the nature of church's unity, namely, a unity that is given by the "convergence, communion, unanimous complementarity of its members . . . sobornicity expresses the position and the complementary work of the members of the Church, as a real body, not its cause as expressed by the term catholicity."[124] Consistent with the christological-pneumatological complementarity, Stăniloae's view sees the church as a dynamic reality expressed by the concept of a body filled with the Holy Spirit and having Christ as her head. Stăniloae adds to the Pauline image of the body,[125] the saying of Basil the Great who considers that the "Holy Spirit is wholly (ολον) in each and is entirely everywhere."[126]

Stăniloae continues by saying that this dynamic presence of the Holy Spirit is seen in the unity and diversity of "different gifts that the Spirit imparts and exercises for the life of the entire body and of every member."[127] The dynamic between individual and communal is seen in the key concepts of sobornicity, namely, communion and plenitude, the two concepts expressing the inner role of a gift for a believer, and the communal role of this gift for the entire community.[128]

Fortunately, Stăniloae does not say anything about clergy versus laity, and what seems to keep him away from this danger of artificial separation in the context of the Holy Spirit's gifts in the church, is the close reading of Pauline texts about the body of Christ. The power of Pauline thought mirrored in the thought of Basil the Great, John the Great and Origen, influences Stăniloae in keeping the dynamic work of the Holy Spirit in the gifts of the church at the level of the entire community.[129] In this way his

---

Stăniloae sees the holiness of Christ infused at baptism and actualized in the daily life of believers through repentance.

124. Stăniloae, *TDO*, 2, 186.

125. Nigel G. Wright, *Free Church, Free State: The Positive Baptist Vision* (Milton Keynes: Paternoster, 2005), 13.

126. Stăniloae, *TDO*, 2, 188.

127. Stăniloae, 187.

128. Stăniloae, 187.

129. Stăniloae, 188–189.

vision of the church's *sobornicity* is in itself an important corrective for his vision of the general priesthood that was under scrutiny above.

Stăniloae continues with the apostolicity of the church, considering rightly and biblically Christ as the foundation of the church (1 Cor 3:11; Eph 2:20), and the apostles of Christ as the pillars of the church (Gal 2:9).[130] There are three components of the church's apostolicity, according to Stăniloae's thought. First, the apostles' non-transmissible apostleship, they being unique witnesses of Christ's resurrection. Second, the apostles were the first to believe, and third, their primacy in the transmission of the teachings of Christ.[131]

Stăniloae seems to be arguing for a distinction between the succession of grace that is conditioned by the continuity of Christ's teachings and the apostolic succession to the bishops as the means for the preservation of apostolic teachings. Yet, Stăniloae continues by insisting that "the Church is apostolic by inheriting the faith, teaching, and grace from the apostles," and that "the apostolicity of the Church unites history with the present."[132] He says, "The apostolicity means the connection of generations in the whole tradition that comes from the apostles, for it is the whole Revelation, but also in the grace and spirituality that comes uninterrupted from the Holy Spirit of Christ through them."[133]

2.4. Summary of Chapter 2

This chapter started with an exploration of the spiritual and intellectual context in which Stăniloae was born, lived, and developed his theology and spiritual practices. I continued with an exploration of his biography, spiritual legacy and general scan of his theology. These three dimensions of his life show the coordinates of Stăniloae's spiritual journey. I argued that the uniqueness of Dumitru Stăniloae in the tapestry of Romanian theological thought is given first by his interdisciplinary, dialogical approach that makes him a theologian of complementarities. His way of working in concentric

---

130. Stăniloae, 193.
131. Stăniloae, 194.
132. Stăniloae, 196–197.
133. Stăniloae, 197.

circles covers the domains of the revelation of God, of the knowledge of God, of Christology, pneumatology and ecclesiology.

Second, Stăniloae is a theologian of ecumenical dialogue. His extensive reading of Catholic and Protestant theology, even though not always acknowledged, is present in every area of his theological construct. Often polemical, radical and sometimes using too much generalization, in his judgments of Catholic and Protestant ideas, Stăniloae proves at least a good knowledge of those different traditions, allowing them to speak into his Orthodox thought.

Third, Stăniloae is a theologian who through his theology opens new avenues for the development of contemporary Orthodox theology, especially, on the direction of recovering the interdependency between theology and spirituality. He also constitutes a good starting point or entrance door for Romanian Baptist theology that could benefit enormously and could be enriched by Stăniloae's integrative way of doing theology. Moreover, there are also many elements in Stăniloae's theological thought that could be taken in account in a formulation of new ways of thinking about the church and her mission in third millennium Romania.

One last note in the end of this chapter is in regard to what is not seen in Stăniloae's thought so far, namely an (over-) emphasis on liturgy as almost constitutive of theology. This is, arguably, a result in part of his biography and his experience in the prison camps, where liturgy was hardly possible, and where the practice of Hesychasm became more than important. This lesser emphasis on the liturgy and insistence on spirituality as a lifelong journey, may prove important for dialogue with Romanian Baptists and can be detected in his view of baptism which will be explored in chapter 3, in his view of the Eucharist, which will be explored in chapter 4 and in his thoughts on spirituality which will be explored in chapter 5.

CHAPTER 3

Trinitarian Theology of Participation in Stăniloae's Thought about Baptism

3.1. The Frame of Stăniloae's Theology of Participation

Stăniloae's theology of participation is framed by his concept of the being of God, with its super-essential and spiritual attributes and inner Trinitarian relations. He starts first with a distinction of the relation between the being of God and the uncreated operations of God that "are flowing from it."[1] In Stăniloae's opinion each operation of God bears features of the being of God, being actually "the attributes of God in motion." In fact, says Stăniloae, "we only know the attributes of God in their dynamism and to the extent to which we participate in them," experiencing God in his operations in the world and in us.[2] This knowledge of God's operations becomes progressively

---

1. Stăniloae, *Revelation and Knowledge*, 125. This distinction between the *esse* and the energies of God that Stăniloae embraces here is the fruit of his engagement with Gregory Palamas (1296–1303), one of the most important theologians of the period between the twelfth and fifteenth centuries, named by Pelikan "the last blossoming of the Byzantine Orthodoxy." See in this regard Jaroslav Pelikan, *Tradiția Creștină, O istorie a dezvoltării doctrinei, 2: Spiritul creștinătății răsăritene (600-1700)* (Iași: Polirom, 2005), 277. Speaking about Palamas, Pelikan argues that "he had the responsibility to articulate a new theology of spiritual life that will include the doctrine of God as light," 286.

2. Stăniloae, *Revelation and Knowledge*, 125–126. An interesting fact is that Stăniloae sees the attributes of God in their perichoretical relationship. He is close here with the same perichoretical view of Karl Barth in regard to the attributes of God. Of course there are differences between the two views but the perichoretical view of the attributes is what they have in common. See in this regard, Eric J. Titus, "The Perfections of God in the Theology of Karl Barth: A Consideration of the Formal Structure," *Kairos Evangelical Journal of Theology*

35

richer "as we develop the capacity to participate in them."³ The possibility of such participation is provided, in Stăniloae's thought, by the Personal character of God as a supreme reality.

> Only as Supreme Person is God "of himself" per se and are all His attributes from himself; he can give to the human person too the possibility of participating in this quality of being per se which belongs to him and of his acts . . . only in relation with such Personal reality do we also feel ourselves overwhelmed by

---

4, no. 2 (2010): 203–222. Titus speaks of the fact that the divine perfections (a term that Barth prefers to use for divine attributes) are perichoretic and dyadic and that:
> the perfections are then divided into six dyads, three belonging to divine love and three belonging to divine freedom. Grace and holiness, mercy and righteousness, patience and wisdom all are affiliated with divine loving. Unity and omnipresence, constancy and omnipotence, eternity and glory are connected with divine freedom. But within this structure of dyads exists also a substructure. For example, within the dyad of the perfections of grace and holiness, which are associated with divine love, a dialectical tension is maintained. That is, for example, that within the divine perfections of love, grace and holiness are further expressed mercy and righteousness as grace and holiness; grace and holiness as patience and wisdom; patience and wisdom as mercy and righteousness, etc. The same construction occurs under the divine perfections of freedom. For example, unity is paired with omnipresence, with unity expressing the divine freedom under consideration and omnipresence bringing the dialectical play of love into the considerations of divine freedom while yet being itself considered a perfection of freedom. This happens then in turn with constancy and omnipotence and eternity and glory. It may further be said that the perfection of divine love and that of divine freedom as wholes also express this same form of perichoretic relationship. Each of these interrelationships point back and interplay with the foundational proposition that God is the One who loves in freedom, and in this is the essence of the life of God, the God who lives as the One who loves in freedom,

Titus, "Perfections of God," 211–212.

3. Stăniloae, *Revelation and Knowledge*, 127. Also, Stăniloae, *Viața și învățătura sfântului Grigorie Palama* (București: Scripta, 1993), 65–78. Also, Lossky, *The Vision of God* (Crestwood, NY: St. Vladimir's Seminary Press, 1983), 131. We find in Lossky's argument the foundation for Palamite distinction between essence and energies. Lossky says that "the distinction between the nature and attributes or between the unknowable essence and the revelatory powers or energies of God is expressly affirmed, following Dionysius and the Cappadocians." Also, Pelikan, *Tradiția Creștină*, vol. 2 (Iași; Polirom, 2005), 294. He comments,
> The systematic justification of this vision of the relation between participative and unparticipative in God, was constituted by the combination between the doctrine of divine works . . . elaborated during the christological controversies, and the doctrine of the divine nature . . . elaborated during the trinitarian controversies. Palamas and his disciples were helped by the controversies with monoenergetism. From these controversies comes the teaching that divine energy is eternal and uncreated, yet being distinct from divine essence.

Pelikan, *Tradiția Creștină*, vol. 2, 294.

his powers which we feel no longer as coming from somewhere else or merely relative.[4]

Stăniloae adds to the personal character of God another important feature of God's being the apophatic character of God. For him, God as a supreme personal being is as such only if he is totally apophatic or super-existent. He follows Evdokimov in considering that because of his super-existence, there cannot be rational proofs of God's existence. Yet he states that it is equally true that the experience of faith in the human soul, as a gift from God, is the frame in which "all become proofs for the existence and activity of God."[5] Stăniloae concludes, "Only the transcendence of the divine Personal reality assures the existence of human persons who are not totally enclosed within nature's system of references . . . Otherwise everything would fall under the rule of the meaningless laws of nature and of death."[6] If the first pillar of Stăniloae's construct of the Trinitarian theology of participation is the being of God, with the distinction between the *esse* and operations, the second pillar is constituted by the super-essential attributes of God, namely, infinity, simplicity, eternity, supraspatiality, omnipotence.

---

4. Stăniloae, *Revelation and Knowledge*, 132.

5. Stăniloae, 135. Also see, Paul Evdokimov, *Vârstele vieții spirituale* (Bucuresti: Christiana, 1993), 45.

6. Stăniloae, *Revelation and Knowledge*, 137–138. Also, Emil Bartoș, *Deification*, 63. Speaking about the trinitarian basis of Stăniloae's distinction between esse and energies, comparatively with Palamas, Bartoș argues that Stăniloae "introduces a more personalist dynamic," (Bartoș, *Deification*, 63). However, one of the reasons Stăniloae found Palamas's thought attractive for that could be Stăniloae's Hesychastic experience in prison, a spiritual personal experience that constituted the platform for his theology, life and ministry. See in regard to Palamas as a theologian of Hesychasm, John Meyendorff, *St. Gregory Palamas and Orthodox Spirituality* (New York: St, Vladimir's Seminary Press, 1974), 75–130. Meyendorff points out the position of Palamas in opposition with that of Barlaam's view derived from Greek philosophy. It might be that here is another reason why Staniloe found Palamas's thought relevant for the Romanian Orthodox Church, whose revived spirituality he was preoccupied with. In Meyendorff's judgment, Palamas:
> integrates the mystical tradition, going back to Evagrius and Macarius, with Christian thought that is based on the Bible and on a vast knowledge of the Fathers . . . Hence Palamas refused to give any credence to what the ancient philosophers said of the knowledge of God. He developed a realistic doctrine of supernatural knowledge, independent of any sense experience but granted in Jesus Christ to man as a whole-body and soul-admitting him even here below to the first fruits of final deification and the vision of God, not by his own powers but by the grace of God,

Meyendorff, *St. Gregory Palamas*, 108–109.

For Stăniloae the infinity of God is paralleled in the created order by finitude. In fact, he says the finitude of the created order exists in the framework of God's infinity, the finitude being conditioned by the infinite, while the participation of the finite in the infinity is possible only through the grace of the infinite God.[7] Stăniloae considers that, the source of God's infinity is the divine super-essence that is expressed in the inner Trinitarian relations of the three hypostases of the Trinity, a relation of which fullness is the cause of a finite human being's longing movement towards it.[8] "Moreover, ... any circling movement of existing things will come to an end in the infinity around God in whom all things that move receive their stability ... Infinity is God's ambiance and through it he makes himself accessible or communicates himself to creatures which have reached union with him as supreme subject."[9] The model of the progress and realization for this participative dimension of the finite in the infinite, Stăniloae concludes, is Christ in whom "after the resurrection, his humanity was raised to the supreme participation in the divine infinity."[10]

The second super-essential attribute in Stăniloae's analysis is God's simplicity. He says that the unity of God is to be seen in the Trinitarian distinction of the three hypostases of God's being, a distinction that means not a composite God, but a God in which "the threefold and common divine subjectivity is simple in itself."[11] Moreover, Stăniloae asserts the unifying importance of Christ's resurrection for the vertical unity of God with human beings and the horizontal unity of human beings between themselves and with the created order, "By acquiring the unity or simplicity which is in God, the composition of creation overcomes the force of decomposition and corruptibility. Hence through the resurrection of Christ, bodies acquire incorruptibility. Corruptibility is overwhelmed by the unitary force of the spirit."[12]

---

7. Stăniloae, *EG*, 141.
8. Stăniloae, 142.
9. Stăniloae, 143.
10. Stăniloae, 144.
11. Stăniloae, 145. See also, Pelikan, *Tradiția creștină*, vol. 2, 294. He says that in maintaining the distinction between the uncreated energies that are many, Palamas, following Basil, also maintained that *ousia* is simple.
12. Stăniloae, *TDO*, 1, 148.

The third super-essential attribute of God in Stăniloae's analysis is eternity. For Stăniloae the eternity of God is the plenitude of the triune communion,[13] the true eternity of God is to be seen in the self-existence of God[14] and in the fullness of the triunic perfect persons' relationships.[15] For Stăniloae, one of the purposes for the created order is to participate in God's eternity. In the case of human beings, eternity is being achieved "through a movement towards God which comes about in time."[16] This is the reason Stăniloae considers time to be the medium in which the progress of a human being, towards God becomes possible.[17] God in his relations within the immanent and economic Trinity experiences simultaneously eternity and time. Stăniloae explains how this simultaneity is possible:

> On this road of ours towards eternity God himself experiences together with us the expectant waiting (and hence time) on the plane of his energies and of his relations with us. And this is so because he himself voluntarily lives out the limitation of the offering of his love . . . God experiences simultaneously his eternity in the inter-trinitarian relations and his temporal relation with created spiritual beings; or indeed in his very relations with creatures he experiences both eternity and time. This is a kenosis voluntarily accepted by God for the sake of creation.[18]

Stăniloae states that even though time is not existent within Trinity, it is explained as having its source in it, as a means to open the possibility of human beings' answer to the love of God.[19] For Stăniloae the incarnation of the Son is the expression of this relation between divine eternity and human

---

13. Stăniloae, 172.
14. Stăniloae, *Revelation and Knowledge*, 150. Also, Barth, *Church Dogmatics*, vol. 2, part 1, 608 (referred to as *CD*, followed by volume then part [e.g. 2.1]). Barth considers that "God's eternity, like His unity and constancy, is a quality of His freedom . . . It is the sovereignty and majesty of His love . . . Eternity is God in the sense in which in Himself and in all things God is simultaneous." (Barth, *CD*, 2.1, 608).
15. Stăniloae, *TDO*, 1, 174.
16. Stăniloae, *Revelation and Knowledge*, 154.
17. Stăniloae, *TDO*, 1, 179.
18. Stăniloae, *Revelation and Knowledge*, 159–160.
19. Stăniloae, 163. Also, Barth, *CD*, 2.1, 611. The same idea is argued by Barth, who says "God is both the prototype and foreordination of all being, and therefore also the prototype and foreordination of time. God has time because and as He has eternity. Thus

temporality.[20] Coming to the supraspatiality of God, Stăniloae affirms that this is an expression of God's apophatic transcendence.[21] In this context space as a medium for the human beings is as time, originated and ended in the Trinity.[22] Moreover space is the medium of God's communion with human beings,[23] God accepting space, in Christ as another form of his *kenosis*.[24] Stăniloae concludes, "The distance between ourselves and God is overcome in Christ not only because God has come down to us, but also because we are raised up to God. In Christ all of us have potentially overcome the distance separating us from God and from one another."[25]

The last super-essential attribute of God, in Stăniloae's analysis is God's omnipotence which is not the power to do whatever he wants, rather it is the power to do good.[26] The power of God manifests outside the life of the Trinity, in creation and towards creation, through God's *kenosis* in regard to human beings. It is manifested in the fact that he offers his power for the human being's ascension towards himself, freely, as an answer in a movement of ascent to the movement of descent from God.[27]

Moreover, for Stăniloae, the manifestation of the omnipotence of God towards creation and human beings is always *for* salvation and deification, not *against* the world.[28] Stăniloae considers that God's power is always first the power of a Father. The "divine paternity" frames all manifestations of God's power, as Creator and Judge.[29] Moreover the power of God is spiritual, a power to love and to open in this way human responses in love to him. He concludes with the centrality of Christ in understanding this reality.

He does not first have it on the basis of creation, which is also, of course, the creation of time." (Barth, *CD*, 2.1, 611).

20. Stăniloae, *Revelation and Knowledge*, 169.
21. Stăniloae, 171.
22. Stăniloae, 173.
23. Stăniloae, *TDO*, 1, 205.
24. Stăniloae, 210.
25. Stăniloae, *Revelation and Knowledge*, 182.
26. Stăniloae, 186.
27. Stăniloae, 189. See also, Barth, *CD*, 2, 522. Barth names God's omnipotence as a perfection of his freedom and that "as omnipotent God, He is constant." (Stăniloae, *Revelation and Knowledge*, 189).
28. Stăniloae, *Revelation and Knowledge*, 190–191.
29. Stăniloae, 192.

In Christ, the Son of God becomes bearer of the perfect Trinitarian love for men and also of human love raised up to the capacity of responding perfectly to that love. In the state of resurrection, moreover, the Son extends unobstructedly this perfect divine-human dialogue of love which has been realized in himself, by drawing us also into it. In Christ, man has received the power to love God within a unique love together with the only begotten Son of God, and to love men with the very love of God.[30]

The spiritual[31] attributes of God – omniscience, justice and mercy, holiness, goodness and love – constitute, in Stăniloae's thought, the third pillar for the theology of participation. Speaking about the omniscience of God, Stăniloae states that God's knowledge of everything does not come from the things themselves, rather it is prior to the things, and therefore it is the cause of all things. Moreover, Stăniloae considers that even though human knowledge is rational, God's knowledge is accessible for participation in it, through human union with God.[32] Stăniloae asserts that God's knowledge of the creatures and God's knowledge of himself should not be seen as separate, following Dionysius the Areopagite[33] (an understanding that seems for Stăniloae more appropriate)[34] in regard to the unity of God. He says, "The

---

30. Stăniloae, 195.

31. It is interesting that in Stăniloae's thought the construct of the perichoretical relation is a reality not only in regard to super-essential attributes of God among themselves but also between them and spiritual attributes. He comes close again with Barth who says that "He is the one, unique and simple God, and as such omnipresent. This clearly raises His grace and holiness, mercy and righteousness, patience and wisdom, above the perfections which . . . could be ascribed to the creature . . . they are all of them omnipresent, omnipresent grace, omnipotent holiness . . . For they are all in themselves the omnipotence of God." Barth, *CD*, 2.1, 523.

32. Stăniloae, *Revelation and Knowledge*, 199.

33. Dionysius the Areopagite, *The Divine Names and Mystical Theology* (London: SPCK, 1975). We have here a possible reason for Stăniloae's appropriation of Dionysus's synthesis between super-essential and spiritual attributes of God, as Dionysius argues that "We must not dare to speak, or indeed to form any conception, of the hidden super-essential Godhead, except those things that are revealed to us for the Holy Scriptures," (Dionysius, *Divine Names*, 51).

34. In asserting this, Stăniloae criticizes the separation between the two kinds of knowledge, as in Karl Barth's opinion the knowledge of God in regard to the creatures is finite for they are finite, whilst the knowledge of God in regard to himself is infinite for he

Eastern Fathers in general declare that full knowledge is the union between the one who knows and the one who is known, just as ignorance causes separation or is the effect of separation."[35]

For Stăniloae, there are three implications for this kind of perichoretical knowledge. First, it implies the personal character of God, second, this knowledge cannot exist outside the full love as expressed in the Trinitarian relationships,[36] and third, this full knowledge opens the possibility for progress in union with God for human beings, as the end of this union of humans is known to God,[37] an end fulfilled in Jesus Christ.[38] "In Christ God knows the humanity of all at its maximum level through its total participation in his life, and God has this knowledge because of his own maximum participation in human life."[39]

For Stăniloae God's justice towards creatures is rooted in the equality of the three persons. This is again a participatory reality opened to human beings based on the fact that God's justice and mercy are united in such a way that "God cannot be just without being merciful and is not merciful without being just."[40] Moreover, to participate in God's justice and mercy, even though incomplete because of human limitations to show horizontally these attributes, is to be part of the ascent of human beings towards God.

---

is infinite. Stăniloae also criticized the Vatican 1 perspective about the knowledge of God as infinite both in regard to the creature and with himself.

35. Stăniloae, *Revelation and Knowledge*, 201. Also, Dionysius, *Divine Names*. He says: "Knowledge unites the knower and the objects of knowledge," 153.

36. Stăniloae, *Revelation and Knowledge*, 202.

37. Stăniloae, 205.

38. Stăniloae, 209.

39. Stăniloae, 210.

40. Stăniloae, 215. Stăniloae is arguing here the dyad of mercy and justice, as they are inseparable reflecting the dyad of mercy and righteousness and their inseparability as well as the inseparability between grace and holiness, in Barth's thought. See in this regard Barth, *CD*, 2.1, 376. Barth is arguing:

> We have seen that there exists a relationship between God's grace and holiness, a relationship of mutual penetration and consummation determined by grace, which necessarily precedes. The relationship between God's mercy and righteousness, is similar. We shall have to emphasize the righteousness of God no less than His mercy . . . The relationship between God's mercy and righteousness will also present itself to us as a relationship of mutual penetration and consummation, but here again it will receive its characteristic stamp from the fact that divine mercy necessarily precedes.

Barth, *CD*, 2.1, 376.

Trinitarian Theology of Participation in Stăniloae's Thought about Baptism

The way and model for this ascent is Christ's perfect justice and mercy, that we can internalize as we identify ourselves with him, "Christ alone as man has attained complete justice. From his justice we absorb power to make progress in assimilating – in the life to come – the justice that belongs to him and is the human form of the divine justice (1 Corinthians 1:30; 2 Corinthians 5:21; Ephesians 6:14)."[41]

God, says Stăniloae, is sustaining and will reward this internal work of harmonization with the right justice that will affect the external status of affairs, with the "full justice that comes particularly in the life to come . . . (Luke 16: 25)." The full expression of this reality is Jesus, "who was most just and suffered the greatest injustice from the world . . . and . . . raised up to heavenly glory because of his justice."[42] The participatory dimension is stated again, "Those who participate in the energies of God (among which is numbered the energy of justice) . . . by which their being is re-established and strengthened – are themselves also animated by the impulse to bring about justice."[43] Another dimension of this participation is the understanding that the spiritual human being should have, that the interior and the external justice are not an ends in themselves but rather "the complete justice" that is, "the reestablishment of the perfect balance between all created things, the full reflection of the justice of God." Only in this way, says Stăniloae, God's justice "will fill the earth . . . radiating both from within us and from above us."[44]

Holiness, for Stăniloae, comes from God in the descent of his revelatory activity and is a participatory reality through the ascent of human persons towards God.[45] Also, the two directions of holiness, the one through which it comes and the one through which it is appropriated, are embodied in Christ, in his divine descent into human form and in his human ascent towards God. This identification of Christ starts for the human in his baptism a reality mirrored in human baptism, deepened and developed, through the

---

41. Stăniloae, *Revelation and Knowledge*, 218.
42. Stăniloae, 219.
43. Stăniloae, 220.
44. Stăniloae, 220–222.
45. Stăniloae, 222.

other sacraments, in their "struggle for purification."[46] Arguing the possibility of this participation in the holiness of God, Stăniloae says, "The Fathers saw in holiness a great likeness of man with God through purification from the passions and through the virtues which culminate in love . . . acquired through the energy of the grace which strengthens human powers . . . a radiation of the presence of God from within man."[47]

Here again the centrality of Christ is underlined, in the fact that the "essence of all virtues is our Lord Jesus Christ himself."[48] Therefore the struggle of the believer against passions, is assisted by the operation of the cross that opens the possibility for the presence of God in Christ to enlighten the human soul,[49] a process that will lead to the human being's "surrender to absolute Person" a surrender that is a "sanctifying self-sacrifice."[50] The participatory dimension is then again stated, "Orthodoxy believes that through spirituality, through the penetration into the world of the uncreated energies, the world is transfigured, a transfiguration which also depends on efforts towards holiness made by believers who are strengthened by these energies. For in these energies, which have come to belong to men also, God in Trinity is made transparent."[51]

Coming to the goodness and love of God, Stăniloae considers that God is "goodness beyond the good" as the supreme goodness God is the source of all good things that he created out of love. This love is supremely expressed in the Trinitarian relationships and is the love that God manifests towards creation and is the one that produces the answer in love from creation.[52]

---

46. Stăniloae, 225. Also, G. L. Prestige, *God in Patristic Thought* (London: SPCK, 1952), 23–24.

47. Stăniloae, *Revelation and Knowledge,* 226.

48. Stăniloae, 227.

49. Stăniloae, 227–228.

50. Stăniloae, 231.

51. Stăniloae, 238.

52. Stăniloae, 238–241. Also, John R. Franke, "God is Love: The Social Trinity and the Mission of God," in *Trinitarian Theology for the Church: Scripture, Community, Worship,* eds. Daniel J. Treier and David Lauber, 115. He says,
> God's love for the world is not that of an uninvolved, unmoved, passionless Deity, but rather that of one who is actively and passionately involved in the ongoing drama of life in the world, one who lavishly pours out this love in Jesus Christ. This lavish expression of love for humanity and creation is revealed in Jesus Christ and points us to the internal life of God as an eternal trinitarian fellowship of

Again, Christ is the supreme embodiment not only of the love of God towards creation but also the maximal manifestation of the answer in love to the love of God. "The fullest loving going out towards creatures was carried out by God through the incarnation of his Son . . . but simultaneously the Son filled human nature with his divine love for the Father."[53] These considerations led Stăniloae to a profound discussion on the Holy Trinity, a construct that will be analyzed in the next section.

3.2. The Heart of Stăniloae's Theology of Participation

The Holy Trinity is the heart of his theology of participation, being a mystery[54] that is revealed in multiple directions. First, the Holy Trinity is the structure of supreme love. Mutual love between the Trinitarian persons originates and explains love in the world.[55] Stăniloae states the importance of the Holy Trinity for our participative progress towards God, being "the foundation, infinite reservoir, power and model of our growing eternal communion."[56]

Second, for Stăniloae, the Holy Trinity is the foundation of our salvation, revealing itself in the work of salvation. The Father restores the relationship with human beings through the incarnate Son and develops progressively through the Spirit the intimate relationship without distance that exists between him and the Son.[57]

Third, the Holy Trinity is the mystery of perfect unity of distinct persons, a mystery that is expressed in the human beings' "unity of being and personal

---

love shared between Father, Son and Holy Spirit. In other words, explication of the triune God in God's self-disclosure in and to creation is at the same time the explication of the triune God in the divine reality.
Franke, "God is Love," 115.

53. Stăniloae, *Revelation and Knowledge*, 243.

54. Also, Louis Berkhof, (*Systematic Theology*, 89) says in line with Stăniloae that "the Church confesses the Trinity to be a mystery beyond the comprehension of man." Also Rahner, *The Trinity*, 21. Rahner argues that "The Trinity is a mystery of salvation."

55. Stăniloae, *Revelation and Knowledge*, 245.

56. Stăniloae, 247.

57. Stăniloae, 248.

distinction."⁵⁸ The difference between the unity of being and persons in regard to God and in regard to human beings is that in God there is no interval between the divine being and its expressions in the three persons, whilst, for humans the interval exists.⁵⁹

From here Stăniloae continues to discuss the divine essence through the concept of inter-subjectivity. This means a "compenetration of the consciousness of each," the three persons being three pure subjects experiencing each other as such, in a total transparency.⁶⁰ Moreover, the inter-subjectivity means that each of the divine persons "experiences the modes in which the others live the divine being,"⁶¹ Stăniloae argues the active aspect of the intersubjectivity between the divine persons.

> The Son is not passive in his generation from the Father, although he is not the subject who begets but the subject who takes his birth. Neither does the term "procession" in reference to the Holy Spirit mark any passivity on the part of the Holy Spirit . . . Moreover, as the Father in incomprehensible fashion is the source of both the Son and the Spirit, each of them together with the Father not only lives the act of his own coming forth from the Father, but also joyfully participates along with the other-though from his own position – in living the act whereby the other comes forth from the Father.⁶²

For Stăniloae this is the model that Christ brings in his personal relationship with us opening the possibility for us to move from sinful individualism,

---

58. Stăniloae, 250.

59. Stăniloae imagines this interval in the metaphor of knots (the distinct persons or hypostasis) and strings (the common nature). When the communion "is a positive one the strings between the knots can grow thicker, whereas distance and struggle between the knots makes the string grow thinner." (Stăniloae, *Revelation and Knowledge*, 253).

60. Stăniloae, *Revelation and Knowledge*, 260.

61. Stăniloae, 261.

62. Stăniloae, 262. Here Stăniloae is close to Calvin in his view of the Trinity. See in this regard, Calvin, *Institutes*, 153. Calvin affirms that "we teach from the Scriptures that God is one of essence, and hence that the essence both of the Son and of the Spirit is unbegotten; but inasmuch as the Father is first in order, and from himself begot the wisdom . . . he is rightly deemed at the beginning and fountainhead of the whole divinity."

towards mutual communion with each other in him.⁶³ Stăniloae continues by saying that the Trinity of persons is a condition of their full personal character and of their perfect communion, for "the number . . . which *par excellence* represents the distinction in unity or unity made explicit in three,"⁶⁴ and makes possible the manifestation of the love of the Father for the Son towards the others.⁶⁵

The Trinity of persons is also a condition of maintaining the distinction of the persons in communion, by overcoming the "dual subjectivity" of two persons and expressing "an objective reality."⁶⁶ Finally, the Trinity of persons "assures the fullness of their communion and makes this communion full with the joy one person finds in another."⁶⁷ Stăniloae concludes:

> as the Son has a distinct position as image of the Father, while the Spirit has been caused to proceed for the purpose of participating in the joy which the Father takes in the Son as image, the Spirit does have a special role . . . that he might make of the joy each person has in the other a joy that is shared by the other.⁶⁸

From the concept of the Holy Trinity as a structure of supreme love, Stăniloae continues with the concept of the Holy Trinity as the foundation of Christian spirituality.⁶⁹ Mirroring the Trinitarian model, Stăniloae imagines the human being as a temple in three parts: body, soul and the inner part where in baptism Christ enters and lives.⁷⁰ Christ enters our lives through

---

63. Stăniloae, *Revelation and Knowledge*, 265. Also, Meyendorff, *St. Gregory Palamas*. Commenting on the Father's view of spirituality, Meyendorff says: "Participation in God is a total participation, in Jesus Christ. In fact there could be no participation in a 'part' of God, for the divine Being is simple and therefore indivisible, and the divine 'energy' is God, not lessened, but freely revealed," 44.

64. Stăniloae, *Revelation and Knowledge*, 266. Also, Dumitru Stăniloae, *Sfânta Treime sau La început a fost iubirea* [The Holy Trinity or in the beginning was love] (București: IBMBOR, 1993), 34.

65. Stăniloae, *Revelation and Knowledge*, 267.

66. Stăniloae, 268.

67. Stăniloae, 275.

68. Stăniloae, 277.

69. Dumitru Stăniloae, *Spiritualitatea Ortodoxă: Ascetica și Mistica* (București: IBMBOR, 1992), 29.

70. Stăniloae, *Spiritualitatea Ortodoxă*, 42.

sacraments (baptism, chrismation, and Eucharist)[71] and from there Christ leads the mortification of the old self and the resurrection of the new self.[72] Baptism is not only the "momentous realization" of this death and resurrection but also the beginning of a long life process. In this process of the "continuation and actualization of baptism,"[73] faith is an essential element. Stăniloae considers that faith is given by Christ through the church "his Body, full with the Spirit of communion."[74] Faith is, says Stăniloae, "the first step in the spiritual life, and as such comes from God through baptism."[75] He continues with some important affirmations:

> All of our virtuous life is a development of this beginning made by God. Of course it is not an automatic development, without us, rather a development willed and helped by us, through all our power. So, before all the virtues we must have the faith received and strengthened at baptism. But its efficacy depends on our participation, to progress on the road of virtues towards perfection.[76]

The strengthening of faith, continues Stăniloae, happens progressively, in the immersion of will, intellect and sentiment in the reality of God.[77] In its progress faith becomes, says Stăniloae, fear of God.[78]

---

71. Stăniloae, 43.
72. Stăniloae, 43–44. Also, Meyendorff, *A Study of Gregory Palamas* (New York: St. Vladimir's Seminary Press, 1998), 151. Speaking about the life in Christ in the hesychatic view of Palamas, Meyendorff says: "the life in Christ in us is, according to Palamas, the foundation of hesychast spirituality . . . For him 'within . . .' does not designate the purely intellectual reality of man . . . but refers to the whole composite human being. It is within our body, grafted on to the body of Christ by baptism and the Eucharist, that divine light shines," (Meyendorff, *Study of Gregory Palamas*, 151). We see again here the influence of Palamas on Stăniloae, reached with a Trinitarian flavour.
73. Stăniloae, *Spiritualitatea Ortodoxă*, 44.
74. Stăniloae, 45.
75. Stăniloae, 45.
76. Stăniloae, 95.
77. Stăniloae, 96–97.
78. Stăniloae, 100.

3.3. Baptism in the Context of the Theology of Participation in the Thought of Stăniloae

Stăniloae considers that salvific work for humanity is a profound Trinitarian reality. He says that the Holy Spirit proceeds from the Father and rests in the Son, in order to show the total unity of reciprocal love between the Father and the Son, and also to mediate the manifestation of this perfect love through the Son towards humanity.[79] The complementarily work of the Son and of the Holy Spirit in salvation is in Stăniloae's opinion a biblical truth, expressed in the Niceo-Constantinopolitan creed. Stăniloae expresses this by quoting Evdokimov:

> During Christ's earthly ministry the relationship of humanity with the Holy Spirit was mediated by Christ. On the contrary after Pentecost the relationship with Christ with humanity is mediated through and in the Holy Spirit. The ascension ends the historical visibility of Christ. But Pentecost opened to humanity the possibility of the internal presence of Christ, revealing Him not face to face, rather inside His disciples.[80]

For Stăniloae, baptism reflects and expresses the salvific work of the Trinity. Baptism expresses this by the complementarity of the work of the Son and of the Spirit that is the foundation for redemptive reality in humans. To argue the inseparability of these two works (of the Son and of the Spirit) in baptism, Stăniloae quotes John 1:11, where is revealed the fact that the ones who receive the Word are united with him by being born anew "from water and Spirit," according to Christ's teaching to Nicodemus in John 3:5–7.[81]

For Stăniloae, Trinitarian participation in the transfiguration of humanity is the basis for humanity's participative answer to God's participation,

---

79. Dumitru Stăniloae, *The Holy Trinity: In the Beginning There was Love* (Brookline, MA: Holy Cross Orthodox Press, 2012), 69.

80. Stăniloae, *Holy Trinity*, 70. Also, Evdokimov, *L'Esprit Saint dans la tradition orthodoxe*, 90.

81. Stăniloae, *Holy Trinity*, 72. Also, Basil of Caesarea, "On the Spirit," in *Nicene and Post-Nicene Fathers,* series 2, vol. 8, eds. Philip Schaff and Henry Wace (Peabody, MA: Hendrickson, 1995), 23, argued: "that the Holy Spirit is in every conception inseparable from the Father and the Son, alike in the creation of perceptible objects, in the dispensation of human affairs, and in the judgment to come."

in baptism, as expressing the birth that is the coming out from spiritual death and it is the entrance into the new life in God.[82] This is seen in the two liturgical questions that the believer or the godparents of the child are to answer affirmatively when they present the child for baptism: Are you renouncing Satan? Are you uniting with Christ? In the context of the two declarative answers, "through the Spirit comes Christ or through Christ comes the Spirit of Christ."[83] The participation of Christ in the act of baptism is stated by Stăniloae who considers that Christ,

> introduces in the water His creative power through which He created human beings in the beginning after the divine image and likeness and He enters first, and is baptized in it. First, for re-establishing the grace that recreates . . . second, to attract the reborn through baptism into the fellowship, becoming Himself the first born from many sons . . . Only through baptism the Lord makes us truly in His likeness and by introducing into the water His deifying power He establishes the basis for our deification . . .[84]

Moreover, baptism is for Stăniloae the start of the participatory journey of salvation for the human being, a journey assisted and empowered by the Holy Spirit. This is argued through the unity between water and Spirit as the "bosom of the new man."[85] He remembers the work of the Spirit in the Son in the act of creation, over the waters, and its direct connection with the re-creation of the new man in Christ's baptism in the Spirit, as he unites in him the entire creation.[86] "The water of Baptism, is in a hidden way the matter of the age to come . . . Immersing in this water the man meets Christ

---

82. Stăniloae, *Holy Trinity*, 71. Also, *Sf. Ioan Gura de Aur: Cateheze baptismale* [St. John Chrysostom, Baptismal homilies] (Sibiu: Editura Oastea Domnului, 2003). He says "baptism is tomb and resurrection," 48.

83. Stăniloae, *Holy Trinity*, 72.

84. Stăniloae, "Drumul cu Hristos prin tainele si sarbatorile ortodoxe" [The way with Christ through the sacraments and Orthodox celebrations], *Ortodoxia*, no. 2 (april-June 1976), 406–407.

85. Stăniloae, *Teologie Dogmatică Ortodoxă*, 3 (București: EIBMBOR, 1997), 25, referred to throughout as *TDO*, 3.

86. Stăniloae, *TDO*, 3, 27.

in it . . . he is framed by His person and is filled with the energies of the Holy Spirit irradiating from Christ."[87]

Baptism is therefore, first, the death of the old man and resurrection, and total submission to God, and in this way, an immersion into the eternal life of God. Baptism is second, in Stăniloae's thought "the power of continual spiritual growth," shown in the cultivation of Christian virtues.[88] For Stăniloae the gift of spiritual power received in baptism is to be followed by the responsible continuation of the development of this gift.[89] In the case that man sins in this process of development for the gift of spiritual power in the virtues, the human being has the possibility to return in the close relationship with Christ through repentance. Moreover, if baptism offers the possibility of cleansing past sins and entering the new life in Christ that is released from the chains of inherited sin, baptism does not offer the possibility of cleansing for sins done after baptism.[90] Stăniloae warns about the danger of considering the sacraments as "magical means" that offer human beings the possibility to enter the Kingdom of God, being just an object on which these are administered.

Rather contrary, argues Stăniloae, the conscious participation of the believer is vital in his effort to assimilate the purity of Christ, in this process of "transformation and perfection," in accord with the image of Christ.[91] However, there is a danger Stăniloae does not warn against, that of considering the water touched by the Holy Spirit, to operate the sacramental cleansing. However, one of the fathers of the church, Gregory of Nyssa warns against this danger when he says:

> If, then, by being "washed," as says the prophet, in that mystic bath we become "clean" in our wills and "put away the evil" of our souls, we thus become better [people], and are changed to a better state. But, if when the bath has been applied to the body, the soul has not cleansed itself from the stains of its passions and affections, but the life after initiation keeps on a level with

---

87. Stăniloae, 27–28.
88. Stăniloae, 28–32.
89. Stăniloae, 33.
90. Stăniloae, 34.
91. Stăniloae, 35.

> the uninitiated life, then, though it may be a bold thing to say, yet I will say it and will not shrink; in these cases the water is but water, for the gift of the Holy Ghost in no way appears in [the one] who is thus baptismally born.[92]

Third, baptism is the reconstruction of Christ's image in a human being. For Stăniloae, sin weakens the human person, reducing the human being to a biological existence, by weakening the divine image in a human being or his relationship with God. This is why baptism has also this dimension of re-establishing the divine image in a human being.[93]

Stăniloae states the participatory dimension of the reality of re-establishment of divine image in a person. A human being enters through baptism in a relationship of "calling – response" with God. This relationship is established through the will of Christ, who resurrects the human being to a new life, and also through the human will, in the responsible response that a human being gives to the personal call to a new life, a manifestation of human will that is not manifested at his natural birth. This is the way in which an individual becomes more and more a unique person imprinted more and more with the form of Christ.[94]

> The image of Christ is a light robe, is Christ Himself. "for all of you who were baptized into Christ have clothed yourselves with Christ" (Gal. 3:26). This robe is not only on the surface as are normal clothes; rather it is imprinted in our entire being. It is Christ Himself, and also at the same time it is a special, personal, and unique relationship with Christ.[95]

Stăniloae continues by saying that the clarification of the image of the human person imprinted by Christ's image happens in a process of continual

---

92. Gregory of Nyssa, "Catechetical Oration," in *Nicene and Post-Nicene Fathers*, series 2, vol. 5, ed. Philip Schaff (Peabody, MA: Hendrickson, 2007), 508. See also, N. T. Wright, *Surprised by Hope* (London: SPCK, 2007). He says "Baptism is not magic, a conjuring trick with water. But nor it is simply a visual aid. It is one of the points, established by Jesus himself, where heaven and earth interlock, where new creation, resurrection life, appears within the midst of the old . . . it should be the foundational event for all serious Christian living," (Wright, *Surprised by Hope*, 285).

93. Stăniloae, *TDO*, 3, 35.

94. Stăniloae, 36.

95. Stăniloae, 37.

positive response to the call of Christ. This call is manifested through the words of the apostles and of the servants of the church. The quality and intensity of this call of Christ through his servants, for the imprint of his image on and in the believers, is illustrated by the passionate and persuasive words of Paul addressed to the believers of the Galatian church (Gal 3:1, 20; 4:8–9, 19; 2 Cor 3:18; Col 3:9–10).[96]

Stăniloae warns again, consistently, in regard to the idea of baptism as part of a participatory process, about the fact that a human is not received in a personal relationship with him starting at baptism, without the response of the human in expressing his desire for this relationship and with the assumption of the lifelong responsibility to answer positively to the call of Christ. He continues by saying that this assuming of responsibility is reflected, on the one hand, in the double baptismal declaration of renouncing Satan and uniting with Christ, and on the other hand, in the confession of faith in the recitation of the Creed. The partnership initiated by God, in Christ, Stăniloae continues to argue, is developed by the coordinates of mutual "fidelity in love," illustrated in the Pauline theology of spiritual freedom (Gal 5:1, 13; Rom 6:18–19; 8:2).[97]

Fourth, baptism is the entrance door to the church. This is so, says Stăniloae, because "personal existence is a form of existence in communion, in which each grows in the originality of his own giving of himself . . . in the service of others."[98] This inclusion in the community of the church is signified, says Stăniloae, by the fact that the act of baptism is done by the priest or bishop, who represents, because of his ordination, Christ and the church in their indissoluble relation.

In this context it is important that Stăniloae states not only the fact that the efficiency of baptism is not rooted in the worthiness of the priest, but also the fact that in Stăniloae's opinion the church recognizes baptism done outside the church with the condition of the three times immersion in water, pouring of water or sprinkling with water in the name of the Holy Spirit. He adds that the church could also baptize again ones baptized outside the church, from a different Christian tradition. The reason the church could do

---

96. Stăniloae, 37–38.
97. Stăniloae, 39–40.
98. Stăniloae, 40.

so is that of the incompleteness of Christ's grace and work in the community from which he comes, an incompleteness coming from the incompleteness of faith in that community.

Stăniloae limits the acceptance of baptism from one tradition to his own (for when he speaks about the church he speaks of the Orthodox Church), based on the form of baptism. The last piece of Stăniloae's thought on baptism is that of the argument for the necessity of baptism for salvation and infant baptism. This necessity is connected with the annihilation of the ancestral sin through the union of Christ in baptism (John 3:3–5). Children also share the imprint of the ancestral sin even though not through personal sin but by birth (Job 14:4).[99]

Stăniloae continues by saying that the new life in Christ cannot be received without baptism, through the confession of faith that opens the being to be entered by Christ.[100] In the case of infants the confession of faith is from the family, a faith that will be shared by the infants at a later time. This is so because the time when infant will start to share the family's spirituality is not known. Stăniloae quotes the texts of the New Testament speaking of baptism as something administered to the entire household (Acts 16:36; 1 Corinthians 1:16), and he quotes also Irenaeus, a spiritual grandchild of the apostle John, as Irenaeus was a supporter of infant baptism.[101]

One last element in the thought of Stăniloae's view of baptism is added, namely the sacrament of chrismation that comes immediately after baptism. Stăniloae discuss first, the connection of chrismation with baptism considering it "a continuation of baptism."[102] This act begins with the recitation of a prayer of invocation for the Holy Spirit to come in the life of the baptized,

---

99. Stăniloae, 42.

100. Stăniloae, 43. Also, Basil of Caesarea, "On the Spirit." Basil says,
Faith and Baptism are two kindred and inseparable ways of salvation: faith is perfected through baptism, baptism is established through faith, and both are completed by the same names. For as we believe in the Father and the Son and the Holy Ghost, as we are also baptized in the name of the Father, and of the Son and of the Holy Ghost; first comes the confession, introducing us to salvation, and baptism follows, setting the seal upon our ascent.
Basil of Caesarea, "On the Spirit," 181.

101. Stăniloae, *TDO*, 3, 44. See also, G. R. Beasley-Murray, *Baptism in the New Testament* (Carlisle, Cumbria: Paternoster, 1962), 312.

102. Stăniloae, *TDO*, 3, 45.

born again in baptism, and now in this act, through the prayer of a priest, empowered and protected by the Spirit. Stăniloae focuses then on the power of the holy oil to start the work of the powers received in baptism, according to the teachings of Nicholas Cabasilas and Alexander Schmemann.[103]

Coming to the Scriptures, Stăniloae considers the teaching of Cyril of Alexandria, who taught that the anointing of Aaron for the priesthood in the Old Testament is the model of the baptized persons' chrismation. In this act, as part of the general priesthood, the baptized persons are "actually" united with the church of Christ, being until now, through baptism, "only virtually" united with it. Second, Stăniloae argues the special work of the Holy Spirit in the sacrament of chrismation. He again uses the Old Testament act of the anointment of "prophets, priests and kings," as a means through which divine power came upon them. He also considers that Christ is the Anointed One, becoming the prophet, priest, and king who "introduces and keeps in the familiarity of God."[104] Third, Stăniloae argues the significance of the seen act of chrismation. He explains the elements of the act, namely, oil, the anointing and the words spoken "the seal of the Holy Spirit." The oil, he says, is imbibed in the body and signifies the assimilation of the new man, whilst the persistence of it on the body signifies the continuous communion of the Holy Spirit with the baptized person. Also, the odor of the oil signifies the intimacy of the work of the Holy Spirit in the baptized persons. This odor, signifies not only the vertical dimension of the work of the Holy Spirit in the baptized person, but also signifies that the person, with the pneumatic new life, will express horizontally the fruit of the Holy Spirit, in the relationships of this person with others.[105]

---

103. Stăniloae, 46. Also, Alexander Schmemann, *For the Life of the Word: Sacraments and Orthodoxy* (Crestwood, NY: St. Vladimir's Seminary Press, 1973). Schmemann argues that:
> In the Orthodox Church, what we call today the second sacrament of initiation – that of chrismation (or confirmation) – has always been an integral part of the baptismal liturgy . . . Confirmation is thus the personal Pentecost of man, his entrance into the new life on the Holy Spirit . . . it is his ordination as truly and fully man . . . his ordination to be *himself*, to become what God wants him to be . . . Confirmation is the opening of man to the wholeness of divine creation, to the true *catholicity* of life.

Schmemann, *For the Life*, 75–76.
104. Stăniloae, *TDO*, 3, 48.
105. Stăniloae, 51.

Stăniloae quotes the apostle Paul in 2 Corinthians 1:14–15, and explains it, through the thought of Cyril of Alexandria, who considers that odor is "the state of sacrifice that the believers live in Christ," in the mortification of the old man.[106] Stăniloae also quotes the apostle John, in regard to the persistence of the Spirit in us, as anointment, especially in the experiential knowledge of God, a knowledge that is to be made known also to others. Stăniloae considers that the anointment of 1 John 2:27 is directly connected with the general priesthood of all believers.[107]

Stăniloae continues by arguing the fact that chrismation is the strengthening of the baptized in order "to develop the new life through working together of the believer with the Holy Spirit." This is signified in the practice of chrismation, with the anointing of all the important members of the body, including the five senses. The anointment of the forehead signifies the fact that the mind is imprinted with the Spirit, the ears' anointment signifies the capacity to hear "the divine mysteries," the nostrils' anointment signifies the protection against the "odours that tempt towards evil." The breast's anointment signifies the capacity to resist evil (Eph 6). Then the anointment is done on the hands and feet an act that signifies the predisposition towards doing and walking in good.[108] Stăniloae continues:

> Through Chrismation the Holy Spirit enters and is imprinted in these members and organs of the body and in the powers of the soul that are at the foundation of them, and persists in them as a good odor like the oil. He is imprinted as a seal not only externally on these members but also internally, giving to man a united spiritual image . . . The Spirit produces an effect or imprints a bigger power accommodated to that organ . . . The Spirit produces a special gift in each man through the strengthening of a certain organ, producing a different gift in each member of the church.[109]

---

106. Stăniloae, 52.
107. Stăniloae, 52–53.
108. Stăniloae, 53.
109. Stăniloae, 54.

3.4. Summary of Chapter 3

I aimed in this chapter to explore the integrative way Stăniloae regards baptism as part of the Christian spiritual journey. I have argued from the understanding of the unique way Stăniloae's thought works in concentric circles, not only in regard to the complementary work of the persons of the Trinity, but also in the complementarity of different stages of the believers' spiritual journey. Therefore, the first dimension that I explored is that of the frame of Stăniloae's theology of participation. I observed that there are three pillars of Stăniloae's theology of participation. I argued that the first pillar is his concept of the being of God, with its super-essential and spiritual attributes and inner Trinitarian relations. The second pillar is constituted by the super-essential attributes of God, namely, infinity, simplicity, eternity, supraspatiality, omnipotence. The third pillar is constituted by the spiritual attributes of God: omniscience, justice and mercy, holiness, goodness and love.

Second, I have argued that the heart of Stăniloae's theology of participation is the Holy Trinity who is a mystery revealed in multiple directions. The first direction is that the Holy Trinity is the structure of supreme love. Second, the Holy Trinity is the foundation of our salvation, revealing itself in the work of salvation. The third is that, the Holy Trinity is the mystery of perfect unity of distinct persons, a mystery that is expressed in human beings, being the foundation of Christian spirituality.

From the understanding of the frame and the heart of Stăniloae's theology of participation I proceeded then to explore his thought about baptism as an important initiatory stage in the Christian spiritual journey. I have argued that for Stăniloae, baptism reflects and expresses the salvific work of the Trinity. This reflection is seen in the complementarity of the work of the Son and of the Spirit that is the foundation for redemptive reality in humans.

For Stăniloae, Trinitarian participation in the transfiguration of humanity is the basis for humanity's participative answer to God's participation in baptism, as expressing the birth that is the coming out from spiritual death and it is the entrance into the new life in God. Moreover, I argued that baptism is for Stăniloae the start of the participatory journey of salvation for the human being, a journey assisted and empowered by the Holy Spirit. Baptism is therefore, first, the death of the old man and resurrection, and total submission to God, and in this way, an immersion into the eternal life of God. Baptism is second, in Stăniloae's thought, the power of continual spiritual growth shown in the cultivation of Christian virtues. Third, baptism is the reconstruction of Christ's image in a human being, and fourth, baptism is the entrance door to the church.

Eventually, I have shown that the consistency of Stăniloae's working in concentric circles in regard with the complementary work of the Christ and the Spirit is seen and reflected in his argument of the complementarity and inseparability of baptism and chrismation, a sacrament that comes immediately after baptism, being in Stăniloae's view a continuation of baptism. How the Eucharist as a consecutive stage of the Christian spiritual journey reflects the reality of divine *perichoresis*, and as such completes and actualizes the reality of baptism and chrismation, will be argued in the next chapter.

CHAPTER 4

Stăniloae's Theology of the Eucharist as a Reflection of *Perichoresis*

It could seem odd to argue the reflection of *perichoresis* in Stăniloae's thought about the Eucharist, when in Eastern thought, and Stăniloae is not an exception, following Palamas, there is a distinction between the being or essence of God and the works or energies of God.[1] Accordingly, the concept of *perichoresis* belongs to the essence of God, and the human participation with or in God is possible by the way of God's energies. Moreover, it has been argued that Stăniloae understands the uncreated energies as "producing sensitivity in the human soul," and as such the energies are "directly connected with the doctrine of *theosis*."[2] Speaking about the way Stăniloae sees the concept of *perichoresis*, Bartoş argues:

> Stăniloae closely follows Maximus's idea of *perichoresis* as the divine penetration into the human level . . . *perichoresis* means a reciprocity within the divine-human relationship, a double penetration . . . Following Maximus, Stăniloae sees in *perichoresis* the real act of the deification of human nature. Stăniloae affirms that the divine nature becomes united with the human nature in the person of the Word by "mutual inherence" or by inter-penetration.[3]

From the Trinitarian and christological levels of the reality of *perichoresis*, Stăniloae is inspired by its reality when he argues the theology of the church.

---

1. Stăniloae, *Viaţa şi învăţătura Sfântului Grigorie Palama*, 65.
2. Bartoş, *Deification*, 59.
3. Bartoş, 182–183. Also, Stăniloae, *TDO*, 2, 90–92.

Considering that the use of Trinitarian *perichoresis* is "more consistent with the way Stăniloae uses the concept of *perichoresis*," than that of christological or deification meanings of *perichoresis*,[4] Mănăstireanu considers as legitimate the use of the *perichoresis* concept as a model for the church in Stăniloae's theology. Mănăstireanu starts from the observation of "the patristic theme of the Church as an icon of the Trinity . . . a community defined in terms of perichoretic terms."[5] He concludes:

> We favour a view of the Church in which the human members are called to relate perichoretically to each other, in Christ and through the Spirit – we called this "the perichoretical model of the Church," a perspective proper to Stăniloae . . . At the same time, we need to keep in mind that this is true only analogically, since a direct transfer from the level of divine to the human level is not legitimate.[6]

---

4. Mănăstireanu, *PM*, 123.

5. Mănăstireanu, 125–127. He argues that according to this concept "the Church has a mimetic relationship with its archetype, the Holy Trinity. That means that the members of the Church are called to imitate in their createdness, in an iconic manner the relationships existing eternally between the divine persons." (Mănăstireanu, 125). Quoting Cyril of Alexandria, *The Commentary on the Gospel of Saint John*, Mănăstireanu argues the meaning of the perichoretical model of the Church: "Being an icon of the Holy Trinity, the Church is called to reflect in her spatio-temporal reality, in Christ and through the power of the Holy Spirit, the dynamic relationships existing eternally between the divine persons, as described by the concept of Trinitarian perichoresis." (Mănăstireanu, *PM*, 127). See also, Ion Bria, *Spațiul nemuririi*, 21. Bria quotes Stăniloae's interpretation of Athanasius, about the church in perichoretical terms: "She is the reciprocal interiority of those abiding in the reciprocal interiority of the persons of the Holy Trinity, which is brought about in us through Christ who became human." (Bria, *Spațiul nemuririi*, 21). Also, Atanasie cel Mare, *Scrieri 2*, trans. Dumitru Stăniloae (București: EIBMBOR, 1988), 85. Also, Ivana Noble, *Theological Interpretation of Culture in Post-Communist Context: Central and East European Search for Roots* (Burlington, VT: Ashgate, 2010). She says that "the whole world with all its diversity has been set on a journey towards greater in God and with each other. This is expressed both in Dionysius and in Stăniloae by a circular movement, not in order to emphasize repetition, but in order to stress the perichoretic nature of relationships that are the image of the *perichoresis* of the Holy Trinity." (Noble, *Theological Interpretation*, 53).

6. Mănăstireanu, *PM*, 265. Also, Colin E. Gunton, *The One, the Three and the Many: God, Creation and the Culture of Modernity* (Cambridge: Cambridge University Press, 1993). Gunton argues that "perichoresis can be developed to serve as an analogical concept," (Gunton, *The One, the Three*, 164). He continues: "it must enable us to . . . begin to explore whether reality is on all its levels 'perichoretic,' a dynamism of relatedness," (Gunton, 165), and asks: "Does the concept enable us to find a framework, or better because of more dynamic, coordinates for our human being in the world?" (Gunton, 166).

With these clarifications and following Mănăstireanu, in the opinion that Stăniloae's view about the ecclesial relationships is inspired by the concept of *perichoresis*, and with Gunton's clarification about the analogical use of *perichoresis*, we will try to explore the way Stăniloae's view of the Eucharist, as a constitutive reality for the life of the church and for the Christian spiritual journey, is a reflection of Trinitarian *perichoresis*.

4.1. The Triad of Baptism, Chrismation and the Eucharist

The first dimension in which *perichoresis* is reflected in the thought of Stăniloae in regard to the Eucharist is the interpenetration between baptism, chrismation and the Eucharist, as three complementary realities of initiatory process in the church. Even though it seems that the three are consecutive stages (having baptism in the beginning of the process, chrismation is the middle stage and the Eucharist in the end of this process)[7] for Stăniloae, as he works in concentric circles, they are simultaneously overlapping, interpenetrated and complementary features of the same reality – that of participation in the divine movement towards humanity, of the Father, in the Son, through the Holy Spirit.

Therefore, for Stăniloae the movement in the Eucharist that is the present impregnation of the final state of perfection, overlaps with the movement of developing, through personal participation, the divine power that is encapsulated within the inner being of the baptized person. This participation is possible through the complementarity between baptism and the Eucharist, baptism being a reality of the death of the old man, and a reality of permanent dedication of the entire being to God. As such baptism is a double reality that opens and facilitates the reality of participation in Christ's resurrection that is the Eucharist.[8]

This is the why for Stăniloae, the Eucharist is not merely a means to be united with Christ who was born and died for our sins, it is also a union with Christ who dies and is resurrected to eternal life. As such the Eucharist for Stăniloae "sows in us the power of total surrender of our existence to God,

---

7. Stăniloae, *TDO*, 3, 56.
8. Stăniloae, 56–57.

in order to receive it back full with His eternal life." From here Stăniloae argues that the Eucharist is not concerned with the present life but with the eternal life, and this is so because, "the new life from Baptism, that follows the death of the old man, cannot exist without the perspective of the eternal life that is sustained by the Eucharist."[9]

The Eucharist, continues Stăniloae, being an act that makes Christ's resurrection a reality interior to us, gives us the power to die to sin and to surrender ourselves to God, and also the power to receive our real death as Christ accepted it, as a way to the eternal life. Moreover, the Eucharist is the "medication for eternity,"[10] and Stăniloae is happy with this remark of the Fathers that he considers is sustained by the sayings of Jesus in John 6:54–58.[11] Stăniloae's thought reflects the theology of *perichoresis* in this complementarity of baptism and the Eucharist, "the mysterious death of Christ, that we share in, through Eucharist, in a more profound way than in baptism, as preparation for our real death and for the full inner death after that, . . . the inner death, the immersion in God, . . . that is not dissolution . . . is immersion in the infinite life that is in God."[12]

The mutual interpenetration between baptism and the Eucharist is seen in Stăniloae's argument in the fact that the initial forgetting of the old man in baptism is indwelled in the repeated deaths of the old man through the repeated eucharistic acts, and that through each we realize a discontinuity with the old man. Moreover, Christ's union with us through his own body and blood happens as we eat his body and drink his blood, and the resurrected quality of his body and blood are permeating our body and blood without being confused with each other.[13] In his own words:

---

9. Stăniloae, 57–58.

10. Stăniloae, 58. Also, Clement of Alexandria, "The Instructor," in *Ante–Nicene Fathers*, vol. 2, *Fathers of the Second Century*, eds. Alexander Roberts and James Donaldson (Peabody, MA: Hendrickson, 2004). Clement argues that "to drink the blood of Jesus, is to become partaker of the Lord's immortality; the Spirit being the energetic principle of the Word, as blood is of flesh. Accordingly, as wine is blended with water so is the Spirit with man. And the one, the mixture of wine and water, nourishes to faith; while the other, the Spirit, conducts to immortality," (Clement, "Instructor," 242).

11. Stăniloae, *TDO*, 3, 58.

12. Stăniloae, 60.

13. Stăniloae, 61.

The union with the Lord in Eucharist is a full union because He is working in us not only through the energy brought to us by the Holy Spirit, but also with His body and blood, imprinted in our body and blood . . . And because we are subject to our own body and blood, and of the works penetrated by the body and the works of Christ, we are together subject with Christ of our own body, that became also His Body or of His body that became our body.[14]

From this vertical dimension of the mutual interpenetration, namely Christ's union with us and our union with him, in the Eucharist, Stăniloae continues with its horizontal dimension. He argues that union with Christ in the Eucharist is the foundation for the union between the members of the church, in the interpenetrating participation of each in the other, without the dissolution of the believers' persons.[15] For this mutual participation, to be a reality in the life of the church, there is necessary, in Stăniloae's opinion, the concept of the real presence of Christ, under the image of bread and wine.[16]

4.2. Real Presence and Human Sacrifice of Submission

The second dimension that mirrors *perichoresis* in Stăniloae's theology of the Eucharist, is that of the interpenetration of the real presence of the

---

14. Stăniloae, 62.

15. Stăniloae, 62–63. See also G. W. H. Lampe, "The Eucharist in the Thought of the Early Church," in *Eucharist Theology Then and Now*, ed. R. E. Clements (London: SPCK, 1968). He says: "Commemoration of his passion and resurrection, participation by faith in his suffering, and through the assurance of hope, in his risen life are the ground and focus of the Church's Eucharist" (Lampe, "Eucharist," 38).

16. Stăniloae, *TDO*, 3, 64. Also Cyril of Jerusalem, "Lectures 22:3, 9," in *Nicene and Post-Nicene Fathers,* series 2, vol. 7, ed. Philip Schaff (Peabody, MA: Hendrickson, 1999), 152. He says that:
> in the figure of Bread is given to thee His Body, and in the figure of Wine His Blood; that thou by partaking of the Body and Blood of Christ, mayest be made of the same body and the same blood with Him. For thus we come to bear Christ in us, because His Body and Blood are distributed through our members; thus it is that, according to the blessed Peter, *we become partakers of the divine nature* . . . the seeming bread is not bread though sensible to taste, but the Body of Christ; and that the seeming wine is not wine, though the taste will have it so, but the Blood of Christ.

Cyril, "Lectures," 152.

body and blood of Christ in the Eucharist, and of the human sacrifice of submission and surrender to God, as enacted in the concluding mediation of the priest and bishop as representatives of both movements, from God to us and from us to God.[17]

First, is the real presence of the body and blood of Christ in the Eucharist that continues the renaissance of man from Christ that started in baptism. The Eucharist is a feeding of man from him, having a double foundation in the sacrifice of Christ on the cross and in the perennial presence of Christ in the Eucharist, through his resurrected body and blood.[18] Stăniloae considers that through the Eucharist we have a perpetual remembering of Christ's incarnation, sacrifice and resurrection, in his unity with us.[19] Moreover, Stăniloae says that through the Eucharist "we proclaim" the incarnation, sacrifice and resurrection of the Son of God, and this reality, constituted by the three acts of Christ, is not only past reality, rather it is a repeated reality. In fact the presence of the pneumatized Christ after resurrection and in the Eucharist is, says Stăniloae, a big mystery because of the mysterious transformation of the bread and wine into the real body and blood of Christ.[20]

The transformation of the bread and wine into the body and blood of Christ is another way in which, in the thought of Stăniloae, the *perichoresis* is reflected in the Eucharist. The union of the bread with the body of Christ, as hypostasis of the Word, transforms the bread into the body of Christ.[21] The body of Christ is deified and pneumatized because of his permanent hypostatic union with God, while our body starts the journey towards

---

17. Stăniloae, *TDO*, 3, 64–82.

18. Stăniloae, 64–65. Also, Joseph Cardinal Ratzinger, *Called to Communion: Understanding the Church Today* (San Francisco, CA: Ignatius Press, 1996), 36–37. Ratzinger argues that "the Lord becomes our bread, our food. He gives us his body, which by the way, must be understood in the light of the Resurrection . . . Christ gives himself-Christ, who in his Resurrection has continued to exist in a new kind of bodiliness." (Ratzinger, *Called to Communion*, 36–37).

19. See also, Paul VI, "Constitution of the Sacred Liturgy (*Sacrosantum Concilium*)," in *The Documents of Vatican II*, ed. Walter. M. Abbott (Baltimore, MD: America Press, 1966), 154. The document says that Christ "entrusted to His beloved spouse, the Church, a memorial of His death and resurrection: a sacrament of love, a sign of unity, a bond of charity, a paschal banquet, in which Christ is consumed, the mind is filled with grace, and a pledge of future glory is given to us." (Paul VI, "Constitution," 154).

20. Stăniloae, *TDO*, 3, 66–69.

21. Stăniloae, 69.

deification and pneumatization, and both remain distinct bodies. Coming to the elements of the Eucharist, Stăniloae states:

> Bread and wine are nature raised to the status of direct food and drink of our body. Through the law of the new being from us, our body transforms his substance in these substances. In the same way Christ transforms these substances, into His body. But through His Spirit He transforms instantly the Eucharistic bread into His body, as a member of manifestation of His hypostasis and of His Spirit.[22]

Moreover, Christ does not transform the bread and wine into his body for himself, but for us, to offer the possibility for us to participate and share in him.[23] Yet, this participation and sharing is conditioned by the way the human persons surrender and desire this sharing. This leads to the second element of the continuum that reflects the *perichoresis* in the Eucharist, namely, our own sacrifice of surrender and submission to God.[24]

---

22. Stăniloae, 70. For a different view see Calvin, *Institutes*, 1362. He speaks of the "spiritual presence of Christ," and about the fact that:
> from the physical things set forth in the Sacrament we are led by a sort of analogy to spiritual things. Thus when bread is given as a symbol of Christ's body, we must at once grasp the comparison: as bread nourishes, sustains, and keeps the life of our body, so Christ's body is the only food to invigorate, and enliven our soul, When we see the wine set forth as a symbol of blood, we must reflect on the benefits which wine imparts to the body, and to realize that the same are spiritually imparted to us by Christ's blood. These benefits are to nourish, refresh, strengthen and gladden.

Calvin, *Institutes*, 1362.

23. John Karmiris, "Concerning the Sacraments," in *Eastern Orthodox Theology: A Contemporary Reader*, ed. Daniel B. Clendenin (Grand Rapids, MI: Baker Academic, 2003), 26. Karmiris argues that "in the Holy Eucharist the faithful truly participate in the real body and blood of Christ. They are mystically united with and incorporated into him" (Karmiris, "Concerning the Sacraments," 26).

24. Stăniloae, *TDO*, 3, 71. Also, Ratzinger, *Called to Communion*, 37, 39. He argues the concept of communion in Eucharist in terms that reflect *perichoresis*:
> The outward action of eating becomes the expression of that intimate penetration of two subjects . . . Communion means that the seemingly uncrossable frontier of my "I" is left wide open and can be so because Jesus has first allowed himself to be opened completely, has taken us all into himself and has put himself totally in our hands, Hence, communion means the fusion of existences. (Ratzinger, *Called to Communion*, 37).

Speaking about this intimate union of the church with Christ, Ratzinger argues it in perichoretical key:

Stăniloae argues the centrality of Christ in the entire process of bringing us to the Father and the Father's grace to us and he also argues that Christ does not see believers as objects but as persons.[25] He says that the blessed bread of the Eucharist is a symbol of the bread that sustains the life of human beings and through the action of the Holy Spirit this bread is transformed into the body of Christ and as such it transforms and deifies the life of believers, and as such the Eucharist is of the church.[26]

For Stăniloae the Eucharist is the meeting place between the two inseparable movements, a descendent movement of God towards believers through his grace, and an ascendant movement of believers towards God, through sacrifice. As such the Eucharist is part of a larger complementarity of the two

---

> the Church is the body of Christ in the way in which the woman is one body with, or rather one flesh, with the man . . . the Church is the Body, not by virtue of an identity without distinction, but rather by means of the pneumatic-real act of spousal love . . . this means that Christ and the Church are one body in the sense in which man and woman are one flesh, that is, in such a way that in their indissoluble spiritual-bodily union, they nonetheless remain unconfused and inmingled. (Ratzinger, 39).

25. Stăniloae, *TDO*, 3, 73.

26. Stăniloae, 74. See also, Gregory of Nyssa, "The Great Catechism," in *Nicene and Post-Nicene Fathers*, series 2, vol. 5, ed. Philip Schaff (Peabody, MA: Hendrickson, 2007), 506. Gregory says that in the Eucharist "He disseminates Himself in every believer through that flesh, whose substance comes from bread and wine, blending Himself with the bodies of believers, to secure that, by this union with the immortal, man, too, may be a sharer in incorruption." (Gregory, "Great Catechism," 506). See also, Ioannis Zizioulas, *Creația ca Euharistie* (București: Editura Bizantină, 1999). Zizioulas argues for a eucharistic vision of the world, (Zizioulas, *Creația ca Euharistie*, 17). Also, Paul Evdokimov, *L'Orthodoxie* (Neuchâtel: Delachaux et Niestlé, 1959). Evdokimov, speaking about remembrance in Eucharist says: "All the holy suppers of the Church are nothing else than one eternal and unique Supper, that of Christ in the Upper Room. The same divine act both takes place at a specific moment in history, and is offered always in the sacrament," (Evdokimov, *L'Orthodoxie*, 241). Ware, *Orthodox Church*, speaking of the Eucharist presents a balanced view when saying that even though "the events of Christ's sacrifice – the Incarnation, the Last Supper, the Crucifixion, the Resurrection, and the Ascension – are not repeated in the Eucharist but they are *made present*," (Ware, 287). Alexander Schmemann, *The Eucharist: Sacrament of the Kingdom* (New York: St. Vladimir's Seminary Press, 1988). Schmemann argues that the Eucharist of the assembly is only the beginning of this sacrament, its culmination being "the manifestation of the presence of the kingdom of God," in the church's "place and ministry in the world," (Schmemann, *Eucharist*, 29). See also Ioan I. Ică Jr, "Împărtășirea continuă pro și contra – o dispută perenă și lecțiile ei" [Continuous Sharing, for and against – a perennial dispute and its lessons], in *Împărtășirea continuă cu Sfintele Taine* [Continuous Sharing with the Holy Sacraments] (Sibiu: Deisis, 2006), 84.

movements present also in the other sacraments of the initiation process, namely, baptism, chrismation, repentance, and priesthood.[27]

4.3. Christ, the Priest and the Church

Stăniloae argues for the concluding mediation of the priest and bishop in the Eucharist. The priest is in Stăniloae's opinion, the seen maker of the Eucharist in his double role as the representative of Christ and of the church.[28] He connects the role of the priest and the church, with the fact that in the Old Testament the paschal Lamb could be sacrificed only in Jerusalem. In the same way he says, the Eucharist cannot happen except in the church through the priest.[29] This is eventually why, says Stăniloae, intercommunion with other faiths (namely other Christian traditions) is not acceptable for the Eastern Orthodox Church.[30]

The essential role of the priest is, in Stăniloae's opinion, rooted in the fact that the Holy Spirit works through his actions and prayers. He says also that the transformation of the elements of the Eucharist (bread and wine) into the body of Christ is the follow-up of the word of institution said by Christ in the Last Supper, words that operate in and because of the priest's prayer called *epiclesis*.[31] To be sure Stăniloae is careful to say that it is not the priest who is *doing* the Sacrament, rather the Holy Spirit, even though the role of the priest cannot be denied, because by denying the role of the priest, implicitly, one denies the concretization of God's salvific work in the "objective seen work of the priest."[32] Stăniloae tries to support this argument with the idea of the consistency between the old and new covenants.

---

27. Stăniloae, *TDO*, 3, 72–74.

28. Stăniloae, 78. Also, Zizioulas, *Being as Communion*, 153. See also, Veli-Matti Kärkkäinen, *An Introduction to Eclessiology: Ecumenical, Historical and Global Perspectives* (Downers Grove, IL: InterVarsity Press, 2002), 97.

29. Stăniloae, *TDO*, 3, 79.

30. Stăniloae, 79–80. See also, Kallistos Ware, "Communion and Intercommunion," in *Primary Readings on the Eucharist*, ed. Thomas J. Fusch (Collegeville, MN: Liturgical Press, 2004). He says that "the technical term 'intercommunion' . . . is a word of modern coinage, not to be found in the Bible, the Fathers or the Holy Canons. The Bible, the Fathers, and the Canons know of only two possibilities: communion and non-communion," (Ware, "Communion and Intercommunion," 195).

31. Stăniloae, *TDO, 3*, 80.

32. Stăniloae, 82.

Or in his own words, "The Law of the New Testament fulfils the one of the Old Testament. In the same way there were necessary objective sacrifices through priests, here must be brought the sacrifice of Christ, through the priest."[33] He concludes by quoting Cyril of Alexandria, with his opinion that based on Numbers 3:6–10, as the office in the inside part of the temple is the exclusive prerogative of the priests, the office of the priests in the new covenant should have also the prerogative of the office inside the church.

Stăniloae considers that if in the case of baptism is added an essential sacrament that completes it, namely the sacrament of chrismation, in the case of the Eucharist it is paired by the sacrament of confession or repentance. For Stăniloae the sacrament of confession or repentance means the forgiveness of sins, of those who confess their sins and are sorry for them, a forgiveness given by the bishop or priest. Stăniloae argues again for the central place of the priest in this sacrament as the seen organ of Christ and as a representative of the church. The reason the priests have this role is that they are already overcomers of human sinful flesh and of its passions.[34]

As in the case of baptism that is complemented by chrismation, Stăniloae argues the complementarity between the Eucharist and repentance includes three elements. The first element is that of confession, the second is that of repentance and the third is that of priestly absolution. For Stăniloae confession is a sacrament of communion between the penitent and the priest, being not a general confession, rather it is an opening of his soul to the priest in order for him to look inside.[35] The role of the priest is seen in the fact that he needs to follow carefully the confession and lead the penitent to the essential elements of his sinfulness in order for the confession to be appropriate. The aim, says Stăniloae is to re-establish the communion between the penitent and the priest, as the seen organ of Christ and as the representative of the church. Stăniloae says, "No other man could fulfill this role to intermediate of the extended communion with other people and with God, except the priest in the sacrament of Confession."[36] From the first element of confession Stăniloae continues with the second element,

---

33. Stăniloae, 82.
34. Stăniloae, 83–84.
35. Stăniloae, 86–87.
36. Stăniloae, 87–88.

that of repentance. Stăniloae considers that this element is again the priests' prerogative. He says, "If in listening to the confession he exercised the role of an understanding friend, and of a judge and doctor who evaluate the nature and the gravity of those who confess, now he exercises especially the role of a judge doubled by that of a doctor, who evaluates the appropriate means to cure the found weaknesses."[37]

Therefore the priest prescribes,[38] or imposes[39] penances or *epitimia*. Stăniloae discusses extensively the practice of imposing penances in the history of the church, some of them connected with the forbidding of sharing in the Eucharist. The third element of the sacrament of confession, in Stăniloae's argument, is that of priest's absolution. The priest is praying for the release of the sinner from their sin. Stăniloae sees in this that Christ is forgiving the sin and that "it is the priest's prayer that effectively makes present the forgiveness that comes from Christ,"[40] the priest exercising his double spiritual interpenetration with the believer, and with Christ.[41]

4.4. Summary of Chapter 4

I aimed in this chapter to explore the way in which Stăniloae, consistently, continues to work in concentric circles, in his though about the Eucharist. I have argued that for Stăniloae the inner Trinitarian relations expressed by the concept of perichoresis, constitute the model of relations between different stages of the Christian spiritual journey.

Therefore, I argued in the beginning that the first dimension in which perichoresis is reflected in the thought of Stăniloae in regard to the Eucharist is the interpenetration between baptism, chrismation and eucharist, as three complementary realities of initiatory process in the church. From here I understood that for Stăniloae the movement in the Eucharist that is the present impregnation of the final state of perfection, overlaps with the movement

---

37. Stăniloae, 91.
38. Stăniloae, *The Experience of God, Orthodox Dogmatic Theology*, vol. 5, *The Sanctifying Mysteries* (Brookline, MA: Holy Cross Orthodox Press, 2012), 125 (henceforth referred to as, *Mysteries*).
39. Ware, *Orthodox Church*, 290.
40. Stăniloae, *Mysteries*, 131. Also, Stăniloae, *TDO*, 3, 95.
41. Stăniloae, *TDO*, 3, 95–96.

of developing, through personal participation, the divine power that is encapsulated within the inner being of the baptized person.

This is why for Stăniloae, the Eucharist is not merely a means to be united with Christ who was born and died for our sins, it is also a union with Christ who dies and is resurrected to eternal life. As such the Eucharist, for Stăniloae, sows in us the power of total surrender of our existence to God in order to receive it back full with his eternal life. From here Stăniloae argues that the Eucharist is not concerned with the present life but with the eternal life, and this is so because, "the new life from Baptism, that follows the death of the old man, cannot exist without the perspective of the eternal life that is sustained by the Eucharist."

The Eucharist, continues Stăniloae, being an act that makes Christ's resurrection a reality interior to us, gives us the power to die to sin and to surrender ourselves to God, and also the power to receive our real death as Christ accepted it, as a way to the eternal life. Moreover, the Eucharist is the medication for eternity. He argues that union with Christ in the Eucharist is the foundation for the union between the members of the church, in the interpenetrating participation of each in the other, without the dissolution of the believers' persons. For this mutual participation to be a reality in the life of the church there is necessary, in Stăniloae's opinion, the concept of the real presence of Christ, under the image of bread and wine.

The second dimension that mirrors *perichoresis* in Stăniloae's theology of the Eucharist, is that of the interpenetration of the real presence of the body and blood of Christ in the Eucharist and of the human sacrifice of submission and surrender to God, as enacted in the concluding mediation of the priest and bishop as representatives of both movements, from God to us and from us to God.

The real presence of the body and blood of Christ in the Eucharist continues the renaissance of man from Christ that started in baptism. As such, the Eucharist is a feeding of man from him, and through the Eucharist we have perpetual remembering of Christ's incarnation, sacrifice and resurrection, in his unity with us. Moreover, through the Eucharist "we proclaim" the incarnation, sacrifice and resurrection of the Son of God.

The transformation of the bread and wine into the body and blood of Christ, is another way in which in the thought of Stăniloae, the *perichoresis* is reflected in the Eucharist. The union of the bread with the body of Christ, as hypostasis of the Word, transforms the bread into the body of Christ. The body of Christ is deified and pneumatized because of his permanent hypostatic union with God, while our body starts the journey towards deification and pneumatization, and both remain distinct bodies.

Consistently, Stăniloae works in concentric circles when he sees the Eucharist as the meeting place between the two inseparable movements, a descendent movement of God towards believers through his grace, and an ascendant movement of believers towards God, through sacrifice. As such the Eucharist is part of a larger complementarity of the two movements present also in the other sacraments of the initiation process, namely, baptism, chrismation, repentance, and priesthood. Consistent with that complementarity, Stăniloae argues for the concluding mediation of the priest and bishop in the Eucharist, as the priest is, in Stăniloae's opinion, the seen maker of the Eucharist in his double role as the representative of Christ and of the church.

Eventually, I have argued that similar with the complementarity between baptism and chrismation, Stăniloae argues the complementarity between the Eucharist and repentance, that includes three elements. The first element is that of confession, the second is that of repentance and the third is that of priestly absolution. For Stăniloae confession is a sacrament of communion between the penitent and the priest, being not a general confession, rather it is an opening of his soul to the priest in order for him to look inside.

CHAPTER 5

Stăniloae's Theology of Spirituality as Actualization of the Trinitarian Christological-Pneumatological Convergence

5.1. The Cruciformity of Christian Spirituality

For Stăniloae, the space where Christian spirituality is embodied is the world as the gift of God[1] to humanity, and as such the world is the first reality in which God imprinted the cross.[2] The reason for this imprint of the cross on the different domains of life in the world, says Stăniloae, is the attachment of humanity to the gift, the ephemeral things of the world, forgetting at the same time the giver, God.[3] Stăniloae argues the universality of the cross that is carried differently by the people of the world. Accordingly, there is a way of carrying the cross, proper to unbelievers, namely, a cross without the hope of transforming resurrection, and a way of carrying the cross, proper to believers, namely, a cross with the hope of resurrection.[4]

---

1. Stăniloae, *TDO*, 1, 234. Also, Schmemann, *For the Life*, 14. See also, Miller, *Gift of the World*, 58–60.

2. Stăniloae, *TDO*, 1, 236. See also, Evdokimov, *Vârstele vieții spirituale*. Evdokimov speaks of the discovery and understanding of your "personal cross" that the spiritual life does provide, "introducing, an order, and discovering a rhythm of your own growth, demanding a progressive walk," (Evdokimov, 63–64).

3. Dumitru Stăniloae, *The Victory of the Cross* (Oxford: SLG Press, 2001), 1.

4. Stăniloae, *Victory of the Cross*, 2. It is here as I mentioned in chapter 4 that Stăniloae argues his theology of the cross that roots the way in which the Christian life means carrying

73

The second reality, on which the cross is imprinted, is that of relationships. Stăniloae argues that there is a cross and consequently suffering, for the loved ones as they are in suffering (he gives the example of the parents who suffer for their children), and for the neighbours, a suffering that mirrors the suffering of Christ "who had pity on those who were suffering, and wept for those who were dead."[5] Then, says Stăniloae, there is a cross and consequently suffering, for the hostile ones, who became our enemies "on account of the noble and high convictions to which we remain faithful."[6] There is also a cross, and consequently suffering, for the erring ones, with them being "our children . . . our brethren . . . our neighbours," as we have to "carry their incomprehension of our good intentions."[7] Arguing the inevitability of the cross and suffering for authentic Christian spirituality Stăniloae affirms:

> without the cross there can be no true growth and no true strengthening of the spiritual life. To avoid the weight of the cross is to avoid our responsibility towards our brethren and our neighbours before God. Only by the cross can we remain in submission to God and in true love towards our neighbours. We cannot purify or develop our own spiritual life, nor that of others, nor that of the world in general, by seeking to avoid the cross . . . The way of the cross is the only way which leads upwards, the only way which carries creation towards the true heights for which it was made.[8]

Stăniloae makes a very important distinction between innocent suffering and suffering because of your own guilt. There has been only one purely innocent suffering, that of Christ, whose purity was proved in the fact that he carried a cross for our sins not because of his own. This is the why, says Stăniloae, in Christ the cross became the power of God for our salvation,

---

the cross towards resurrection, that is an important element in keeping together in their mutual synthesis the incarnation, life, death and resurrection of Christ.

5. Stăniloae, *Victory of the Cross*, 3–4.
6. Stăniloae, 3–4.
7. Stăniloae, 3–4.
8. Stăniloae, 4–5.

as in us "purity is always mixed with impurity, innocence with guilt and the cross comes to us in great part because of our fault, because of our sin."[9]

Moreover, from the personal level, that of accepting responsibility for suffering because of your own sinfulness, Stăniloae brings into attention another important element that defines the responsibility for the cross in relationships. Many times the suffering of someone is due to his limitation in regard to others with whom a relationship is not good. There is, says Stăniloae, almost always a double reason for enmity in relationships, therefore "I bear the cross for myself . . . and for them as well, since I carry this cross on account of the kind of person I am." For Stăniloae, in this context acceptance of the cross means acceptance of our own responsibility for others, acceptance of our own guilt, for only as such can one find his true humanity, be in a dialogical relationship with God, keeping "the ability to hear the word of God . . . and his neighbours word to him."[10]

The third reality on which the cross is imprinted is that of pleasures of the body and flesh that lead to pain. Stăniloae compares and contrasts the fleshly mechanism to overcome suffering in life, and the Christlike attitude to suffering. The first is indulgence in pleasure as a way to evade pain that produces a new pain,[11] the second is overcoming pleasure through bearing the cross, meaning a balancing in the human nature between "excessive sensibility, and re-establishing the power of the spirit." Stăniloae keeps Christ as the model:

> He did not overcome pleasure and pain by a sort of stoic insensibility, an inability to feel; he mastered them through the strengthening of his spirit . . . preserving yet transfiguring our full human sensibility . . . His cross means that the spirit is victorious over matter without making matter of no effect . . . but by transfiguring the material world through the response of a will wholly given to God.[12]

---

9. Stăniloae, 5.
10. Stăniloae, 6–8.
11. Stăniloae, 8.
12. Stăniloae, 9.

To be sure Stăniloae distinguishes, following Maximus the Confessor, the type of pleasure he is speaking of. It is "blind pleasure" characterized by the absence of "the vision of the spirit." Such pleasure will "inevitably bring sorrow," even though, being realistic, all human pleasures "tend to be blind pleasures," being self-oriented and lacking a horizon beyond themselves. The pain that comes as a consequence of such blind pleasure is characterized by a "spiritual feeling of weakness . . . of matter in the spiritual realm," as opposed to the cross that produces transparency of matter for the spirit and has as a consequence an opening of the "eyes of the spirit." This as such provides an understanding of the fact that "the cross is given to all of us to lead us towards the life of the spirit and as a means of re-establishing the dialogue of man with God."[13]

From the three realities over which Stăniloae sees the imprint of the cross, namely, the gift of the world, the relationships between human beings, and the pleasures of the body, he continues with three meanings of the imprint of the cross on the above realities that are overlapped in human existence. First, in Stăniloae's thought, one of the meanings of the cross' imprint on human existence is the revelation of God's transcendence over the gifts that he offers to the world and humanity. This is especially important in the face of suffering of the innocent, as reflected in the book of Job. In Stăniloae's perspective, Job's attitude, in his quest for an answer in regard to his suffering, reveals an important dimension of a human being's relationship with God. That is the necessary attachment to God as the giver instead of promoting an excessive concern for what he gives, a concern that "puts the gifts above the giver."[14]

> The point of view of Job's wife is basically the same as the point of view of Job's friends who say that God gives things to those who remain faithful to him and takes away his gifts when they become unfaithful. They say essentially the same thing because both affirm that man remains faithful to God on account of his gifts . . . Satan is a cynic and says that man loves God merely for the gifts . . . But God wishes to show by the example of

---

13. Stăniloae, 9–11.
14. Stăniloae, 11–13.

Job that there is such love, that man is capable of remaining attached to God himself even if he no longer receives his gifts.[15]

The second meaning of the cross' imprint on human existence, argues Stăniloae, is the revelation of God's sovereignty that provides an understanding of God's uniqueness. Continuing his reflection on Job's experience, Stăniloae uses the expression "to see God in all his greatness and wisdom and marvelous nature."[16] Like Job, argues Stăniloae, believers need to travel the road of making an "abstraction of the things of this world in order to think of God who is above all human understanding."[17] Stăniloae continues by saying that sometimes God himself intervenes in order to interrupt a human being's attachment to things or to his gifts, an intervention that is regarded many times, from the human perspective as his abandonment. In fact it is God's hiddenness, in order to provide a revelation at a superior level. Only in these coordinates, says Stăniloae, "we enter into a relationship with God, which is truly personal, a relationship which is above all created things."[18]

The third meaning of the cross' imprint in human existence is the revelation of the true love for God as person, despite the presence or absence of his gifts. It is the love that is, says Stăniloae, perfectly expressed by Christ, the one who loved humanity when she was in enmity and rebellion towards God. Stăniloae considers that only a love such as Christ's is "true love" because in true love, "a man should transcend himself, go beyond himself."[19] In the light of the three realities on which the cross is imprinted and of the three meanings for that imprint, Stăniloae concludes,

---

15. Stăniloae, 13.
16. Stăniloae, 16–18.
17. Stăniloae, 16–18.
18. Stăniloae, 16–18.
19. Stăniloae, 19–20. Also, Christos Yannaras, *Elements of Faith: An Introduction to Orthodox Theology*, trans. Keith Schram (Edinburgh: T & T Clark, 1991), 5. Yannaras speaks of a "religious need . . . that is in within man . . . to relate to something which surpasses him, to some existence much superior to his own." (Yannaras, *Elements of Faith*, 5). This would be very similar to what the Catholic theologian Karl Rahner calls supernatural existential, the gift of God which enables us to respond to God's call to us. See in this regard Karl Rahner, *Foundations of Christian Faith: An Introduction to the Idea of Christianity* (New York: Crossroad, 1978), 126–128. In Rahner's words: "God's self-communication is given not only as a gift, but also as the necessary condition which makes possible an acceptance of the gift," (Rahner, *Foundations*, 128).

> We cannot think of the cross without the world as the gift of God. But on the other side we cannot think of the world without the cross . . . The cross completes the fragmentary meaning of this world . . . The cross reveals the destiny of the world as it is drawn towards its transfiguration in God by Christ . . . By the cross the tendency of the whole cosmos to transcend itself in God is accomplished.[20]

5.2. The *Telos*, the Foundation and the Way of Christian Spirituality

Stăniloae seems to refuse any divorce of theology from spirituality, the union of the two being so profound, as it mirrors the profundity of the divine person's communion. For Stăniloae Christian spirituality has a *telos*, a *way* and a *foundation*. He considers that Christian spirituality is the process of progressing on the road of perfection in Christ.[21] In this regard the *telos* of Christian spirituality is the union of a believer with God in Christ,[22] through the work of the Spirit. For this union to become a reality in the life of believers, there is necessary, says Stăniloae, a series of ascetical efforts, those representing the active dimension of the spiritual life, whilst the passive dimension is the work of God's grace to which the believer needs both to be open to and to follow.[23]

Ascetical efforts have, in Stăniloae's opinion, a double role. First those efforts assure the mortification of the old nature of a believer, being as such a prolongation of baptism. Second, those efforts assure the participation in Christ's resurrection. The practical consequence of this double role of ascetical efforts is purification from passions and consequently the possession of virtues, through a double process of unlearning the vices and learning of virtues. For Stăniloae, the entire human being is involved in this process, human reason and will being permanently illuminated by a

---

20. Stăniloae, *Victory of the Cross*, 20–22.
21. Stăniloae, *Spiritualitate Ortodoxă*, 5.
22. Dumitru Stăniloae, "Desăvârşirea noastră în Hristos după învăţătura bisericii Ortodoxe," part 1, *Mitropolia Olteniei* 32, nos. 1–2 (1980), 76.
23. Stăniloae, *Spiritualitate Ortodoxă*, 7–8.

pneumatic understanding of all things, towards more and more harmony with the work of the Holy Spirit.[24]

The union with God that is the *telos* of spirituality is not for Stăniloae total identification with God.[25] Rather it is a process of coming on the coordinates of the relationship with God, a relationship that would be impossible if it would not be initiated and maintained by God himself. For Stăniloae this is, "a confirmation for the thesis of Christian spirituality, that the vision of God is impossible without a special grace from Him . . . and excludes the possibility for our being . . . to be absorbed into the being of God."[26] The spiritual believer understands the truth that makes him humble, the truth of his total dependence on God for all the things of his life. Stăniloae considers that real spirituality is that living of the human "I" through Christ without being replaced by Christ's "I," Christ's life being the power through which my life is lived. For Stăniloae, this is the culmination of spirituality in the experience of a believer.[27]

From the vertical dimension in regard to the *telos* of spirituality, namely, union with God, Stăniloae continues with the horizontal dimension, that of a believer's responsibility in regard to the created order. He considers that instead of promoting an indifferent withdrawal from the world or from among people of the world, true spirituality is conditioned by such participation in the preserving and sustaining work of divinity over creation. The aim of such participation of the believer in creation as a whole or in the life of other human beings is that of "actualization of the spiritual potencies built in him or in us." This actualization is produced, says Stăniloae through a permanent "disciplining" of our behavior based on a sustained "carefulness to everything we do, think, and through the good we do to others."[28] Stăniloae says that:

---

24. Stăniloae, 10–20.
25. Stăniloae, 21–22.
26. Stăniloae, 22.
27. Stăniloae, 23. See also, Dumitru Stăniloae, *Filocalia sfintelor nevoinţi ale desăvârşirii*, 1 (Bucureşti: Harisma, 1993), 9. Here Stăniloae says that "the road of purification from passions . . . is the way constituted by the life of Jesus Christ . . . He himself is 'the way' and progressing on it is the same as progressing in Him towards the telos of perfection to which He raised humanity assumed through victory with patience of our weaknesses and passions" (Stăniloae, *Filocalia sfintelor*, 9).
28. Stăniloae, *Spiritualitatea Ortodoxă*, 24–27.

> The activity through which we help the formation of our fellows and of us is crystallized in virtues that culminate in love . . . Nobody should consider that his work is an end in itself, but it has the purpose to beautify his nature with the virtues of patience, of self-control, of love for people, of faith in God, and to open progressively the eyes to see the meanings created by God in everything.[29]

The fact that spirituality is union with God, in Christ, through the Holy Spirit, is for Stăniloae the reason why the Holy Trinity is the foundation for Christian spirituality. This is so, asserts Stăniloae, because the personal God is not to be conceived in singularity but always in a unity of persons in a relation of love.[30] For Stăniloae spirituality in the life of God as the Holy Trinity is the foundational base on which Christian spirituality is possible, "Only a perfect community of Supreme Persons could feed with an unending and perfect love, our thirst of love for it and between us. This feeding cannot be only thought, it should be also lived."[31] In order to avoid the danger of confusing the believer with God in the process of union, Stăniloae asserts that the Trinity cannot be experienced without its uncreated energies, love being such an energy that irradiates from God toward believers.[32]

> God wanting to spread progressively the gift of His infinite love, to a different order of conscious subjects, namely, created, wants to spread this love in its paternal form, as for sons, united with His Son. This is the reason why, after the creation of man, He wants His Son to become man, for His love towards His Son, as man, to be a love that directs itself towards any human face, in the likeness of His Son . . . Together with the love of the Father towards us and with our love towards the Father, in Christ, overflow upon us the paternal love in the form of the Holy Spirit overflowed over His Son.[33]

---

29. Stăniloae, 27–28.
30. Stăniloae, 29. Also, Stăniloae, *Revelation and Knowledge*, 245.
31. Stăniloae, *Spiritualitate Ortodoxă*, 35.
32. Stăniloae, 36.
33. Stăniloae, 37.

If the *telos* of Christian spirituality is union with God in Christ, through the Holy Spirit, and *the foundation* of such spirituality is the communion of the persons of the Trinity, then third, *the way* of this union is Christ. For Stăniloae the christological character of Christian spirituality is vital. He considers that "any union with divinity that is not through Christ and in Christ is an illusion." Christ is the way of our union with God, says Stăniloae, being "contemporary" with us at any moment of this process. Christ is present in our lives through a profound participation in the actualization of his death and resurrection in our lives. The christological character of Christian spirituality is completed in Stăniloae's thought by its pneumatological character. If baptism and the Eucharist are the elements of Christ's contemporaneity with us and the force for our ascent in union with God, the Holy Spirit is the one who brings us into the space where communion with Christ is possible, namely, the church.[34]

5.3. The Stages of Christian Spirituality

Starting from the classical division of the process of spiritual life, in Eastern thought, namely, *praxis* (work) and *teoria* (contemplation), he considers that there are three phases of the spiritual life: the active one or the work, the contemplation phase of nature, and the theological one or the contemplation of God.[35]

Purification

The first stage in spiritual life, considers Stăniloae, is that of purification from vices. Considering the vices as being the lowest level where a being can fall, Stăniloae argues that it is exactly the fallen human nature that is the source for vices,[36] and defines them as being something irrational, some of them being connected with the body, some with the soul and that they are in a relationship of inter-conditionality with each other. Also, the essence of the vices, in Stăniloae's perspective, is that they produce a turning towards

---

34. Stăniloae, 38–44. Also, Stăniloae, *Mysteries*, 2.
35. Dumitru Stăniloae, *Ascetica și Mistica Ortodoxă* (Alba Iulia: Deisis, 1993), 51.
36. Stăniloae, *Ascetica și Mistica*, 55–57. Also, Stăniloae, "Desăvârșirea noastră în Hristos după învățătura bisericii Ortodoxe" [Our perfection in Christ according to the teaching of the Orthodox Church], part 2, *Mitropolia Olteniei* 32, nos. 3–6 (1980): 401.

himself, namely "an egocentric self-love," and a pre-eminence of the carnal dimension over the spiritual dimension of existence.[37]

From here Stăniloae continues by distinguishing between vices and affects, considering that affects are connected with our basic necessities because they contribute to the "preservation of our nature." On the other hand, Stăniloae considers that affects are not proper to human nature from the design of creation, rather they became part of the human nature after the fall, and this is the reason affects could become vices,[38] they will not survive in eternity, and therefore the ascetical efforts have a double aim, to keep the affects under control and to enhance spiritual growth. He concludes, "Ascetics means, in the Eastern thought, to stop and discipline the biological, not fight to exterminate it. Moreover, ascetics means 'sublimation' of this element of bodily affection not its abolition. Christianity does not save man from a certain part of his being, rather it saves him entirely."[39]

Moreover, Stăniloae elaborates on the causes and effects of the vices, and he distinguishes three overlapping causes of vices. First, "the weakening of the mind in its own and autonomous work," second, the exacerbation of sensual work escaped "from the control of the mind," and third, the production of "an exclusive and irrational running towards pleasure and running from pain." The effects of a vice over the life of a human being are, in Stăniloae's opinion, on the coordinates of disorder at the level of a weakening of human nature, a fracturing of the harmony between mind and senses that leads to a "dissipation of mind," to "forgetting of God," and to "conflicts with others," all of them rooted in a egoistic preoccupation with one's self.[40]

Considering with the fathers that "heart" is an expression that refers to the "soul itself," Stăniloae, sees similarities between the Christian doctrine of the soul and modern psychology. He speaks of the subconscious part of

---

37. Stăniloae, *Ascetica și Mistica*, 58–60. Stăniloae follows the classical classification in Eastern tradition about the passions: Gluttony, Fornication, Avarice, Anger, Accidie (spiritual sloth or sluggishness), Dejection, Vainglory, and Pride, (Stăniloae, 58–60).

38. Stăniloae, 61–62. Stăniloae names the needs: appetite for food, pleasure of eating, fear and sadness (Stăniloae, 61–62).

39. Stăniloae, 63.

40. Stăniloae, 67–70. Stăniloae considers that the "dissipation of the mind" could be overcome only through the "guarding of the mind" of the Christian ascetics (Stăniloae, 67–70).

the soul as the inferior place of the soul, where exists the negative content of the being, and about the upper place of the soul that he names, the *transconscious* or supraconscious part of the soul, the part that not only contains the "virtual human energies" but also is an open door for the divine energies.[41]

For Stăniloae the spirit of the soul, or of the mind, the heart (νους) is the one who makes contact with the subconscious part and with the external reality as well as the locus where Christ, through the Spirit, lives.[42] He says:

> "The spirit" is an aspect and *nous* another of the same simple soul. "The spirit" or the heart contains in itself "the mind" or "the understanding" and "the reason" as the Holy Spirit contains the Father and the Son. "The understanding" contains as well in itself "the heart" or "the love," and "the reason," as well as "the reason" contains "the understanding" and "the love."[43]

In this context the vices are simultaneously the "effect and the cause of a mind that lacks true understanding," and of the weakening of the will, that leads to a fracture of reason, with the result that both mind and will become servants of vice, being transformed in "unwise reason" and respectively "irrational will."[44] Stăniloae concludes:

> The vices are born by the contribution of all faculties of the soul, through their wrong activity, indicating an illness of the entire being. They are a turn of the entire being towards external reality, towards living according to the feelings, a transformation of the entire being in "body," in bodily feeling. Vices . . . represent therefore, a living through the superficial part of our being . . . an exit of our being from the region of ontological truths, from connection with the springs of existence, a party on the margin of the nothing abyss, from which is coming,

---

41. Stăniloae, 72–73. For Stăniloae, the supraconscious part of the being as "the spirit of the soul or of the mind" is in fact the heart (Stăniloae, 72).

42. Stăniloae, 74. Stăniloae sees the similarity between the human spirit with the capacity to go deep in the human being with the Holy Spirit who has the capacity to go in the deepness of the Divinity.

43. Stăniloae, 75.

44. Stăniloae, 76–80.

when we wake up from the fire of the vice, a sensation of emptiness, of false, of nothingness of our existence.[45]

From the diagnosis, the description and the features of vices, Stăniloae continues by saying that purification from them is not simply their elimination through ascetical efforts; rather it happens by the replacement of vices with virtues. Stăniloae insists that, of vital importance is the order to be followed in this process of replacing the vices with the virtues. He considers that the primordial condition for this process is faith, obtained and strengthened at baptism, a faith whose efficacy, admits Stăniloae, depends on our cooperation on the journey of perfection through virtues. To be sure, Stăniloae affirms, faith is the gift of God's grace, and has the role of strengthening the reason, considering the fact that the start of every sin is a departure of the reason from the truth. This is the reason faith is to become a life style, being an intellectual-volitional synthesis, an act that is a solution to the other intellectual-volitional act that is the fall into sin. Faith is therefore the first act of purification that responds to the beginning of every fall into sin.[46]

Second, in its progress, says Stăniloae, "faith becomes *fear of God* that is the opposite of the fear of the world." For Stăniloae, the virtue of authentic fear of God (in accordance with the Heideggerian classification), is the rediscovery of the primordial, spiritual fear that was in the beginning simultaneously a fear of separation from God into an empty way of existence and a "fear united with the trust in God."[47] Therefore, the fear of God is the fear to sin through union with the world, a revelation of a higher authority than that of the world (the imminent danger), namely God, and the consciousness of the future danger, that of an "eternal existence that is unauthentic and unfulfilled," as the result of the last just judgment of God.[48]

Third, the fear of God, leads to the virtue of repentance for past sins and self-control to avoid future sins. Considering with the fathers that repentance

---

45. Stăniloae, 81–82.
46. Stăniloae, 91–99.
47. Stăniloae, 100–102. Stăniloae says that there are two types of the fear of God, "The first is the fear of the slaves, fear of His punishment, and the second is the fear of love, the fear of being without his (master's) kindness . . ." Heidegger distinguishes, says Stăniloae, between the fear "of something from the world (Furcht) and the fear of the universal emptiness of the world (Angst)" (Stăniloae, 100–102).
48. Stăniloae, 102–103.

is the second grace, a second reborn and a renewal of baptism, Stăniloae argues for permanent repentance with a continuous confession of sins, and the patient overcoming of present sorrows, a repentance that is to be directed to our vices and sins as well as to "our virtues always unfulfilled." There is a danger of confusing repentance with discouraging discontentment that is filled with doubt. Rather, repentance is an acknowledgment of the actual limits, not the declaration of the final limits. In fact, says Stăniloae, discouragement is the opposite of repentance, as repentance should be always superior to every moral achievement and as such "a hand of God" that raises us and keeps us in an authentic relationship with God.[49]

Fourth, the next step in the process of purification from vices is the virtue of self-control that helps the believer to see the world in its true light, as a dynamic and transparent means from God to help him towards God, and not as a world of things and objects. From here Stăniloae speaks of two forms of self-control, a radical one, practiced by monks, and a partial one, that of the believers in the world. Of note is the fact that even if Stăniloae considers radical self-control, that implies an exit from the world as being real, he does not exclude the possibility of self-control for those believers who are in the world as well. However, he says that in order to compensate the limits of the second type, God will permit more troubles to overtake the believer which he will need to overcome in patience in order to continue the process of purification from vices in his life. Stăniloae differentiates, "If self-control is the virtue more found in monks, patience is more found in the layman, even though none of them should forget entirely the virtue of the other." Stăniloae sees in the three vows of a monk: that of poverty, chastity, and obedience, the medication for the vices of gluttony, fornication, avarice and pride, through the practice of fasting.[50]

Fifth, in the process of purification from vices comes the virtue of the guarding of the mind or of thoughts. Stăniloae considers that the mind contains good thoughts coming from the supraconscious part of the soul that is open to God, as well as wicked thoughts coming from the subconscious part of the soul connected with the biological which is under the influence

---

49. Stăniloae, 104–108.
50. Stăniloae, 116–120.

of evil spirits. The guarding of the mind aims in Stăniloae's argument for the "complete predominance of the good thought produced by the good heart," namely the supraconscious part of the soul, in such a way that the wicked heart, namely the subconscious part of the soul will be under the control of the first. This is to be done, says Stăniloae, through a permanent bringing of our thoughts in connection with the mind of Christ, an idea that mirrors closely Pauline concepts from Philippians 4:7 and 2 Corinthians 10:5, even though Stăniloae does not connect his argument with that text – the idea is to train your discernment and that of the peace of Christ that guards the mind. The permanent bringing of our thoughts to the mind of Christ is rather, for Stăniloae, done through the permanent remembering of the name of God in our minds through concentrated and uninterrupted prayer.[51]

Sixth, in the process of purification from vices comes the virtue of patience in grief. Speaking about grief Stăniloae differentiates between two forms of God's assistance to human beings in the process of perfection. The first is the providence of God and the second is the judgment of God. One is positive and one is negative. One has to do with the beauty and the good we experience, being in obedience to God, and the second is the punishment that we experience as the result of our sins, in order to depart from sin and to stop sinning. Stăniloae is referring to griefs provoked by other people to a person who is in the process of spiritual growth, or after some spiritual achievement. For Stăniloae the first way in which we meet the providence of God, is the way towards God, the way of ascetical efforts, whilst the second way is the way of returning to God after departure from him.[52] He summarizes:

> If self-control and the guarding of the mind . . . address the vices of lust (gluttony, fornication and avarice), patience in regard with the sorrows that are provoked by people and different griefs that come over us address especially the vice of anger

---

51. Stăniloae, 123–134. See also Meyendorff, *St. Gregory Palamas*. He says about Palamas: "The hesychast doctor justifies the psyco-physical method of prayer in this context, rejecting the Platonic spiritualism of Barlaamite anthropology for the Biblical concept of man; the body is so far from being a prison of the soul, for the body itself receives the grace of the sacraments and the pledge of final resurrection," (Meyendorff, 109).

52. Stăniloae, *Ascetica și Mistica*, 134–135.

(acidy and dejection) . . . Usually, the successes that somebody obtained through self-control and through achieving of more virtues, exposes him to vainglory and pride. This is why God permits over this person troubles from different people and griefs, in order to heal him of this vices.[53]

Seventh, in the process of purification from vices comes hope, as a result of the understanding that comes from the practice of patience in grief. Stăniloae considers that if "faith is the certainty of some unseen actual realities," hope is "the certainty of participation in future realities." Moreover, for Stăniloae hope is a different way of "being oriented forward toward the future," than worrying, even though both have "a common root," namely, "preoccupation with the future."[54] He concludes:

> Comparing carefully hope and worry, we acknowledge the impossibility of their coexistence due to the fact that as much evidence as hope contains, so much uncertainty worry contains. This is the reason why the uncertainty of worry is present where the evidence of hope is missing. For the kind of concern that serves hope is not fueled by the uncertainty of worldly worry, rather it is only careful not to lose any part of the sure hope. The assurance of future good from God and the uncertainty of worldly worry are shown in the tranquility that comes from the first and the unstopped turmoil given by the latter.[55]

Eighth, in the process of purification come kindness and humbleness, which are "flowers that rise from the patience in grief and from hope." Kindness, says Stăniloae is that "unmoved disposition of mind in face of critics or praise . . . it means to be unaffected by the evils that someone is producing which are directed toward you."[56] For Stăniloae kindness, as opposed to anger, produces simplicity from the inner capacity of "transposing yourself into the situation of the other" and that it is actually "a wisdom" to judge unpassionately. Humbleness, on the other hand, is the opposite of

---

53. Stăniloae, 135–136.
54. Stăniloae, 143–144.
55. Stăniloae, 144.
56. Stăniloae, 144.

pride, and unlike pride that is "the spring of all vices," humbleness is the "concentration of all virtues," and as such is the "most complete reestablishment of the true understanding of natural reality, love being the understanding of the ones who are above the natural."[57] Stăniloae considers that humbleness is "the supreme consciousness and living of the divine infinity and personal smallness."[58] He concludes:

> Humbleness is in fact a coming back of our nature to the state of being a window of infinity and of being an empty room meant to be filled with the divine light. The window in fact does not exist for itself, and the room to which God is sending the light does not see anything without the light. In the same way, man, only accepting this role to be nothing else than a reflector and receiver of the divine light has a great destiny, that of living with the infinity.[59]

Ninth, in the process of purification comes the state of no vices, as the culmination of the progress through virtues. For someone in this state, says Stăniloae the vices are not, "an ontological impossibility, as for God. Rather they are a moral impossibility . . . a freedom from all vices and the possession of all virtues."[60]

The tenth point[61] as preparation for the process of purification, is failure, shame and despair. Stăniloae speaks of the disillusion consequent to the vices that could open "the spirit to the truth," and consequently there is the possibility of a "awakening of conscience, that could lead to the starting point towards freedom." But with the revelation of sin, says Stăniloae, comes shame, as on one hand "a warning from God," and on the other hand, "an instinctive reaction of the soul."[62] Stăniloae concludes, "Shame not only punishes for past sins, rather it equips one against future sins . . . Its pain

---

57. Stăniloae, 144.
58. Stăniloae, 145–149.
59. Stăniloae, 150.
60. Stăniloae, 150–152.
61. In the one volume called *Spiritualitate ortodoxă: Ascetica și Mistica* (Bucuresti: IBMBOR, 1992) this tenth step does not appear. In the two volumes called *Ascetica și Mistica* (Deisis, 1993) this tenth step closes the process of purification.
62. Stăniloae, *Ascetica si Mistica*, 194–196.

on one hand followed sin is in remembering, on the other hand it burns sin, keeping it in memory as an abomination."[63]

Illumination

The second stage in spiritual life, Stăniloae considers is that of *illumination*, when the gifts of the Spirit received in the sacrament of chrismation, are seen fully after full purification, through all the virtues. To be sure the Holy Spirit is at work in all the process and Stăniloae distinguishes between the power of the Spirit in the process of purification and the light of the Spirit that comes at the end of the purification process.[64]

Stăniloae follows the classical number of seven gifts of the Spirit, connecting the first two with the process of purification and the last five with the process of illumination.[65] For Stăniloae the journey mediated by the gifts of the Spirit is a progressive journey from a partial knowledge towards a more and more profound knowledge of God, namely, knowledge *through* the Spirit and *in* the Spirit that opens the possibility of seeing the hidden reasons of human beings and their destiny. Moreover, this adequate and true knowledge about yourself is followed by the profound knowledge of God within the created order, and consequently an understanding of the divine design for the world, and the reasons "hidden in the things" by God the Creator, an awareness of the "structure as symbol of the world."[66] Stăniloae affirms two reasons for the creation of the world, reasons that become clear in this process of simultaneous illumination (in the Spirit and through the Spirit), "This is the meaning of the world as a road to God. The existence of the world proves itself to have, besides other meanings, that of exercising the powers of our soul in our ascent towards God."[67]

---

63. Stăniloae, 196.
64. Stăniloae, *Ascetica si Mistica* (1992), 157–158.
65. Stăniloae, 158–159. The seven gifts of the Spirit in Stăniloae's view are the gifts of fear, of strength, of advice, of science, of knowledge, of understanding, of wisdom. The classic list of the gifts of the Spirit is drawn from Isaiah 11:2–3. See in this regard, D. S. Dockery, "Fruit of the Spirit," in *Dictionary of Paul and His Letters*, ed. Gerald F. Hawthorne and Ralph P. Martin (Downers Grove, IL: InterVarsity Press, 1993), 317.
66. Stăniloae, *Ascetica si Mistica* (1992), 160–167. For Stăniloae knowledge in the Spirit makes possible a turning inside to the spirit and therefore knowledge in the Spirit.
67. Stăniloae, 168–169.

In fact Stăniloae affirms that the first step in the ascent of illumination is that of the spiritual understanding of the world, and of its reasons, a knowledge that is not "an irrational act, rather one that is supra-rational," meaning not reducing reason to silence, rather it means to transcend reason, having as a base the intuitive knowledge in which is involved the reason that is exercised in knowing and doing. Because there is an objective truth attached to everything, a deed says Stăniloae, is rational only if it is in congruence with the reason it serves, otherwise it is irrational. This is the tension a human being faces because the tendency of the fallen nature is towards the fulfillment of the irrational egoistic desires of the ego, and in the process, reason is disturbed as it is forced to find fabricated reasons for these egoistic actions. The necessary thing is to replace the subjective reasons produced by the egoistic nature, with the objective one of the purified nature, in order to hope for a healthy development in connection with the universal truth that is "beyond our subjective truths."[68] In Stăniloae's words:

> This exit from yourself in objectivity in order to refind the truth and to practice it as something proper to the most subjectivity of your own, or better say, with this integral identification of the self with the objective logos, means at the same time, an exit from isolation and entrance into the universal, in relation with the Person who encompasses everything . . . This is the reason we can speak of a threefold knowledge of the Logos: in nature, in Scripture and in His individual human body.[69]

The illumination process consists in the inner illumination of your own status and of the meaning of created order, and also, in the spiritual illumination of the Scriptures, meaning to understand the "living words" through the written words of the Scriptures, which is in its turn a symbol, a medium that reflects the "infinite depths of the spiritual meanings communicated by God as Persons." The spiritual understanding of Scriptures is available to persons who have the Spirit in them and are reading the Scriptures through the Spirit. Stăniloae considers that is the same light of the Spirit that illumines the interior of the being and the meaning of the

---

68. Stăniloae, 169–172.
69. Stăniloae, 174–182.

Scriptures, that has the role to help us in our ascend towards the infinity of God. This is the why Scriptures are actualized in a personal address by the Spirit, in discovering new actual meanings that are in harmony with its old meanings.[70] Stăniloae concludes, "For the spiritual man, in the depths of Scriptures, of nature and of creation's development in time, is present and active the same Spirit that is present and active in man's interior, sustaining his efforts of purification and illuminating all the things around him to become transparent symbols of divinity."[71]

At this stage of entering into the reality of the transparent symbols of divinity, the ascent of illumination is expressed in pure prayer that is an "ecstasy of the interior silence." Stăniloae considers that prayer itself has different qualitative stages that are intimately connected with the stages of spiritual ascend, from the "inferior prayer that asks for material goods" to the superior prayer characterized by a more and more profound concentration and a transcendence of all images and objects, the mind becoming full with the reality of God.

The coordinates of such prayer consist not only in emptying of the mind and filling it with the divine reality, a returning says Stăniloae "of the mind in the heart," the heart being the superior dimension of the soul, where, says Stăniloae, "Christ has been hidden from the time of Baptism."[72] Therefore, a returning of the mind from external objects and preoccupation to an inner place (the heart) where Christ lives is for Stăniloae the essence of pure prayer as mediator of a different and superior knowledge of God:

> Pure prayer or mental prayer does not mediate a knowledge of God through beings but through the depth of our own soul, through "the heart." This means actually to sense Him directly, for man forgets even the heart when collected in it, he feels himself in the presence of Jesus Christ, in the atmosphere of the heavenly Kingdom, found in his interior.[73]

---

70. Stăniloae, 183–188.
71. Stăniloae, 188.
72. Stăniloae, 211–216.
73. Stăniloae, 216.

Stăniloae differentiates between mind and reason, considering the mind as being the personal subject and the reason the source of concepts. The human mind is the image of the Father (the divine *nous*), and human reason is the image of the eternal Logos emanating eternally from the Father. From here he continues by arguing the necessity of transcending all objects (all things that could be defined through reason) to get to our own interiority in order to understand God, an understanding that is not a comprehension, rather it is a revelation of divine reality. The mind enters the heart, says Stăniloae, and therefore contemplates itself, becomes a mirror in which is contemplated God. This experience is possible only when this disconnection from the worldly things that is the returning of the mind into the heart happens, and also, equally important because the heart is filled with the presence of Christ, from baptism, kept totally safe by him.[74] He concludes:

> In reality the subject returning towards himself does not find only himself, and this experience excludes the distance and also the identification with God. Exactly when we put off the clothes of the created world, expecting to contemplate our own subject revealed (γυμνος νους) and to experience the feeling of full sovereignty, we realize that we are facing a power whose authority over us reveals itself more mightily and more overwhelmingly than the authority of the world . . . Arriving at our own pure intimacy, we experience the infinite but personal presence of God.[75]

There is then, a last step in the ascend of illumination, following the transcendence of the outside objects, and the transcendence of our own subject, and that is the experience of the love of God, as a form of knowledge that will not be achieved through the "direct personal subject and the indirect divine object," but rather is the seeing of the revealed light of God, that is love.[76] This is the first step into the third stage of a spiritual life that is union with God.

---

74. Stăniloae, 239–242.
75. Stăniloae, 244.
76. Stăniloae, 252.

Union with God

The third stage of spiritual life is that of union with God, which one can get through pure prayer, a union that is beyond pure prayer, being the pure love that can not come from man himself but from God. Love for Stăniloae is the confirmation of purification, for the vices are an expression of egoism that is the opposite of love.[77]

Also for Stăniloae, love is the answer coming from God to the pure prayer coming from man, and this love is actually one of God's uncreated divine energies,[78] and as such is the one that roots the love of people, that is "the fruit of the love of God." Moreover love from God is for Stăniloae the factor of perfect union for people. The model of this love between God and man is a perichoretical one and Stăniloae speaks of love without dissolution "as free subjects," without separation and with a communication of energies.

This communication is not unidirectional, from God to man, rather it is bidirectional, including communication from man to God, a communication of God's love that was appropriated by the human being as personal subject, that is in the process of transformation in the likeness of the person whose love he experiences.[79] Stăniloae reflects again the perichoretical love of divine persons as a model for human love, "So, love is realized when two subjects meet in a full mutual experience, in their quality as subjects, so without mutual reduction to the status of objects, but discovering at maximum, as subjects, but in spite of that, mutually self-giving into total freedom."[80] For Stăniloae, love is not only the supreme union and mutual promotion but also a supreme kind of knowledge, a knowledge that cannot be contained in concepts.[81]

Stăniloae admits that the stages of spiritual life cannot be separated except for methodological reasons, when in fact the reality of such a life is that we are not in an uninterrupted ascend, as we go back many times to

---

77. Stăniloae, 254–255.
78. Stăniloae, 255–256. Stăniloae is in agreement with the Palamite tradition that considers that participation in the life of the Trinity is possible in the divine uncreated energies, coming from the triune activity, not sharing the being as the three persons share. See also Meyendorff, *Study of Gregory Palamas*, 202.
79. Stăniloae, *Ascetica si Mistica* (1992), 256–261.
80. Stăniloae, 266.
81. Stăniloae, 266–267.

inferior steps in the ascend, because of our weakness and the limitations of human nature. But recovery towards the superior steps of ascent is easier as we keep the experience of them in our life. Also, love is possible in human communities and communion because of God who is "the spring of such plenary love." Stăniloae argues the unifying role of love in inter-human relationships, a love that facilitates union with God and as such union with others. For Stăniloae the way towards the reality of union through love is that of practicing the love of people which is a constant separation from the egoistic way of living, and as such it is a "strengthening of the sentiment of our union with them and with God."[82]

For Stăniloae the best expression of the convergence between love from God and love for people is life in the home, the reality that is inhabited by the loved one. But "the house" is the mirroring of God's house that is his heart in which all people meet unified by his love, this being the "most superior and the purest structure of love" in whose image Moses was to build the tent, and later were to be built the temple and then the church.[83]

Stăniloae insists on the fact that the experience of God is like light, and the danger is that in the replacement of this light of God with concepts of God, and the transformation of those in the reality of God, comes idolatry. The light that is the experience of God, says Stăniloae is not "a plain uniformity or lightening chaos, rather it is an implicit fullness."[84] This is why when Stăniloae speaks about the structure of love he does not refer to a concept, rather he refers to a spiritual reality:

> This is the way the loving relationship is structured between him and light, or this is the form taken by his experience. As he is progressing more and more in light, he feels that he progresses in a holy temple, in a loving intimacy, but that there remains in it eternally a hidden depth from where all the light, all the love start as a mysterious infinite, that make possible an infinite progress of our knowledge, of love between Christ and us.[85]

---

82. Stăniloae, 269–274. See also, John Climacus, *The Ladder of Divine Ascent* (New York: Paulist Press, 1982).

83. Stăniloae, *Ascetica și Mistica* (1992), 275–276.

84. Stăniloae, 294–297.

85. Stăniloae, 298.

Moreover, this structure of love means intimacy with the reality of "the tent that is not made by human hands; that is Christ who is also the 'Church not made by hands,'" the reality that fulfils and encompasses everything. This the "greater and more perfect tabernacle" in which Holy of Holies Christ entered. It means in fact, says Stăniloae, the divinity in which Christ fully entered as man, being our forerunner, "in which all were created."[86]

Coming to humans, Stăniloae states that our soul and body in the totality they represent constitute the "lower tabernacle" made in the image of the "upper tabernacle" that is the divine Logos. Here steams the reason for the Son's incarnation, in which the light of the "upper tabernacle" flooded the "lower tabernacle" of humanity who had become darkened.

Moreover, in his resurrection and ascension and in our participation in them is the "recollection of all in Him . . . a coming home," of humanity, that constitutes itself in a "spiritual structure" that models the entire progress of "eternity's pilgrims." Therefore, in this continuous process of purification, illumination and union by seeing the divine light, the believer, says Stăniloae, "becomes transparent and spiritualized, being filled with love for God whose heat transforms in light, having at the same time its spring in the work of the Holy Spirit."[87]

Finally, for Stăniloae at the end of the process the full spiritualization of humans is possible through "divine penetration of man by God," called *theosis* or deification, through divine energies.[88] Stăniloae concludes:

> Divine energies are nothing else than rays of the divine being shining from the three divine Persons. And since the Word of God was incarnated, these rays irradiate through His human face. On the other hand, it could be said that the entities of the world are images of divine Logos' reasons, which are in the same time energies. Through creation God put a part of His infinite possibility of thought and work in existence, in specific form at the level of human understanding and work, in order to realize

---

86. Stăniloae, 299–300. Stăniloae quotes the text in Hebrews 9:11–12 corroborating it with 2 Corinthians 5:4, 12:4 and with Colossians 1:16

87. Stăniloae, *Ascetica si Mistica* (1992), 300–307.

88. Stăniloae, 309, 317.

with men a dialogue in which they will ascend more and more towards the likeness with God and towards union with Him.[89]

5.4. Summary of Chapter 5

I have aimed to explore in this chapter the way in which Stăniloae consistently working in concentric circles develops his theology of spirituality as actualization of christological-pneumatological convergence. I have argued that one of the characteristics of Stăniloae's view of spirituality is its cruciformity. He argues for the universal imprint of the cross on three realities of humanity, namely, the world, relationships and pleasures of life. From here we observed the preoccupation of Stăniloae with distinguishing between the innocent suffering of Christ and human suffering that is rooted always in the mixture between innocence and one's own guilt. Stăniloae continues by showing the way the three realities on which God imprinted the cross, correspond to three meanings of such an imprint of the cross, namely, the revelation of God's transcendence over the gifts that he offers to the world, the revelation of God's sovereignty that provides an understanding of God's uniqueness, and the revelation of the true love for God as person, despite the presence or absence of his gifts.

From the centrality of the cross for Stăniloae's view of spirituality, I have aimed to explore the *telos*, the foundation and the way of Christian spirituality. In this regard the *telos* of Christian spirituality is the union of a believer with God in Christ, through the work of the Spirit. This union with God has not only a vertical dimension, but is expressed in a horizontal dimension, that of a believer's responsibility in regard to the created order. The fact that spirituality is union with God, in Christ, through the Holy Spirit, is for Stăniloae the reason the Holy Trinity is the *foundation* for Christian spirituality, and *the way* of this union is Christ. For Stăniloae the christological character of Christian spirituality is completed in its pneumatological character. If baptism and the Eucharist are the elements of Christ's contemporaneity with us and the force for our ascent in union with God,

---

89. Stăniloae, 319. See also, Dumitru Stăniloae, "The Faces of Our Fellow Human Being," *International Review of Mission* 71, no. 281 (1982): 29–35. Also, Stăniloae, "Image, Likeness, and deification in the human person," *Communio* 13 (1986): 72.

the Holy Spirit is the one who brings us into the space where communion with Christ is possible, namely, the church.

Eventually, I aimed to explore the stages of Christian spirituality in Stăniloae's view, namely, purification, illumination and union. From the diagnosis, the description and the features of vices, Stăniloae continues by saying that purification from them is not simply their elimination through ascetical efforts; rather it happens by the replacement of vices with the virtues. The second stage is that of *illumination*, when the gifts of the Spirit received in the sacrament of chrismation, are seen fully after full purification, through all the virtues. For Stăniloae the journey mediated by the gifts of the Spirit is a progressive journey from a partial knowledge toward more and more profound knowledge of God, namely, the knowledge *through* the Spirit and *in* the Spirit, a spiritual illumination that mediates the spiritual understanding of Scriptures and of the meaning of created order. At this stage of entering into the reality of the transparent symbols of divinity, the ascent of illumination is expressed in pure prayer that is an ecstasy of the interior silence. There is then, a last step in the ascend of illumination, the experience of the love of God, as a form of knowledge that is the seeing of the revealed light of God, that is love. This is the first step into the third stage of a spiritual life that is union with God which one can get through pure prayer, a union that is beyond pure prayer, being the pure love that cannot come from man himself but from God. Finally, for Stăniloae at the end of the process the full spiritualization of humans is possible through divine penetration of man by God.

Part 2

The Dynamic of Spiritual Journey in Paul Fiddes's Theology

In part 1 of the present project I aimed to explore the reasons supporting why Dumitru Stăniloae could be considered the entrance door for enhancing the conversation between Baptists and Orthodox in contemporary Romania. I believe that I proved that Stăniloae is a proper partner for this conversation as a theologian who is systematic, Trinitarian and ecumenical.

The aim of part 2 is to show the reasons Paul Fiddes could be considered a valuable Baptist partner for a theological conversation with the Orthodox theologian Dumitru Stăniloae, on the subjects of baptism, the Eucharist and spirituality, as essential elements of the lifelong spiritual journey. Therefore, in chapter 6, I will explore the place of Paul Fiddes within the Baptist world, as well as the dominant influences on Fiddes's spirituality and theology. In this context then, I will explore the way Fiddes's view of theology was built by the development of his understanding of God's relationship with the world and of his understanding of the dynamics of salvation.

In this framework in chapter 7, I will explore Fiddes's theology of participation in his thoughts about baptism, trying to see the way Trinitarian participation roots human participation, the place of baptism in the process of Christian initiation, in the context of Fiddes's theology of participation. In chapter 8, I will explore the way Fiddes's perichoretical theology roots his thought about the Eucharist, as an essential part of the lifelong spiritual journey. In the last chapter of part 2, chapter 9, I will explore the way Fiddes's covenantal theology is reflected in his thought about spirituality, as a lifelong reality.

CHAPTER 6

Paul Fiddes's Spiritual Journey

6.1. Place of Paul Fiddes within the Baptist World

Paul Stuart Fiddes (born on 30 April 1947), is considered today one of the most important Baptist theologians. He started his education in Oxford at Dayton Manor Grammar School, and because of his early preoccupation with the relation between theology and literature he decided to focus his studies on Literature and Theology. In 1976 after completing his doctoral dissertation he spent a year in Germany for post-doctoral study at the Eberhard Karls University of Tubingen where he studied with Jürgen Moltmann and Eberhard Jüngel.

After he was ordained as a Baptist minister in 1972, he became Fellow and Tutor in Christian Doctrine at Regent's Park College in Oxford in 1975, he was later also the Principal of this institution between 1989 and 2007.[1] He was the chairman of the Board of Oxford Theological Faculty, becoming also in 2002 Professor of Systematic Theology at the University of Oxford. His recognition as one of the leading scholars in the fields of theology and literature was endorsed in 2004 with his election as Honorary Fellow of St Peter's College in Oxford.[2] In 2004 he became an Honorary Doctor of Divinity of the University of Bucharest and in 2007 Principal Emeritus, Professorial Research Fellow, and Director of Research, at the Regent's Park College in Oxford.[3]

---

1. Paul S. Fiddes, "Contributors," *Ecclesiology* 7, no. 2 (2011): 137.
2. Fiddes, "Contributors," 137.
3. Bill J. Leonard, *Baptist Ways: A History* (Valley Forge, PA: Judson Press, 2003), 374.

Fiddes's worldwide recognition as a leading Baptist theologian can also be seen in the way his scholarship is valorized today, by important institutions. Therefore, he is a member of the editorial board of *Ecclesiology*,[4] *The Journal for Ministry, Mission and Unity*, a consultant editor for *Studies in Baptist History and Thought,* published by Paternoster Press, and a series editor of *New Critical Thinking in Religion, Theology and Biblical Studies*. He is also general editor of the *Regent's Study Guides Series*. In addition, Fiddes is a member of ecumenical study commissions of Churches Together in Britain and Ireland, chairman of the Doctrine and Worship Committee of the Baptist Union of Great Britain, convenor of the Division for Theology and Education of the European Baptist Federation, and vice chair of the Baptist Doctrine and Inter-Church Cooperation Study Commission of the Baptist World Alliance. Fiddes is also an Ecumenical Representative to the General Synod of the Church of England.

Another reason for Fiddes's worldwide recognition as one of the most important Baptist theologians today is his significant volume of writings. By 2013 Fiddes had written eleven books, a significant number of chapters in books, an important number of papers in academic journals, as well as a number of publications as editor.[5] From a look at Fiddes's impressive bibliography one can have a glimpse of the interdisciplinary characteristics of Fiddes's scholarship as well as the vast range of subjects that his theology and thought aim to explore. From these few characteristics Fiddes's spiritual and intellectual journey can be detected, and these are the subjects of the next section.

6.2. Fiddes's Spiritual and Intellectual Journey

We have seen in the previous section that from his biographical data one could understand the way Paul Fiddes has evolved in his academic career, an evolution that made him become a worldwide recognized Baptist theologian of today. In this section I aim to explore some of the influences of Fiddes's spiritual and intellectual journey. These are important, in my

---

4. Paul S. Fiddes, "A Journey of Discovery: Christian Initiation, Archbishop Rowan Williams and Ecumenism," *Ecclesiology* 8, no. 2 (2012): 153.

5. See Appendix A for a full list of his published works.

opinion, because they are foundational for the features of Fiddes's thought and theology.

One important influence that proves to be foundational, not only for his academic career but also for his spiritual and intellectual journey, is that of the Oxford ecumenical *ethos*. Or in Fiddes's words describing it, "In my own situation, in Oxford, candidates are formed for Baptist ministry in a university faculty, which includes not only a good number of Baptists, but members of the United Reformed and Methodist churches, Anglicans . . . Roman Catholic theologians . . . and a Greek Orthodox bishop."[6] Fiddes himself confesses that his personality was shaped by this ecumenical context in Oxford, and he also believes that a multi-denominational rather than a non-denominational setting is more appropriate for theology in a university in England, in order to preserve the necessary connection of theology with the life and mission of the church in society.[7]

Another important influence that proved to be foundational for Fiddes's spiritual and intellectual journey is that of Protestant theology, starting with his post-doctoral studies with Eberhard Jüngel, a leading German Lutheran theologian, and with Jürgen Moltmann, a German Reformed theologian, both of them leading theologians of the University of Tubingen, Germany. The encounter with the two German theologians facilitated for Paul Fiddes the encounter with the theology of Friedrich Schleiermacher and of Karl Barth, the latter a theologian who exercised a significant influence on the

---

6. Paul Fiddes, "Theology and a Baptist Way of Community," in *Doing Theology in a Baptist Way*, ed. Paul S. Fiddes (Oxford: Whitley, 2000), 20–21.

7. Fiddes, "Theology and a Baptist Way," 21. Fiddes says "For my own part I must say that this ecumenical context has been a major influence in shaping my writings of Christian doctrine, while at the same time it has sharpened my awareness of the distinctive features of Baptist life and witness, and has made me more and not less a Baptist," (Fiddes, "Theology and a Baptist Way," 21). Interesting in this context the argument of David Tracy argues that there are "three publics of theology: society, academy and church" (David Tracy, *The Analogical Imagination: Christian Theology and the Culture of Pluralism* [London: SCM Press, 1981], 3). See also, Vladimir Lossky, *The Mystical Theology of the Eastern Church* (Cambridge: James Clarke, 1973). Lossky arguing the inseparability between mysticism and theology affirms that "if the mystical experience is a personal working out of the content of the common faith, theology is an expression, for the profit of all, of that which can be experienced by everyone" (Lossky, *Mystical Theology*, 8–9). Also see, Stăniloae, *Revelation and Knowledge*. He says that "theology is reflection upon the content of faith inherited from that witness and initial living out of revelation which we possess in the Scripture and in apostolic tradition," (Stăniloae, 84).

thought of the two German theologians, and whose theology became one of the most important influences for Fiddes himself.

Under the influence of Jürgen Moltmann's Trinitarian theology, the doctrine of the Trinity became paramount for Paul Fiddes. As well the importance of patristic theology for contemporary theology became more and more acknowledged. Therefore, Fiddes starts his construct of the theology of the Trinity by reminding us of the fact that from the beginning it was the experience of the church in regard to the three persons of the Trinity that led to the crystallization of the doctrine.[8]

He states from the beginning the relevance of the internal procession in the life of the Trinity, as the basis for the triune persons' processions in the world, and that an adequate image of God is fundamental for the efficacy of the pastoral work of the church.[9] It is therefore clear, in Fiddes's approach that we can speak of a double influence, first of the pastoral experience of the doctrine of God, and second, of the view of the triune God and the participation in him, on the way our pastoral practice is conceived.[10]

Fiddes considers that in the process of the development of the doctrine of the Trinity there were four contributions that the patristic thinkers made to the understanding of the dynamic of the life of the Trinity. First, is that of defining the Trinity as one essence in three persons,[11] and second, that of rooting the distinctiveness of the three persons in their relationships with each other.[12] The third contribution is that of affirmation of the freedom of the personal God and also of human persons,[13] and the fourth is the

---

8. Paul S. Fiddes, *Participation in God: A Pastoral Doctrine of the Trinity* (London: Darton, Longman and Todd, 2000), 5.

9. Fiddes, *Participation in God*, 7.

10. Fiddes, 8.

11. Fiddes, 13. See also, Jaroslav Pelikan, *The Christian Tradition: A History of the Development of Doctrine*, vol. 1 (Chicago, IL: University of Chicago Press, 1971), 218. See also, Stephen R. Holmes, *The Holy Trinity: Understanding God's Life* (London: Paternoster, 2012). Holmes says, referring to the Council of Nicea, that "The Son was confessed to be 'from the *ousia* of the Father'; the council highlights an unusual word, *homoousios* (of the same ousia), to describe the relation of Son and Father," (Holmes, *Holy Trinity*, 87).

12. Fiddes, *Participation in God*, 14. Holmes, resuming the Cappadocian fathers' (Basil the Great, Gregory of Nyssa, and Gregory of Naziansus) view of Trinity, insists that, "The Godhead is simple, and exists thrice-over, in *hypostases* distinguished by relation of origin . . . This is Cappadocian Trinitarianism" (Holmes, *Holy Trinity*, 116).

13. Fiddes, *Participation in God*, 15.

affirmation of the distinct identity and otherness of the three persons as having its meaning in their relationships.[14]

From here Fiddes identifies "four pastoral concerns." First, is that of the acknowledgment of the distance between the concept of person and the concept of personage, namely the being and the roles that it embodies in relationship. Second, is the need for "balance between the integrity of the self and openness to others." Third, it is the relation between dependence on others and independence from them, namely the relation between relationship understood as mutuality, and relatedness understood as relating through social roles, and, the fourth concern is the need for balance between "unity and diversity."[15]

Fiddes considers that the idea of the imitation of God should be completed by the idea of participation in God,[16] with its relevance for the experience of God, and for pastoral work, through an engagement in God's relation, exemplified by Fiddes with two Trinitarian practices, the sign of the cross and baptism.[17] Moreover, the engagement in God is the basis for engagement in community through *perichoresis*, in personal relationships, by the way of participation.[18]

On these foundations Fiddes promotes what he calls an "ecclesiology of participation," showing that the church is called to mirror the life of the Trinity. The deep involvement of the three persons of the Trinity in the constitution and life of the church is argued by Fiddes, by reminding the reader of three biblical metaphors of the church, namely, the body of Christ, the temple of the Holy Spirit, and the people of God.[19] He says, "The metaphor of the body begins with the Son, as the church is identified with Christ. The image of the temple directs our attention first to the Spirit, indwelling

---

14. Fiddes, 16. Also, Zizioulas, *Being as Communion*, 17.
15. Fiddes, *Participation in God*, 19–25.
16. Fiddes, 28–29.
17. Fiddes, 30–34.
18. Fiddes, 46–50. Similarly, Colin E. Gunton argues in the same line with Fiddes that the concept of *perichoresis* as it "opens up all kinds of possibilities for thought . . . can be developed to serve as an analogical concept . . . the concept of perichoresis is of transcendental nature status, it must enable us . . . to explore whether reality is on all its levels 'perichoretic,' a dynamism of relatedness." (Gunton, *The One, the Three*, 163–165).
19. Fiddes, *Participation in God*, 65–68.

the church. The image of the people of God begins from a relationship to God the Father, Father now not of one nation alone but of all humankind."[20]

The influence of German theology, via Schleiermacher and Barth, is seen in the way Fiddes underlines three features of theology in its vital connection with the life of the church.[21] First, following Schleiermacher,[22] Fiddes considers that theology is shaped by the experience of the community, in its practice mirroring the values of the kingdom of God.[23] The presence of the kingdom in community, says Fiddes, is embodied in the unique rule of Christ over the church, a rule that in fact makes the church as the body of Christ to be the embodiment of *episcopate*, or general spiritual oversight of all over all, even though this will not exclude the ministry of an individual.[24] Fiddes argues for a balance between "corporate and individual oversight," in order to avoid disastrous disequilibrium in the life of the church.[25]

Then, Fiddes analyzes the life of discipleship of the church, as expressed in baptismal practice in which the believer confesses his dedication to a life of participation in Christ. For Fiddes this is connected with the prophetic ministry of the community that through its confession of the lordship of Christ over all, challenges the powers.[26] Finally, Fiddes points to the *diakonia* of all members of the community through the *charismata* given to all for all, for assistance in the worship of God.[27] The authority of Christ as the base

---

20. Fiddes, 70.

21. Here we have another meeting place between Fiddes and Stăniloae, as the second considers that "Orthodox theology is a theology of spirituality and of communion, and inasmuch as it is theology of the Church, it is at the same time a theology of the mystery of God's activity in men and of the growth of men into God," (Stăniloae, *Theology and the Church*, 218).

22. Friedrich Schleiermacher, *Christian Faith* (Edinburgh: T & T Clark, 1968), 88–93.

23. Edward Schillebeeckx, *Church: The Human Story of God* (New York: Crossroad, 1990), 116–118. He speaks of "Jesus' praxis of the kingdom of God," as the model for his followers (Schillebeecks, *Church*, 116).

24. Speaking about the exercise of authority in the church, Jonathan Lamb argues "the model of authority: the gentleness of Christ . . . the foundation for exercising authority: the gospel of Christ . . . the purpose of authority: building up the body of Christ . . . the context of authority: a life like Christ's," (Jonathan Lamb, *Integrity: Leading with God Watching* [Nottingham: Inter-Varsity Press, 2006], 69–74).

25. Fiddes, "Theology and a Baptist Way," 22.

26. Fiddes, 22. This confessional dimension of baptism will be explored extensively in chapter 7 of the book.

27. Fiddes, 23. These diakonal and charismatic dimensions of Christian life will be explored in chapter 9 of the books.

for the mutual pastoral ministry of the church, the discipleship life of the church and the togetherness of the worship of the church, are all dimensions of the experience of the church that shapes its theology.

From the connection of theology with the *experience* of the community, Fiddes continues with the connection of theology with the *confession* of the community. Fiddes agrees with Karl Barth in affirming that theology "is the confession of the church in response to God's self-revelation."[28] From Barth, Fiddes understands the need of differentiation between "the first-order theology that is church confession, and the second-order theology that is an examination of the confession of the church."[29] Fiddes also notes the distinction between the confession and the creed of the church, the creeds being "seen as binding belief and conscience," and confessions as being "associated with the covenant" of members of a community, without being a condition for "walking together."[30] Third, Fiddes connects theology with the *stories* of the community. In this regard Fiddes, following McClendon's insight about the immediacy in which a community lives the biblical story, says that theology is about "interaction of the story of scripture with the story of the community."[31]

Stating the Baptist way of doing theology as "a continual re-making, a collegiality, a living in the biblical story, a generous pluralism."[32] Fiddes af-

---

28. Fiddes, 24. See also, Karl Barth, *Church Dogmatics*, vol. 1, part 1, 2nd ed. (Peabody, MA: Hendrickson, 2010), 4 (referred to hereafter as *CD*, 1.1, 2nd ed.).

29. Fiddes, "Theology and a Baptist Way," 24. See also Barth, *CD*, 1.1, 2nd ed., 71–86.

30. Fiddes, "Theology and a Baptist Way," 24–25.

31. Fiddes, 26. Also, James W. McClendon, Jr, *Systematic Theology*, vol. 1, *Ethics*, rev. ed. (Nashville, TN: Abingdon, 2002), 31.

32. Fiddes, "Theology and a Baptist Way," 32, See also, McClendon, *Ethics*. McClendon in fact defines theology as being: "The discovery, understanding, and transformation of the conviction of a convictional community including the discovery and critical revision of their relation to one another and to *whatever else there is*." (McClendon, 23). Ivana Noble speaks of theology as a:
> triple critical reflection: Theology originates in experience. In continuity with the patristic tradition, we can say that it is an experience of encounter with God, and an experience of the believing community that, with all available help, strives to hold together orthodoxy (the correct way of belief) and orthopraxis (the correct way of life). Theology reflects on that experience, and on the tradition that the experience both initiates and continually challenges. Furthermore, this reflection is critical. It means that theology not only collects data about the experiences but also examines the patterns or norms implicit in the experiences and measures them against its own accumulated principles . . . Theology as a triple critical

firms what he believes is the central theme of Baptist theology, namely, the concept of the covenant,[33] that intersects and mirrors in the community life the characteristics of the eternal covenant of God with humanity.[34] Fiddes lists three characteristics, "First it is God's making peace with humanity, through the sacrifice of Christ; second it is God's agreement to take the Church as God's own people; and third . . . it is the agreed purpose within the very triune life of God, the intention established between Father, Son and Spirit, to create and redeem humanity."[35]

The concept of the covenant, concludes Fiddes, roots the role of theology to "reflect" the vital connection "between human community and divine communion."[36] Also, the concept of covenant circumscribes the concern of theology with the "relation between divine grace and human freewill,"[37] and finally, it opens the possibility for theology to explore "the theme of promise in society and foster a renewal of mutual trust."[38] How the influences explored above shaped the development of Fiddes's theology will be explored in the next section.

6.3. Paul Fiddes's Theology

For Paul Fiddes, God is not a reality disconnected from the world and the problems of humanity. He starts the discussion of God's relation with the world with the concept of the suffering God. Fiddes points out the presuppositions of his theological construct of the suffering God. First, the

---

reflection seeks, deciphers, and puts together traces of God in the transfiguration of human ways of being.
Ivana Noble, *Tracking God: An Ecumenical Fundamental Theology* (Eugene, OR: Wipf & Stock, 2010), 5, 14.

33. Fiddes, Theology and a Baptist Way," 32. See also, Nigel G. Wright, *New Baptists, New Agenda* (London: Paternoster, 2002), 79.

34. Fiddes, "Theology and a Baptist Way," 33. Also, Barth, *CD*, 4.1, 22.

35. Fiddes, "Theology and a Baptist Way," 33.

36. Fiddes, 34. Also, Alan J. Torrance, *Persons in Communion: Trinitarian Description and Human Participation* (Edinburgh: T & T Clark, 1996). Analyzing a Moltmannian way of integrating doxology and theology, Torrance affirms that "Christian worship shares in a human – Godward movement that belongs to God and which takes place within the divine life. It is precisely into and within this that we are brought by the Spirit to participate as a gift of grace," (Torrance, *Persons in Communion*, 314).

37. Fiddes, "Theology and a Baptist Way," 34.

38. Fiddes, 35.

supremacy and universality of God's suffering,[39] second, the particularity of God's suffering in the cross of Christ[40] and third, the entire suffering of the world that is taken into God through the death of Christ.[41]

In Fiddes's thought construct there are four answers to the question of the necessity for believing in a suffering God. The first answer is connected with the meaning of the love of God that cannot be conceived outside its relationship with the suffering of God for the loved one, namely, humanity.[42] The second answer, in Fiddes's thought is connected with the central place of the cross,[43] as it is "the most dense concentration of the suffering of God,"[44] and also "the actualisation in our history of what is eternally true of God's nature."[45] Fiddes's third answer is connected with human suffering, namely, the affirmation of God's suffering "*with* humanity."[46] For Fiddes this idea has two effects. First, it provides a consolation in human suffering due to the fact that God "understands it from within," and second, will prevent any "theological argument of God directly causing suffering," even though "he may allow it."[47] Third, the idea of God's suffering with the world will assure "credibility to a defense of the world as God's creation."[48] The fourth answer to the question of why to believe in a suffering God is connected with the picture of the world today.[49] For Fiddes "the model of the world as organism" opens the possibility to speak of God as a "suffering

---

39. Paul Fiddes, *The Creative Suffering of God* (Oxford: Clarendon, 1988), 2.

40. Fiddes, *Creative Suffering*, 3.

41. Fiddes, 10. See also Jürgen Moltmann, *The Crucified God: The Cross of Christ as the Foundation and Criticism of Christian Theology* (London: SCM, 1974). Moltmann argues that "In the passion of the Son, the Father himself suffers the pains of abandonment. In the death of the Son, death comes upon Himself, and the Father suffers the death of his Son in his love for forsaken men" (Moltmann, *Crucifies God*, 192).

42. Fiddes, *Creative Suffering*, 16.

43. Fiddes, 25. See also, Stăniloae, *Victory of the Cross*, 1–5. Here is one of the meeting places of Fiddes with Stăniloae as the latter is also arguing for the centrality of the cross in the world, mirroring the innocent suffering of Christ.

44. Fiddes, *Creative Suffering*, 10.

45. Fiddes, 29.

46. Fiddes, 31.

47. Fiddes, 31–32.

48. Fiddes, 33.

49. Fiddes, 37.

God as its creator and sustainer."[50] The presupposition for this possibility is explicated by Fiddes:

> Through his work both in the cross and creation God can manifest himself as "the one who is hidden in suffering" and thus theology of nature and "theology from the Cross" ought to join hands, though so far they hardly seem to have touched fingertips. There can also be an integration between natural theology and existential theology which begins from reflection upon human experience since both are concerned with forms of organic community.[51]

The second question that Paul Fiddes discusses is "How does God suffer?" The issue in discussion is that of the change in God that the suffering seems to presuppose.[52] Fiddes discusses the concepts of God's immutability and impassibility,[53] on the coordinates of this suffering as feeling and constraint. He is challenging the separability of feeling and constraint in regard to God's

---

50. Fiddes, 40.

51. Fiddes, 39–40.

52. Fiddes, 46. The argument about a God who is not passible to the suffering of humanity, in Fiddes's thought, is a sample of engaging, as a Baptist in England, with Protestant-Anglican theology. See in that regard, Thomas G. Weinandy, *Does God Suffer?* (Edinburgh: T & T Clark, 2000). He says, "The passibility of God, was first advocated within an English Anglican setting of the nineteenth-century and early twentieth centuries. With the demise of nineteenth-century optimism and in the face of the social suffering caused by the Industrial Revolution and the agony of World War I, the passibility of God found a cultural climate in which to sprout." (Weinandy, *Does God Suffer?*, 2)

53. Constantin Galeriu, *Jertfă si răscumpărare* (București: Harisma, 1991), speaking about God's immutability he says that "God is immutable in the sense that he is absolute stability in good, truth, but not immobility . . . he is unmoved, unchanged in his nature, but he is movement, is activity, as a living and vivifying principle, as person," 127.

suffering, in traditional theology,[54] considering that perhaps the view of "an apathetic God" makes apathetic believers.[55]

Fiddes affirms the "unity of suffering and change" in God,[56] discussing his affirmation in conversation with patristic and process theology in regard to the issues of potentiality and actuality in God. Accordingly, he compares Aquinas and Hartshorne, and considers that if Aquinas "forbids the movement of suffering in God because it is a movement from potentiality to actuality,"[57] for Hartshorne this movement is crucial. Fiddes concludes:

> God grasps all potentialities and all actualities, but he does not grasp potentials as actuals. This idea is basic to process theology, but it is also an insight which I believe is basic to any assertion of the suffering of God . . . A suffering God is one who has potentialities within him which he has not actualized; only in this way we speak of God who suffers change in suffering.[58]

The second layer of the discussion on the issue of potentiality and actuality is that of the knowledge of God. Fiddes proposes a distinction between what "God knows perfectly in potentiality, and what he knows perfectly in

---

54. Galeriu, *Jertfă și răscumpărare*, 19–20. Also Weinandy, *Does God suffer?*. Weinandy is summarizing the argument of the theologians who argue for the "passibility of God," against the theologians who argue the "impassibility of God": "The static, self-sufficient, immutable, and impassible God of Platonic thought, hijacked, via Philo and the early church Fathers, the living, personal, active, and passible God of the Bible . . . The Fathers of the church too uncritically accepted the immutable and impassible God of the Greeks and in so doing distorted the Christian God of revelation," (Weinandy, 19, 20). See also, Pelikan, *Christian Tradition*. Speaking about the relation of Greek philosophy with Patristic theology, in regard to God's immutability, Pelikan says: "Whether theologians found Platonic speculation compatible with the gospel or incompatible with it, they were agreed that the Christian understanding of the relation between Creator and creature required the concept of an entirely static God, with eminent reality, in relation to an entirely fluent world, with deficient reality – a concept that came into Christian doctrine from Greek philosophy" (Pelikan, *Christian Tradition*, 53).

55. Fiddes, *Creative Suffering*, 48. See also Dorothee Söelle, *Suffering* (Philadelphia, PA: Fortress, 1975). She is arguing that the view of an apathetic God roots "the apathy Christians practiced," and the fact that in the contemporary world of suffering "Christianity has become a stranger to pain" (Söelle, *Suffering*, 41).

56. Fiddes, *Creative Suffering*, 49.

57. Fiddes, 52. Also, Thomas Aquinas, *Summa Theologiae* (London: Eyre & Spottiswoode, 1964), 12:9.1–2.

58. Fiddes, *Creative Suffering*, 52.

actuality as it happens."[59] In this way Fiddes considers that we can describe the suffering love of God as a "pilgrimage of trust and risk," without which "there will not be reconciliation."[60] Moreover, in the context of creation Fiddes affirms that God "creates one who is other than himself, a stranger of his being, and goes on pilgrimage with him. The very act of creation is a kenotic event for God."[61] Fiddes is opposed to the idea of imaginative suffering that "suggests that God feels suffering, but is not changed in any way at all,"[62] the idea of the redemptive suffering, that suggests that God "is under constraint from suffering, but it has not power to overwhelm him because he has freely chosen it as part of his being. He triumphs over suffering because he chooses it for a purpose."[63]

Besides the affirmation of the unity between feeling and constraint, between potentiality and actuality, and the affirmation of the freedom of God in choosing to suffer for the world and with the world, Fiddes affirms also the unity of the will and nature of God,[64] considering "that the key to divine suffering lies in God's desire for fellowship beyond himself."[65] Fiddes concludes:

> If God suffers then he is changed by the world, and he can only be changed to become more truly himself; but he opens himself to this suffering because he chooses mankind for fellowship, and so chooses to be fulfilled through his creation. While this suffering love is a matter of free choice of God, it is at the same time a desire in which there can be no question of God's not longing for our love.[66]

---

59. Fiddes, 55. See also, Wayne Grudem, *Systematic Theology: An Introduction to Biblical Doctrine* (Leicester: Inter-Varsity Press, 1994). He says: "God's knowledge may be defined as follows: God fully knows himself and all things actual and possible in one simple and eternal act" (Grudem, *Systematic Theology*, 190).

60. Grudem, *Systematic Theology*, 56.

61. Fiddes, *Creative Suffering*, 55.

62. Fiddes, 58.

63. Fiddes, 62.

64. Fiddes, 68.

65. Fiddes, 71.

66. Fiddes, 75. See also, John M. Frame, *No Other God: A Response to Open-Theism* (New Jersey: P & R, 2001). Admitting that the Scripture speaks of a change in God's attitude, Frame illustrates the way this happens. He says: "When God 'changes' his attitude

Speaking about the future of a suffering God,[67] Fiddes brings the perspective of the glory of God, namely the "fulfilled desire" of God in regard to his desire for fellowship with humanity. For God suffering means, in Fiddes's opinion, "the unfulfilled desire" in the present for this fellowship with humanity,[68] connected with his protest against this present situation.[69] Fiddes also speaks of God's defeat of suffering,[70] through experiencing it in present time, "redeeming the past and anticipating the future in a new harmony."[71] Fiddes concludes that instead of being fulfilled by the suffering

---

from wrath to favor, it is because the creature has moved from the sphere of Satan to the sphere of Christ," (Frame, *No Other God*, 171). Yet he continues to argue the fact that "God is unchanging in his *essential attributes*," (Frame, 172) "is unchanging in his *decretive will*," and "is unchanging in his *covenant faithfulness*," (173). See also, Grudem, *Systematic Theology*. He differentiates between the incommunicable attributes of God, namely, independence, unchangeableness, eternity, omnipresence, and unity, (Grudem, *Systematic Theology*, 150–180). The communicable attributes of God in Grudem's argument are systematized under three rubrics: Attributes describing God's being (spirituality, invisibility), Mental attributes (knowledge or omniscience, wisdom, truthfulness and faithfulness), Moral attributes (goodness, love, mercy or grace, patience, holiness, peace or order, righteousness or justice, jealousy, wrath), Attributes of Purpose (will, freedom, omnipotence or power, and sovereignty), and Summary Attributes (perfection, blessedness, beauty, glory), (Grudem, 160–221). He defines the unchangeableness of God, arguing that: "God is unchanging in his being, perfections, purposes, and promises, yet God does act and feel emotions, and he acts and feels differently in response to different situations. This attribute of God is also called God's immutability," (Grudem, 163). Grudem, as a Baptist theologian, is influenced in his systematization of the attributes of God by the Reformed theologian Louis Berkhof. See in this regard Louis Berkhof, *Systematic Theology* (London: Banner of Truth, 1958). He speaks also of the incommunicable and communicable attributes of God, (Berkhof, *Systematic Theology*, 57–81). For an Orthodox view see Dumitru Stăniloae, *The Experience of God: Orthodox Dogmatic Theology*, vol 1., *Revelation and Knowledge of the Triune God* (Brookline, MA: Holy Cross Orthodox Press, 1998) (referred to as *Revelation and Knowledge* throughout). Stăniloae speaks of super–essential attributes of God (infinity, simplicity, eternity, supraspatiality, and omnipotence) and of spiritual attributes of God (omniscience, justice and mercy, holiness, goodness and love), (Stăniloae, *Revelation and Knowledge*, 141–243). A more detailed analysis of Stăniloae's view of God's attributes and the way they root his theology of participation, will be provided in chapter 4 of the present project.

67. Dorothee Sölle, *Christ the Representative: An Essay in Theology after the "Death of God"* (London: SCM, 1967). She argues in regard to the future of a suffering God that "In Christ God himself left the immediacy of heaven, abandoned the security of home, forever," (Sölle, *Christ the Representative*, 141), and that "God has a future in Christ," "as Christ took over God's role in the world, but in the process it was changed into the role of the helpless God," (Sölle, 148,150).

68. Fiddes, *Creative Suffering*, 85.
69. Fiddes, 88.
70. Fiddes, 100.
71. Fiddes, 104.

in the world and with the world, God is fulfilled by the fulfillment of his desire to bring humanity into fellowship with him, even though this could be realized *through* his suffering.[72]

Trying to answer the question of how God can suffer and remain God, Fiddes, brings in discussion Barth's thought of the Trinity, comparing it with the thoughts of process theology and of Jürgen Moltmann. Fiddes observes that Barth makes space for immutability in God, in what is called immanent Trinity, as well as for mutability in God in the economic Trinity, preserving the unity of the Trinity by arguing "the whole Trinity in God himself, and the whole Trinity in action in the world, in order to speak of the worldly suffering of both the Father and Son."[73] This patristic principle of the indivisibility of the Trinity, that Barth adopted, is the basis for the dialectic of impassibility and passibility of God, "God can immerse himself in the finite, God can suffer, God can die. The God who is impassible in himself can also be passible in the world . . . God suffers in his divine being when he takes on the 'form of a servant' in the world."[74]

The process theologians, says Fiddes, assert that God "suffers in his contingent nature, but remains untouched by the world in his transcendent nature,"[75] a separation in God that makes room for a concept of "a dipo-

---

72. Fiddes, 109. Also, Clark Pinnock, "Systematic Theology," in The *Openness of God: A Biblical Challenge to the Traditional Understanding of God*, eds. Clark Pinnock, Richard Rice, John Sanders, William Hasker, and David Basinger (Carlisle, Cumbria: Paternoster, 1994), 118. Pinock affirms that "The suffering or pathos of God is a strong biblical theme . . . God suffers when there is a broken relationship between humanity and himself." (Pinnock, "Systematic Theology," 118).

73. Fiddes, *Creative Suffering*, 115. Also, Barth, *CD*, 4.1. Barth says:
Even in the form of a servant, which is the form of His presence and action in Jesus Christ, we have to do with God Himself in His true deity. The humility in which he dwells and acts in Jesus Christ is not alien to Him, but proper to Him . . . It is His sovereign grace that He wills to be and is amongst us in humility, our God, God for us, as that which He is in Himself, in the most inward depth of His Godhead . . . The One who reconciles the world with God is necessarily the One God Himself in His true Godhead. (Barth, *CD*, 4.1, 193).
It is interesting that this distinction in God between essence and work in Barth's theology, that Fiddes detects, is mirrored in the distinction of Stăniloae between "the being and the operations of God," probably under the same influence of patristic theology. See in this regard also Stănilaoe, *Revelation and Knowledge*, 125.

74. Fiddes, *Creative Suffering*, 115.

75. Fiddes, 124.

lar God."[76] God is in process thought, "impossible within himself, and supremely possible for us."[77] Fiddes's own opinion in this regard is that a Trinitarian understanding of "the personal analogy of God," rather than a dipolar understanding of God, proposed by process thought, avoids the danger of equating "transcendence with immutability and impassibility," with the consequence of "diminishing the reality of suffering."[78]

Commenting on Moltmann's view of the unity between immanent and economic Trinity,[79] Fiddes acknowledges the similarity of Moltmann's view with that of Karl Rahner.[80] The direct consequence of Moltmann's view is that the experience of economic Trinity is experienced in the immanent Trinity.[81] Moreover, to the Moltmannian view of the "social analogy of the Trinity," and his insistence on the "inter-personalness"[82] in the detriment of the "persons as relations" of Augustine and Aquinas,[83] Fiddes prefers the Barthian view of "persons in God as modes of being characterized by their mutual relationship,"[84] and the reason for that preference is the fact that in this way we are able "to think of God as a complex relationship," including "our participation in God."[85] Moreover, Fiddes is arguing that the Barthian concept of "God as event" described "in terms of personal relationship,"[86]

---

76. Fiddes, 124. See also, Weinandy, *Does God suffer?*, 23.

77. Fiddes, *Creative Suffering*, 125.

78. Fiddes, 131. See also, Bruce A. Ware, *God's Lesser Glory: The Diminished God of Open Theism* (Wheaton, IL: Crossway, 2000). He warns about the danger of an excessive immanentism and argues that even though God "is intimately involved in the affairs of human history," we should regard his immanence "from the standpoint of undiminished and fully glorious transcendence," (Ware, *God's Lesser Glory*, 141).

79. Fiddes, *Creative Suffering*, 135. See also, Moltmann, *Crucified God*, 240.

80. Rahner, *Trinity*, 22.

81. Moltmann, *Crucified God*, 241.

82. Fiddes, *Creative Suffering*, 139. See also, Jürgen Moltmann, *The Trinity and the Kingdom of God: The Doctrine of God* (London:CSM, 1981), 171, 174–178.

83. Augustine, *The Civitate Dei* (Turnhour: CCSL, 1953), 11:10. Also, Aquinas, *Summa Theologie* (London: Blackfriars, 1964), 12:40.

84. Fiddes, *Creative Suffering*, 140. See also, Karl Barth, *Church Dogmatics*, vol. 1, part 1 (Peabody, MA: Hendrickson, 2004), 375, and Alan Torrance, "The Trinity," in *The Cambridge Companion to Karl Barth*, ed. John Webster (Cambridge: Cambridge University Press, 2000), 81.

85. Fiddes, *Creative Suffering*, 141.

86. Fiddes, 142.

opens the possibility for an understanding of God's transcendence as "transcendent suffering not transcendence beyond suffering."[87]

For Fiddes, the concept of a suffering God is a corrective for what he calls "the concept of a dominating God."[88] The power of God instead of being one of domination, is according to Fiddes, that of "persuasive influence,"[89] expressed through "the story," and "the situation" of a suffering God. The story of a suffering God, on one hand, is a story that provides a meaningful perspective on human suffering,[90] and the situation of the suffering God, on the other hand provides the possibility of inclusion of the human history of suffering.[91]

Fiddes states that "the cross is 'the moment when the distance separating Father and Son has been widened to embrace the whole world,'"[92] and this inclusion of humanity "takes form in forgiveness."[93] In this loving giving of himself, God opens the possibility of human beings to "share in his own love of himself within the Trinity."[94]

There are another two dimensions of the connection of God's suffering in, for and with the world. The first in Fiddes's thought is the experience of death and the second is the experience of alienation. The experience of death for God is, for Fiddes, the experience of "non-being," in entering through the death of Christ in "human desolation and estrangement."[95]

---

87. Fiddes, 143.

88. Fiddes, 145. Also, Sallie McFague, *Models of God: Theology for an Ecological, Nuclear Age* (Philadelphia, PA: Fortress, 1987), 63, 65. She speaks of a monarchical model of God and argues that "in the monarchical model, God is distant from the world, relates only to the human world, and controls that world through domination and benevolence."

89. Fiddes, *Creative Suffering*, 146. Also, Fiddes, *Participation in God*, 37.

90. Fiddes, *Creative Suffering*, 147.

91. Fiddes, 151. Also, Söelle is arguing that
God in the world has been, and still is, mocked and tortured, burnt and gassed: that is the rock of the Christian faith which rests all its hope on God attaining his identity. In this faith, Christians know that God is helpless and needs help. When the time was fulfilled, God had done something for us for long enough. He put himself at risk, made himself dependent upon us, identified himself with the non-identical. From now on, it is high time for us to do something for him.
Söelle, *Christ the Representative*, 151–152.

92. Fiddes, *Creative Suffering*, 151.

93. Fiddes, 169.

94. Fiddes, 171.

95. Fiddes, 205.

The second dimension of the connection of God's suffering with humanity is the participatory aspect of suffering in the experience of alienation. The suffering of this experience takes two forms. The first is that of God's relation with creation and the second is that of the inner life of God. Suffering in connection with the alienation of creation takes the form of total identification with the creation, that has as a consequence God making the alienation of creation his own, through what could be called God's *kenosis*.[96] Fiddes concludes that assuming death and alienation through Christ's cross, God conquered death and alienation generated by sin, through resurrection, opening the possibility of human response. For Fiddes, "It is true that resurrection happens, overcoming death, because death has entered into the being of God . . . by responding to the self-giving love displayed in God's encounter with death, we are enabled to co-operate with God in new possibilities for life which he eternally offers to human personalities in this life and the life to come."[97]

Paul Fiddes starts his journey of exploring the dynamics of salvation by a diagnosis of the human condition. In his description of the human condition in relation to God, Fiddes points out three elements that are in interdependence with each other. First, the "sense of alienation and estrangement," translated in the expression of human beings as "lost," second, the "loss of potential" of human beings in fulfilling the purpose of God for them, and third, the rebellion of human beings that takes the form of breaking down of the horizontal relationships between human beings, and of the vertical relationship between humans and God.[98]

Fiddes continues by naming the generic term that describes the human condition circumscribed by the three elements of alienation, loss, and

---

96. Fiddes, 230. Also, Galeriu mentions the fact that Russian Orthodox theologians "see in creation the manifestation of the Trinity's *kenosis*," (*Jertfă și răscumpărare*, 50).

97. Fiddes, *Creative Suffering*, 267.

98. Paul Fiddes, *Past Event and Present Salvation: The Christian Idea of Atonement* (London: Darton, Longman & Todd, 1989), 6. Stăniloae argues the consequence in a fashion close to Fiddes: "Christian teaching maintains that through the fall into sin, creation has changed from being a transparent means of love between humans and God into what is now largely an opaque wall separating humans from one another, and all humans together from God." Dumitru Stăniloae, *The Experience of God, 2: The World: Creation and Deification* (Brookline, MA: Holy Cross Orthodox Press, 2005), 198 (referred to as *World: Creation and Deification* hereafter).

rebellion, namely, sin. He also analyzes the understanding of this concept of sin and salvation in a historical perspective. He affirms that if in the New Testament period, sin was seen as impurity and atonement "was portrayed as sacrifice," in the period of the church fathers, sin was seen as caused by the hostility of negative powers and salvation was seen as rooted in Christ's victory over "the devil and the hostile powers."[99]

Fiddes continues his analysis of the understanding of sin and atonement in a historical perspective in the period from the early church fathers to the Enlightenment. The first period under scrutiny is that of the centuries up untill the Middle Ages. In this period, due to the influence of Platonism, the human condition in sin was regarded as rooted in the pressure and captivity of the mortal body on the immortal soul, and salvation was regarded as renewal of "the image of immortal God in the whole human being."[100] In the Middle Ages, sin was regarded as caused by "a disturbance of order" imprinted by God into the world, and salvation was regarded as a payment of the debt impossible to be paid by human beings.[101] In the twelfth century the cause of the human condition was "a loss of love," consequently, salvation was regarded as "returning human beings to love."[102] The Reformation saw the cause of the human condition as rooted in the breaking of the law given by God to humanity, and salvation was seen as satisfaction of God's Law.[103] In the Enlightenment period the cause of the human condition was seen as the failure to reach moral standards "to which the mind bore witness, and salvation meant the change in human beings."[104] The last period to which Fiddes refers, is that of modern times, where the cause of the human condition is seen as the conflict between freedom and limitations that generate anxiety, and salvation is regarded as healing of the fragmentation and alienation.[105]

---

99. Fiddes, *Past Event*, 7.
100. Fiddes, 7–8.
101. Fiddes, 8.
102. Fiddes, 9.
103. Fiddes, 9.
104. Fiddes, 10.
105. Fiddes, 10–11.

From here Fiddes focuses his discussion on the vital connection between the past event of the cross and the present reality of salvation. He starts by affirming that salvation happens "here and now," being a "continuous process,"[106] and there are four reasons for that. The first reason is the truth of salvation as restoration of relationships that involves healing, and the response of human beings in the present is vital.[107] The second reason is the unity of creation and redemption,[108] as reflected in the permanent work of God in history to redeem creation,[109] and expressed continuously in the meaning and elements of the eucharistic event.[110]

The third reason for the view of salvation as a continuous process is, in Fiddes's opinion, the continual suffering of God for human beings.[111] The dimensions of God's suffering are expressions for the acceptance of the cost of redemption of humankind, together with God's total identification with the estrangement of human beings, his being there with and for human beings.[112] The fourth reason for the present reality of salvation is the answer to the proclamation of the cross that facilitates transformation in the present of human thoughts, views and lifestyles in connection with God and the surrounding world.[113]

Stating the vital connection of the decisive act or event of the cross and the continual process of the Spirit's work of reconciliation,[114] Fiddes consid-

---

106. Fiddes, 14.
107. Fiddes, 14–15. David Peterson says: "Genuine repentance, however, is not simply a matter of turning from evil with sorrow. It is a matter of turning to God in Christ and placing one's life under his rule and control." David Peterson, *Possessed by God: A New Testament Theology of Sanctification and Holiness* (Grand Rapids, MI: Eerdmans, 1995), 131.
108. Fiddes, *Past Event*, 17.
109. Fiddes, 19.
110. Fiddes, 21.
111. Fiddes, 22. Jon Sobrino, argues that "The Father suffers the death of his Son and takes upon himself all the sorrow and pain of history. This ultimate solidarity with humanity reveals God as a God of love in a real and credible way rather than in an idealistic way." Jon Sobrino, *Christology at the Crossroads: A Latin American Approach* (London: SCM, 1978), 371.
112. Fiddes, *Past Event*, 23.
113. Fiddes, 24.
114. Fiddes, 25. The preoccupation to argue Christology in a vital connection with Pneumatology is a common feature of Stăniloae's and Fiddes's thought. The a way this synthesis is a meeting point between Fiddes and Stăniloae, and the way this christological-pneumatological synthesis is foundational for their view of spirituality is explored in chapter 6 of the present project.

ers that the starting point of discussion about salvation, namely, the objective dimension of salvation, is to be located in the past event of the cross, as an event that is the foundation of the subjective dimension of salvation, that is its experience in the present.[115] Affirming the need to integrate the two dimensions of salvation, Fiddes speaks about "the power of the cross" to enable the present experience of salvation.[116] He also connects the past, present and future dimensions of salvation by saying that "the power of future salvation is the present," as expressed in the Eucharist.

> Eucharist . . . celebrates the three tenses of salvation. There is a remembrance of God's redemptive act in the past, an encounter with the crucified and risen Christ who shares table-fellowship with his disciples in the present, and a longing for the final coming of the kingdom of God, expressed in the words of institution that the celebration is to continue "until he comes."[117]

Fiddes identifies the key element for the harmonization and integration of the objective and subjective dimension of salvation which is the permanency of faith, a reality that is not disconnected from history, yet not enslaved by history.[118] Rather, says Fiddes, "we should place historical facts . . . *alongside* the insights of faith."[119] Fiddes continues on these lines showing the fact that the historical revelation of God in Scriptures with its culmination in the life and ministry of Jesus Christ,[120] redefines and reinterprets, in the light of the reality of God's kingdom,[121] the way in which God's relationship with

---

115. Fiddes, *Past Event*, 26.

116. Fiddes, 27.

117. Fiddes, 30. See also, Jürgen Moltmann, *The Church in the Power of the Spirit: A Contribution to Messianic Ecclesiology* (London: SCM, 1992). He says that "the Lord's Supper is the sign of the actualizing remembrance of the liberation suffering of Christ (*signum rememorativum*). As such it is the prefiguration of Christ's redeeming future and glory (*signum prognosticum*). In the coincidence of remembrance and hope, history and eschatology, it is the sign of present grace, which confers liberty and fellowship (*signum demonstrativum*)" Moltmann, *Church in the Power*, 243.

118. Fiddes, *Past Event*, 36.

119. Fiddes, 38. Christopher J. H. Wright writes that "salvation is experienced through faith," (Christopher J. H. Wright, *Salvation Belongs to God: Celebrating the Bible's Central Story* [Nottingham: Inter-Varsity Press, 2008], 123).

120. Fiddes, *Past Event*, 42–43.

121. Fiddes, 44.

humanity is intensified. For Fiddes, the event of the cross of Christ "sums up and completes the whole course of Jesus' life."[122] Moreover, the unique relation, communion and identification of the Father with the Son in the Christ event and in the cross reveal the real communion desired by God with humanity and also reveal a God deeply involved and participating in the suffering of the world.[123] The proof for this participation is the common suffering of the three persons of the Trinity, in the cross.

> The cross reveals the nature of God, not as an invulnerable Absolute, immune from all suffering and change in our world, but as a Father who suffers the loss of His son, a son who is forsaken by his Father, and the Spirit of love and self-giving that moves through this event . . . If we let this shape our faith, we must understand atonement as the bringing of many human sons and daughters into the fellowship of God's own life. This confirms once again that happens here and now.[124]

There are four images that Fiddes identifies as being key elements for a complete view of salvation. First, is the image of *sacrifice*, seen in a biblical and patristic perspective. Fiddes prefers the concept of expiation instead of the concept of propitiation, arguing that in the case of expiation the cost of sacrifice is on "God as well as man," while propitiation points to an allegedly "hostile attitude" of God towards human beings.[125] Moreover, the expiatory sacrifice of Christ is the means that enables the human being's right answer to God.[126]

The second image for a complete view of salvation is that of *justice*. Fiddes considers that the demand of justice makes necessary the condemnation and death of Christ as the foundation of our acquittal and new life in relation with God.[127] Christ assumes in his death on the cross, the judgment of God as a consequence of God's wrath, which is not a penalty of God, rather it

---

122. Fiddes, 47.
123. Fiddes, 57.
124. Fiddes, 58.
125. Fiddes, 75.
126. Fiddes, 79.
127. Fiddes, 88.

is God's acceptance of the consequences or results of human sin.[128] In this regard, Fiddes prefers the view of atonement as a response to "the aims of justice"[129] rather than a payment of "a debt to justice,"[130] for the former view is in harmony with the concept of God's continuous suffering in and with the world, in his identification and sharing in the human condition with the desire for its healing and transfiguration.[131]

The third image for a complete view of salvation is that of threefold *victory* of Christ over sin, satan and powers.[132] Fiddes discusses the victory of Christ over sin in its connection with the internal dominion over human beings, of its connection with the bondage of human life to the law,[133] and in its connection with the tyranny of death.[134] Christ's victory over satan and powers is analyzed by Fiddes in the light of the gospel, first in the direct

---

128. Fiddes, 93. Karl Barth insists that in Christ's crucifixion,
God is supremely God . . . in this death He is supremely alive . . . there is fulfilled in it the mission, the task and the work of the Son of God. There takes place here the redemptive judgment of God on all men . . . We are dealing here with sin . . . the corruption which God has made His own, for which he willed to take responsibility in this one man. Here in the passion in which as Judge He lets Himself be judged, God has fulfilled this responsibility. In the place of all men He has Himself wrestled with that which separates them from Him.
Barth, *CD*, 4.1, 247.
129. Fiddes, *Past Event*, 104.
130. Fiddes, 96.
131. Fiddes, 109.
132. Fiddes, 114. Also, in Barth's thought:
The passion of Jesus Christ is the judgment of God in which the Judge Himself was the judged. And as such it is at its heart and centre the victory which he has won for us, in our place, in the battle against sin . . . As the passion of the Son of God who became man for us it is the radical divine action which attacks and destroys at its very root the primary evil in the world; the activity of the second Adam who took the place of the first, who reversed and overthrew the activity of the first in this place, and in so doing brought in a new man, founded a new world and inaugurated an new aeon-and all this in His passion.
Barth, *CD*, 4.1, 254.
133. Fiddes, *Past Event*, 115.
134. Fiddes, 116. For Dietrich Bonhoeffer,
God's love has become the death of death and the life of man . . . The miracle of Christ's resurrection makes nonsense of that idolisation of death which is prevalent among us today. Where death is the last thing, fear of death is combined with defiance. Where death is the last thing, earthly life is all or nothing . . . But wherever it is recognized that the power of death has been broken, wherever the world of death is illuminated by the miracle of resurrection and of the new life, there no eternities are demanded of life but one takes of life what is offers, not all or nothing but good and evil, the important and unimportant, joy and

conflict and provocation that the life and ministry of Christ brought to the kingdom of evil, and in the final defeat of satan and powers on the cross.[135] Fiddes concludes by underlying the uniqueness of God's victory in Christ, circumscribed by the truth of the victory through suffering,[136] and the truth of victory through weakness.[137]

The fourth image for a complete view of salvation, in Fiddes's view is that of *love*. Fiddes speaks of the redemptive power of God's love,[138] in its sacrificial dimension of this love that is, in Fiddes words, "the means as well as the motive of redemption."[139] For Fiddes the cross is the event "that reveals the love of God,"[140] a God who "loves in freedom,"[141] and opens himself to humanity,[142] for the "transformation of humanity through Christ,"[143] is in the "power of the Spirit."[144] The corollary of the present experience of salvation is the permanency of the reality of forgiveness, acts of political engagement and the protest against, presence in, and the acceptance of suffering.

Fiddes explores the issue of forgiveness, acknowledging the aim of forgiveness as reconciliation, the blockages to forgiveness, namely the barriers which hinder the relationship, and the need for healing of relationships.[145] For these to be realized, says Fiddes, a reciprocal journey of forgiveness is

---

sorrow . . . It is from beyond death that one expects the coming of the new man and of the new world, from the power by which death has been vanquished. . . Dietrich Bonhoeffer, *Ethics* (New York: Macmillan, 1955), 59–60.

135. Fiddes, *Past Event*, 118.
136. Fiddes, 125.
137. Fiddes, 126.
138. Fiddes, 141.
139. Fiddes, 143.
140. Fiddes, 148.
141. Fiddes, 158. Fiddes takes this expression from Barth, see Barth, *CD*, 2.1, 257.
142. Fiddes, *Past Event*, 160.

143. Fiddes, 166. Fiddes is close here with Stăniloae's argument of this transformative identification of God with humanity. Stăniloae says: "In Christ we see how God overcame death by uniting Himself with humanity through love, rather than arbitrarily using omnipotence to defeat death, He made us beloved by God and capable of receiving His power so that we too can defeat death through His love." Stăniloae, *Holy Trinity*, 43; also, Stăniloae, *Sfânta Treime sau La Început a fost Iubirea*, 52.

144. Fiddes, *Past Event*, 167.

145. Fiddes, 172. Also, Trudy Govier, *Forgiveness and Revenge* (London: Routledge, 2002). She defines forgiveness as "a matter of dealing with anger and resent(ment) and attitudes while reconciliation is a matter of dealing with remaking a relationship," (Govier, *Forgiveness and Revenge*, 77).

necessary,[146] that involves two dimensions, an active dimension, that of "sympathy" that comes from an understanding of the reasons and resorts of the offence, and a passive one, that of "endurance," coming from "a submitting to the consequences" of the offence.[147]

This practice of forgiveness mirrors the vertical dimension of forgiveness that implies a journey of the offended God for and with the offending fallen humanity. Fiddes exemplifies the twofold journey of forgiveness in the way of God's offering of reconciliation in Christ through the cross.

> Through the twofold journey of forgiveness, through the stages of awakening awareness and absorbing hostility, the forgiver is learning how best to win the offender to himself. The fruit of agonizing journey is the ability to draw a hostile and stubborn heart into forgiving love . . . God's Spirit is able to wrestle with human spirits today and draw them into reconciliation because he has made the journey of discovery in the cross. God's approach to us is shaped to our needs because it is marked by the experience of Calvary; the God who comes to us here and now is the one who was *then* in the cross and who has been marked eternally by it.[148]

For Fiddes this vertical dimension of forgiveness is of paramount importance not only because it is a model for the horizontal dimension, but also because it is a resource for overcoming guilt. This guilt is expressed in not accepting forgiveness for oneself, leading to hostility and anxiety.[149] Fiddes argues for

---

146. Fiddes, *Past Event*, 173.

147. Fiddes, 174.

148. Fiddes, 178.

149. Fiddes, *Past Event*, 179. The way Fiddes argues the synthesis between vertical and horizontal dimensions of forgiveness is important, for the risk is that of captivity of the concept in its vertical dimension. See in this regard, Geiko Muller-Fahrenholz, *The Art of Forgiveness: Theological Reflections on Healing and Reconciliation* (Geneva: WWC Publications, 1996). The author signals the same danger: "This vertical reduction of forgiveness between sinner and God" ignores "its effect and impact in the social and natural realms," "placing the sinner at the centre of theology and spirituality, not the victim, the one who is sinned against . . . This reductionism led to the privatisation and spiritualisation of sin and forgiveness," "it left the concerns of salvation, including forgiveness, to the realm of the gospel, whereas the concerns of the 'world' including economics and politics, belonged to the realm of the law," (Muller-Fahrenholz, *Art of Forgiveness*, 12–13). See also, Christopher Jones, "Loosing and Binding: The Liturgical Mediation of Forgiveness," in *Forgiveness and Truth: Explorations in Contemporary Theology*, eds. Alister McFayden, Marcel Sarot, and Anthony Thiselton

the need to overcome the temptation of refusing responsibility of true guilt, by finding justifications,[150] or the temptation of being trapped in a false guilt and feeling responsibility for the effects of our limits.[151]

Fiddes considers that the way God offers his forgiveness, "for a life of freedom from our past history and our present character," should be a resource for distinguishing between true and false guilt, and should lead to the courage to assume our true guilt, namely, "the sense that 'I' am less than I can be," and "I need not have done what I did," and repent,[152] understanding that in spite of our guilt we are accepted by God "being generous in our penitence, as God is generous in his forgiveness."[153]

If the experience of salvation here and now is a reality, based on the past event of the cross, then this experience has as its consequence social involvement in addressing the injustices and evil in the world. Fiddes argues that this is a natural participation in the way God is related to the actual world.[154] The model for this attitude is God's own "immersion into the situation of human sin,"[155] having as a result the crucifixion of the Son "by human hands."[156]

(Edinburgh: T & T Clark, 2001). Jones points out the same major problem of contemporary Christian communities that is reflected in Fiddes's preoccupation for arguing the horizontal dimension of forgiveness as a resource for overcoming guilt, namely, "the Churches failure to mediate forgiveness in their worship and corporate life," (Jones, "Losing and Binding," 31). See also, Lesley Carroll, "Forgiveness and the Church," in *Forgiveness: Embodying Forgiveness* (Belfast: Centre for Contemporary Christianity in Ireland, 2002). She is arguing that "Unforgiveness in the life of the church, lack of teaching about forgiveness and lack of community in which forgiveness can be facilitated either formally or informally, damages the relationship of the community to its God. Unforgiveness also disables relationships between community members and ultimately the ability to continue Christ's mission of forgiveness in the world," (Carroll, "Forgiveness and the Church," 6).

150. Fiddes, *Past Event*, 179–180.
151. Fiddes, 181.
152. Fiddes, 182.
153. Fiddes, 183.
154. Fiddes, 190–192.
155. Haddon Willmer, "Jesus Christ the Forgiven, Christology, Atonement and Forgiveness," in *Forgiveness and Truth: Explorations in Contemporary Theology*, eds. Alister McFayden, Marcel Sarot, and Anthony Thiselton (Edinburgh: T & T Clark, 2001). Meditating the same reality described by Fiddes as the immersion of God into the situation of sin, Willmer focuses the discussion on the concept of Christ made sin for us, and connects this reality with the possibility of forgiveness: "If 'being made sin' calls those who live within that 'making' to take responsibility for sin, they are eligible for forgiveness . . . The forgiven one forgives and in forgiving his being forgiven is actualized," (Willmer, "Jesus Christ the Forgiven," 26–27).
156. Fiddes, *Past Event*, 193.

Moreover, the entire life of Christ shows the coordinates of God's involvement in society, in the "dialectic of action and submission," where the silence of the cross was "preceded by a ministry of action."[157] In our participation in this dialectic is the understanding of the "meaning of atonement," that enables us "to find the meaning of reconciliation."[158] Fiddes concludes, "God gives the cross meaning, as he reveals himself to have been present there, making the furthest journey of discovery into his creation. He makes this story, written in human flesh and history, available so that all other human stories can acquire meaning also. This past event has a creative power upon the present."[159]

6.4. Summary of Chapter 6

I aimed in this chapter to argue first, the place of Paul Fiddes in the contemporary Baptist world. In this regard we have seen that the recognition of Fiddes, as one of the most important contemporary Baptist theologians, can be seen in the development of his academic career and the positions he has been appointed to during this career. I have also argued that the recognition of Fiddes as one of the most important contemporary Baptist theologians is shown by his significant number of books, articles, and chapters written on various subjects that are connected with the relation between theology and literature, church and society, and Trinitarian and ecumenical theology.

Second, I aimed in this chapter to show several influences that shaped Fiddes's spiritual and intellectual journey. I argued that one important influence is that of the Oxford *ethos* with its interdisciplinary, ecumenical dimensions. Another important influence is the encounter with leading Protestant theologians such as Karl Barth, Friedrich Schleiermacher, Eberhard Jüngel and Jürgen Moltmann,

Following these formative encounters and influences, Fiddes developed progressively as a systematic, Trinitarian and ecumenical theologian. His systematic theology evolved in the way his perspective on God roots his view of human beings and salvation, and of the way in which he views

---

157. Fiddes, 201.
158. Fiddes, 203.
159. Fiddes, 220.

the development of God's relationship with the world and of the world with God. Fiddes tries to build his theological construct on two pillars, namely, Scripture and tradition and he tries to avoid the often present sterile Biblicism of many theological systems. Fiddes's ecumenical thought developed based on his ecumenical perspective on theology, namely the multi-denominational, pluralistic and inclusive way of doing theology, in dialogue between Scriptures and tradition and in conversation with other traditions from the Christian family.

Fiddes tries to argue a concept of God that is not disconnected from the suffering of God. In spite of his critique of impassibility of God understood as immobility, Fiddes seems to be aware of the fact that the fathers, by maintaining the doctrine of the immutability and impassibility of God, preserved the truth of the transcendence and immanence of God, without undermining one for the other. Also, they preserved the doctrine of creation *ex nihilo* as opposed to the Platonic philosophy,[160] affirming the dependence of the created order on God, without God being dependent on the created order. They affirmed the eternity, perfection, omnipotence and goodness of God, and the incorporeality, incomprehensibility, infinity and omnipresence of God.[161] All these attributes are speaking in the fathers' thought of the mystery that God is, in his otherness.[162] Yet, one could detect some possible issues that are pointed out, rightly, by Fiddes's doctrine of God.

First, Fiddes's construct of the doctrine of God, based on the present situation in the world today, is a sample of the necessary permanent struggle of theology to proclaim a God who is not disconnected from the suffering of the word. Second, even though Fiddes could be categorized among the process theologians,[163] the way he argues proves that he is not captive to process theology and he still continues a theological dialogue with theologians who are not process theologians even though they argue the pathos of God, in, for and with humanity.[164] For Fiddes, God, instead of being defeated by suffering as he is not defeated by sin, is permanently responding to these

---

160. Weinandy, *Does God Suffer?*, 109.
161. Weinandy, 109–110.
162. Weinandy, 112.
163. Weinandy, 21.
164. Barth, *CD*, 4.1, and Moltmann, *Crucified God*.

issues transforming evil into good[165] and "Jesus and His redemptive work is the Father's full and decisive response to human suffering and its causes."[166]

Fiddes, as a Trinitarian theologian, evolved from his perspective on the life of the triune God, characterized by a perichoretical movement that opens the divine life towards the world – a movement that became the basis for the human perichoretical movement towards God, and towards each other, in a world that is the body of God having the church as the sacrament of the entire world. And the church as the embodiment of the triune life[167] is an instrument of the Father's continual assistance and address of the suffering in the world, an assistance based on the redemptive work of Christ, through the body of Christ the church, is the context of the Father's invitation for the entire world to return in relationship with him. Jürgen Moltmann, for example, states that:

> In the movements of the Trinitarian history of God's dealings with the world the church finds and discovers itself, in all the relationships which comprehend its life. It finds itself on the path traced by this history of God's dealings with the world, and it discovers itself as an element in the movements of the divine sending, gathering together and experience.[168]

The church as the embodiment of the Trinity's openness in the perichoretical movement is also an offer of God to the entire world to enter the restoration and the process that amplifies this relationship through the participatory dimension of Christ's death and resurrection as celebrated in the Lord's Supper. Moreover,

> the persons of the Trinity perfectly possess all goods as fully actualized, they are incapable of suffering within their divine

---

165. This pattern of God's act in regard to the evil is seen in Exodus 8, in the impossibility of Pharaoh's magicians to stop the evil of the plague (yet they could amplify it, verse 7), only God could stop it (verse 8).

166. Weinandy, *Does God Suffer?*, 214–216. He says that "The Son did not assume some generic, antiseptic or immunized humanity, which would quarantine him from sinful human history and condition, but rather he assumed a humanity which bore the birthmark of sinful Adam, and so entered into our human history as one like ourselves." (Weinandy, 216).

167. Miroslav Volf, *After Our Likeness: The Church as the Image of the Trinity* (Grand Rapids, MI: Eerdmans, 1998), 204.

168. Moltmann, *Church in the Power*, 64.

nature for they never suffer, unlike human beings, the loss of some good . . . this lack of suffering within the Trinity actually purifies their love of all selfish concerns, and so allows it to be thoroughly altruistic. The Trinity loves freely and never in a manner that would benefit themselves – such as to relieve their own suffering . . . Thus all facets of love are fully in act – goodness, commitment, affection, joy, kindness, as well as mercy, compassion, grief, and sorrow.[169]

How Fiddes spiritual journey developed along the systematic, Trinitarian and ecumenical characteristics of his theology are reflected in his view of baptism, the Eucharist and spirituality as vital elements of the lifelong spiritual journey, will be explored in the following chapters of part 2.

---

169. Weinandy, *Does God Suffer?*, 226–227.

CHAPTER 7

Fiddes's Theology of Participation in His Thought about Baptism

7.1. Trinitarian Participation as the Atmosphere for Human Participation

Fiddes considers the life of the Trinity as being of paramount importance for the Christian life. He acknowledges the fact that the issue of human participation in the life of the Trinity has been a perennial preoccupation in the Christian thought, from the fathers to contemporary days. By showing the hesitation of many fathers to affirm the possibility for human beings to participate in the inner life of the Trinity, Fiddes appreciates the fact that there was a unitary reaction of the fathers towards the Arian conception of the inferiority of the Son in regard to the Father under the influence of neoplatonism.[1]

Moreover, Fiddes notes the fact that the fathers preferred to use the concept of generation in describing the relationship between the Father and the Son, whilst the concept of participation was used in regard to the relationship of creatures with God.[2] The debate was somehow concluded

---

1. Paul S. Fiddes, "Participation in the Trinity," *Perspectives in Religious Studies* 33, no. 3 (2006): 375–376. Also, Athanasius, "Defence of the Nicene Definition," in *Nicene and Post-Nicene Fathers*, series 2, vol. 4, ed. Philip Schaff (Peabody, MA: Hendrickson, 1999). Athanasius argued concerning the Son that: "He was of the essence of the Father . . . being alone truly for God . . . in all things exact and like the Father." Athanasius, "Defence of the Nicene Definition," 163).

2. Fiddes, "Participation in the Trinity," 377. Also, Meyendorff, *Study of Gregory Palamas*. He describes Palamas's view of participation in God, "Thus, also, through each of

by Gregory Palamas with his distinction between the essence of God, in which human beings cannot participate, and the uncreated energies of God, the only reality through which human beings could participate in God.³

Besides the Eastern formulations, Fiddes continues, there are also Western attempts to explain the concept of participating in God. He notes that Aquinas tried to understand this concept in a different manner than the Eastern tradition, arguing for the possibility of human beings to share in the essential life of God, by the way of knowledge, in a "space of encounter," superior to mind, since the mind cannot contain what cannot be contained, namely God. Aquinas speaks of that movement in which intellect is "raised above its nature" by the "created grace" of God, and in this way opening the possibility "of a direct vision of the uncreated essence."⁴ But even with Aquinas's view, the possibility for direct participation, says Fiddes, remains only an eschatological hope. With this acknowledgment, Fiddes proposes that a real Trinitarian understanding of participation means that, "Human persons are involved . . . in the interweaving, mutual relations of the Trinity. It is as if God 'makes room' within God's own self for created beings to dwell, in the midst of eternal relations of self – giving and other-receiving love between the Father, the Son, and the Holy Spirit."⁵

Fiddes notes the actuality of the discussion of the participation in Trinitarian life in the thought of Alan Torrance who speaks of "doxological and semantic participation in God,"⁶ and Miroslav Volf's opinion that there is no interior participation of human beings in the divine life, rather "human beings indwell the life – giving ambience of the Spirit."⁷ In his turn Fiddes considers that a key concept for the problematics of participation is that of

---

his energies one shares in the whole of God . . . the Father, the Son and the Holy Spirit," 220. See also, Stăniloae, *Viața și învățătura Sfântului Grigorie Palama*, 244.

3. Fiddes, "Participation in the Trinity," 378.

4. Fiddes, 378. See also, Thomas Aquinas, *The Summa Theologica* (Chicago: Encyclopedia Britannica, 1952). He argues that "in order to see God, there must be some likeness on the part of the seeing power whereby the intellect is made capable of seeing God. . . . Therefore it must be said that to see the essence of God there is required some likeness in the seeing power, namely, the light of divine glory strengthening the intellect to see God . . ." Aquinas, *Summa Theologica*, 52.

5. Fiddes, "Participation in the Trinity," 379.

6. Fiddes, 380. See also, Torrance, *Persons in Communion*, 362.

7. Volf, *After Our Likeness*, 211.

divine persons as "subsistent relations,"[8] or a concept of God as an "event of relationships,"[9] and Fiddes argues that mirroring the Barthian concept of God as "event."[10] "Talk about God as 'an event of relationships' is not therefore the language of a spectator, but the language of a participant . . . Thus, through our participation, we can identify three distinct movements of speech, emotion and action which are like relationships 'from father, to son,' 'from son to father' and a movement of 'deepening relations.'"[11]

Fiddes continues by exploring the way in which mystical theologians bridged the gap between the divine being and human beings, in their synthesis between "positive and negative, affirmations and denials, word and silence," and he notes that for them the two approaches, namely, *kataphatic* and *apophatic* are in a direct interaction.[12] From here Fiddes argues that the concept of *perichoresis* is the best way to express the theology of participation.[13] The concept of *perichoresis* describes the uniqueness of communion between the three persons of the Trinity, their participation in each other, their reflection in each other, without the dissolution of one in the other and without confusion of one with the other. It also prevents, Fiddes says, any concept of God "as a dominating authority whose power lies in immobility and in being secure from being affected by the changing world."[14] Moreover, the unique dynamics of the communion in the inner Trinitarian life is expressed in Eastern tradition by the *perichoresis* as a dance, whilst the Western tradition goes so far as to consider the common nature of the three persons as the *perichoresis* of persons.[15] Fiddes seems to favor the view of the Eastern tradition, in his understanding of the Western tradition's view as being followed by a dangerous possibility to regard the inner Trinitarian communion a "closed circle," not open to any partners from outside, namely,

---

8. Fiddes, *Participating in the Trinity*, 380.
9. Fiddes, 381.
10. Barth, *CD*, 2.1, 263.
11. Fiddes, *Participating in the Trinity*, 382.
12. Fiddes, 384. Also, Denys Turner, *The Darkness of God: Negativity in Christian Mysticism* (Cambridge: Cambridge University Press, 1995), 160–163.
13. Fiddes, *Participating in the Trinity*, 385
14. Fiddes, 386
15. Fiddes, 387. Also, Mănăstireanu, *PM*, 77, says that "perichoresis derives from the Greek noun *chora*, meaning 'space' or 'room' and from the verb *chorein* . . . which can be translated as 'to contain,' 'to make room' or 'to go forward.'"

humanity.[16] However, Fiddes affirms the contribution of both traditions, Eastern and Western, to the understanding of the theology of participation, understanding the way the two complement each other, "Tracing the Western pattern, we find ourselves participating in a movement of mutual giving and receiving; following the Eastern pattern we find ourselves involved in the mission of God to the world."[17]

From here Fiddes argues the participation of all creation in the divine perichoretical dance,[18] not through an authoritative intervention of God in creation, but through his embracing of the world in the divine persuasive influence, through the Holy Spirit. Fiddes sees this reality expressed in God's covenant with creation (Genesis 9:8) and in the expectation of the entire creation for God's redemption (Romans 8:19–22).[19]

However, this participation of the entire creation in God, initiated and sustained by the persuasive influence of God in the entire creation, through the Holy Spirit, is differentiated, by what Fiddes calls, "a conscious relationship of trust, expressed in the 'yes' to the Father through the Son," and the relationship with God of those who continually say "no" to God. It is the "humility of God" in the world that allows human beings to say "no" to him, and if these movements of saying "yes" or "no" to God are realized in the encompassing movement of the Trinitarian life in creation, the "yes" or "no" is spoken in the Trinity.[20] However, the "yes" of human beings to God, is spoken in the "yes" of the Son to the Father, and mirrors his self-giving and obedience to the Father, opening the way in which the participation in God informs and frames the participation of human beings in each other.

> Wherever, then, in the world people give themselves to others or sacrifice themselves for others, these actions match the movement in God which is like a Son going forth on mission

---

16. Fiddes, *Participating in the Trinity*, 387.

17. Fiddes, 388.

18. Mănăstireanu, *PM*, 78–79, says that the metaphor of "divine dance" is "based on a confusion or, at best, on a play of words. Thus the verb chorein . . . meaning 'to contain' is confused with the Greek word choreuo . . . meaning 'to dance,' from which is derived perichoreuo . . . meaning 'to dance around.'" However, he says, agreeing with Fiddes, that the metaphor is a good illustration of the dynamism of the perichoretical reality.

19. Fiddes, *Participating in the Trinity*, 388.

20. Fiddes, 389.

Fiddes's Theology of Participation in His Thought about Baptism 135

in response to the purpose of a Father; their acts share in the patterns of love of God, and so in them we can discern the body of Christ . . . At the root of participation in others there is participation in God. To see another object or another person without attempting to control them is to share in the triune life of God. The turning of the self towards an object, and the return to oneself, takes part in those eternal movements in God that we call the mission of the Father and the obedience of the Son. Yet knowledge is always at the same time mystery, since the depths of the beauty in the world derive from the fathomless depths of the personality of God.[21]

7.2. Baptism and the Process of Christian Initiation

In regard to baptism, Fiddes considers that a holistic understanding of it could be achieved through a bifocal lens provided by the tandem of creation and redemption.[22] This bifocal view opens the possibility for a plurality of images that in their togetherness will give a deeper understanding of baptism.[23] The first image that describes baptism, in Fiddes thought, is that of birth "often associated with a return to the womb, and so with regeneration and the renewal of life."[24] The image of birth from and through the water is in Fiddes's opinion, vitally connected with the birth of creation "from the cosmic womb," in the act of creation, with the redemption of Israel through God's "pains of childbirth," and is explicated fully in Jesus's baptism that confirms him as the begotten Son of the Father.[25]

The second image that describes baptism, in Fiddes's thought, is that of spiritual cleansing, that points to the universal need of humans for cleansing, expressed in the "universal use of water for washing."[26] Starting from the

---

21. Fiddes, 390–391.
22. Paul S. Fiddes, "Baptism and Creation," in *Reflections on the Water: Understanding God and the World through the Baptism of Believers*, edited by Paul Fiddes (Macon, GA: Smyth & Helwys, 1996), 47.
23. Fiddes, "Baptism and Creation," 48.
24. Fiddes, 49.
25. Fiddes, 49–50.
26. Fiddes, 51.

centrality of washing in all aspects of Israel's worship life, in the tandem of water and blood, Fiddes shows how the expiatory sacrifice of Christ, through his blood, maximizes, completes and concludes the theme of washing, starting from the inner life and continuing with the external life.[27]

The third image that describes baptism, Fiddes considers, is that of conflict. Baptism is an evocation of the spiritual conflict with the hostile powers, as well as an evocation of the believer's victory over them in Christ.[28] He shows the way in which the Old Testament connection between conflict, victory and redemption is clarified in Christ's victory over the principalities and powers, named by Fiddes as the "idols and the tyrants that they are."[29]

With the fourth and fifth images in describing baptism, those of journey and refreshment, Fiddes shows the vital connection and continuity between the reality of our past salvation, described by the previous images, and the reality of our present salvation. The image of journey speaks of a clear separation between the life of the past life characterized by alienation from God and the present life, characterized by a life of fellowship with God, as an expression of "a new covenant relationship."[30] The image of refreshment on the other hand, points to another dimension of the present salvation that is the permanent "renewal of energies," in the actuality of the "pouring out" of the Spirit.[31]

Fiddes describes baptism as a "boundary-marker,"[32] underlying the fact that believers' baptism is "an act which includes and embraces the professing disciple in fellowship life." This inclusion does not, says Fiddes, mean

---

27. Fiddes, 51–52. See also, Calvin, *Institutes*, 1325, he says that, "Scripture declares that baptism first points to the cleansing of our sins, which we obtain from Christ's blood; then to the mortification of our flesh, which rests upon participation in his death and through which believers are reborn into newness of life and into the fellowship of Christ."

28. Fiddes, "Baptism and Creation," 53.

29. Fiddes, 53–54.

30. Fiddes, 55. Richard L. Pratt, Jr, "Baptism as a Sacrament of the Covenant," in *Understanding Four Views on Baptism*, ed. John H. Armstrong (Grand Rapids, MI: Zondervan, 2007). He says: "the covenant of grace was initiated immediately after the fall into sin, extending from the point in the OT to the end of the NT . . . Baptism administers the NT dispensation of the covenant of grace," Pratt, "Baptism," 64–65. See also, Berkhof, *Systematic Theology*, 272.

31. Fiddes, "Baptism and Creation," 56–57.

32. Paul S. Fiddes, *Tracks and Traces: Baptist Identity in Church and Theology* (Carlisle, Cumbria: Paternoster, 2003), 125.

an exclusion of those on the way to faith, namely, children and adults who were baptized as children.[33] Fiddes argues for a theology of integration based on a view of salvation as process, the key concept being that of initiation.

> If we are to speak of a process of initiation in which baptism may stand either near the beginning (infant baptism) or near the end (believers' baptism), we need constructively to develop a theology of initiatory process . . . The boundary then does not seal off the community of the baptized from others . . . Baptism is indeed a boundary, but is also a witness that crosses all boundaries.[34]

Considering the fact that in accepting the concept of "common baptism," even if it shows the starting point of a believers' union with Christ and with each other in the body of Christ, it proved unproductive for the application of this "commonality" for other areas where Christians from different tradition are still separated. From this reality he considers that there is still much to be said about the potential the "common baptism" concept could have, if one moves from the common *moment* of initiation, namely, baptism, to the common *process* whose start baptism should be.

Fiddes points out the fact that for the Eastern Orthodox (especially the Romanians) this is exactly the meaning of the process of initiation that is intimately connected to chrismation and the Eucharist. For Baptists too it is clear that between conversion, a reality initiated by the grace of God the Father, through the Holy Spirit into communion with Christ, and baptism, there is a process that should be acknowledged.[35] From this participation of the Trinity in the life of believer, we can speak of the believer's participatory response to God's saving grace:

> . . . a strong and continuing stream within the Baptist tradition has regarded baptism in a sacramental way as an encounter between the faith of the believer and the transforming grace of God . . . Placing saving faith before baptism is bound therefore

---

33. Fiddes, *Tracks and Traces*, 126–139.
34. Fiddes, 145, 155–156.
35. Paul S. Fiddes, "Baptism and the Process of Christian Initiation," *The Ecumenical Review* 54, no. 1 (Jan–Apr 2002): 48–49.

to result in an understanding of "becoming a Christian" as something characterized by process.[36]

However Fiddes is prudent, understanding the differences in regard to the elements contained in the process of initiation, differences that exist in the views of Protestant paedobaptist churches and of Baptists, but he thinks that it could be possible to "affirm theologically a 'completeness' in baptism . . . which does not exclude its being only a part of a complete journey of initiation."[37] Fiddes analyzes what he calls "the language of process," in different ecumenical documents[38] as he aims to discuss "baptism as process"[39] towards a "theology of process."[40] Baptism as process means that baptism is not only a moment but also a "life-long growth into Christ."[41] This reality is encompassed by the idea of Christian discipleship, that includes "the formation in faith,"[42] in order to follow Christ in his mission through the church in the world: "While baptism at whatever age, certainly contains some aspects of formation in faith, initiation requires a more extended process of this formation which includes personally owned faith."[43]

7.3. Baptism in the Context of the Theology of Participation

Fiddes speaks of what he calls "a theology of initiatory process," as a necessary framework for the concept of "baptism as process." Here, in the developing of the theology of initiatory process is one of the dimensions of Fiddes's

---

36. Fiddes, "Baptism and the Process," 49.

37. Fiddes, 50.

38. Fiddes, 55. He analyzes the following documents: *Baptism, Eucharist and Ministry 1982-1990: Report on the Process and Responses*, Faith and Order, paper 149 (Geneva: WCC Publications, 1992); David R. Holeton, ed., *Christian Initiation in the Anglican Communion. The Toronto Statement "Walk in Newness of Life": The Findings of the Fourth International Anglican Liturgical Consultation, Toronto 1991*, Grove Worship Series no. 118 (Bramcote, UK: Grove Books, 1991); *Baptism and Confirmation: A Report Submitted by the Church of England Liturgical Commission to the Archbishop of Canterbury and York in November 1958* (London: SPCK, 1959).

39. Fiddes, "Baptism and the Process," 56.

40. Fiddes, 58.

41. Fiddes, 56.

42. Fiddes, 57.

43. Fiddes, 58.

theology of participation. Fiddes's proposal for the elements of this theology of process is summarized in what he calls the "three dynamics," namely, the "interplay of grace and faith," the "interplay of spirit and water," and the "interplay of Christ's body and church."[44]

First, Fiddes considers the interplay of grace and faith in the journey of Christian initiation, a journey initiated by God through God's prevenient grace.[45] This grace is a deep desire of God to be in fellowship with humans. The proper answer of humans to this movement of God's prevenient grace is that of faith. In the case of infant baptism or the blessing of a child this faith is the corporate faith of the community or the vicarious faith of parents, godparents etc. Prevenient grace and corporate/vicarious faith are two concentric realities that overlap being "aspects of participation in God," indicating the participatory movements from God to human beings and of human beings towards God.[46] Prevenient grace and corporate/vicarious faith are continued in the journey of Christian initiation with what is called "transformative grace" and faith of the community and "owned faith," of the individual believer, all these being realities that overlap and are expressed either in believer's baptism or in a practice of confirmation or commitment.[47]

Moreover, as the prevenient grace and transformative grace are to be seen as "continuum," in God's participation in human beings, so vicarious faith and owned faith together with the faith of the community should be seen as stages of the initiatory process of the journey of a believer towards the status of being a disciple. Adding the fact that the daily "baptismal process," is a journey of salvation,[48] Fiddes concludes:

---

44. Fiddes, 58–61.

45. T. C. Hammond, *In Understanding be Man: A Handbook of Christian Doctrine* (Leicester: Inter-Varsity Press, 1968), 137. Hammond defines prevenient grace as meaning "anticipating, predisposing . . . It describes a special work of the Spirit of God whereby, before there is any human will to good, the Holy Spirit recreates in a man the desire to be reconciled to God and to do His will." (Hammond, *In Understanding*, 137).

46. Fiddes, "Baptism and the Process," 58–59.

47. Fiddes, 59.

48. Fiddes, 59–60. Fiddes differs here from Augustine who considered baptism as nothing else than "salvation" and the sacrament of the body of Christ nothing else than "life." See St Augustine, "Treatise on the Merits and Forgiveness of Sins and on the Baptism of infants," in *Nicene and Post-Nicene Fathers*, series 1, vol. 5, ed. Philip Schaff (Peabody, MA: Hendrickson, 1995), 28.

> In the case of infant baptism the later moment of freely accepted discipleship will belong to the foundation of the beginning of the Christian life, Eucharist and confirmation (or some other rite of laying-on of hands) will not complete baptism, but they will complete *initiation*. In the case of believer's baptism, the apprehending of the person by God's grace before baptism, prior faith and first communion are all part of the process.[49]

Second, Fiddes considers the interplay of spirit and water, starting with the tradition of interpretation of relationship between "the seal of the spirit" and water baptism.[50] From here Fiddes considers the continuum of God's participation in the process of salvation in Christ through the Spirit, and considers that is logical to think of "different comings of the Spirit," appropriate to various stages of the process of initiation. Fiddes insists that this is the heart of participation in God's triunic life, a continual, progressive, and deeper immersion in the life of the Trinity that opens the possibility for God to equip the believer, through *charismata*, in order to participate in God's mission in the world. He concludes:

> Just as in baptism the Spirit takes an element of in the natural world – water – and uses it as a place of encounter with God for renewal of life, so the Spirit takes natural human faculties and opens them up as a place to manifest spiritual gifts. When this begins to happen it is the end of the "beginning," the end of laying foundation: a woman or man has become a disciple.[51]

---

49. Fiddes, "Baptism and the Process," 60. In arguing these vital connections and mutuality between God's actions and human's faithful response, Fiddes mirrors a Petrine theological idea: "His divine power has given us everything we need for a godly life. . . For this very reason, make every effort to add to your faith goodness; and to goodness, knowledge; and to knowledge, self-control; and to self-control, perseverance; and to perseverance, godliness; and to godliness, mutual affection; and to mutual affection, love." (2 Peter 1:3, 5–7).

50. Fiddes, 60. Fiddes starts with the Pauline concept of the "seal of the Spirit" showing that most New Testament theologians consider the sealing as happening in the water baptism. Yet, there are theologians (such as Karl Barth and James Dunn) who consider the sealing and water baptism as separate stages, with the precedent of either over the other. For the Eastern Orthodox tradition, the sealing is something that comes after baptism, in chrismation, the same for the Pentecostal-Charismatic tradition, the sealing comes after baptism as "a second blessing." (Fiddes, 60).

51. Fiddes, "Baptism and the Process," 61.

Yet, giving preeminence to the action of the Spirit, Fiddes is close to Stăniloae when arguing that the water is "a place of encounter with God for renewal of life." However, Fiddes tries to keep the balance by the discussion about the interplay of Christ's body and church that will be analyzed below. Third, Fiddes considers the interplay of Christ's body and church, remembering the fact that in the New Testament the concept of the body of Christ has "three meanings," describing three realities "interweaving, overlapping and conditioning each other,"[52] and we can see here a correspondence of the perichoretical dimension of the Triune life as a model for the life of the church. Fiddes develops further on this venue of the theology of participation stating that according to the first meaning of the concept of "body of Christ," that of the risen Christ, the believer enters the participatory reality of "being drawn more deeply into the interweaving movements of the triune life."[53] According to the second meaning, that of the community of the church, the theology of participation is expressed by the fact that the believer/believers are "being conformed to the movement of relationship in God which is like a Son relating to a Father, characterized by a self-giving . . . and a newness of life."[54] According to the third meaning, that of the eucharistic bread shared in the community, Fiddes considers that all who are members of the body and "on the way to being disciples, may share in the Eucharistic body."[55] Fiddes concludes, "At the end of the process of initiation . . . a person relates to the body of Christ as a disciple, commissioned for service. The disciple is in a covenanted relation with other disciples in the community of the church, and exercises the spiritual gifts."[56]

---

52. Fiddes, 61. The three meanings of the biblical concept of the "body of Christ" are: the risen and glorious body of Christ who was crucified, the community of the church and the Eucharist bread in which the community shares.

53. Paul S. Fiddes, "Baptism and the Process of Christian Initiation," in *Dimensions of Baptism: Biblical and Theological Studies*, eds. Stanley E. Porter and Anthony R. Cross (London: Sheffield Academic Press, 2002), 302.

54. Fiddes, "Baptism and the Process," 302.

55. Fiddes, 302.

56. Fiddes, 302.

7.4. Summary of Chapter 7

I aimed in this chapter to explore Fiddes's theology of participation in his thought about baptism. I argued that for Fiddes, Trinitarian participation is the atmosphere for human participation, having *perichoresis* as a key reality. I observed that Fiddes argues the participation of all creation in the divine perichoretical dance, not through an authoritative intervention of God in creation, but through his embracing of the world in the divine persuasive influence, through the Holy Spirit. This giving of the Father in the Son through the Spirit opens the way in which the participation in God informs and frames the participation of human beings in each other.

In this framework I observed that Fiddes considers that a holistic understanding of it could be achieved through a bifocal lenses provided by the tandem of creation and redemption, rooting the possibility for a plurality of images for a deeper understanding of baptism.

He uses the images of birth, spiritual cleansing, conflict, journey and refreshment, considering baptism as a boundary-marker in the life of believers. He argues for a theology of integration based on a view of salvation as process, the key concept being that of initiation. Therefore baptism could be regarded not only as a moment but also as lifelong growth into Christ.

From here I explored Fiddes's view on baptism in the context of the theology of participation, I observed the developing of the theology of initiatory process is one of the dimensions of Fiddes's theology of participation. Fiddes's proposal for the elements of this theology of process is summarized in what he calls the "three dynamics," namely, the interplay of grace and faith, the interplay of spirit and water, and the interplay of Christ's body and church.

CHAPTER 8

Fiddes's Perichoretical Theology in His Thought about the Eucharist

8.1. The Framework of Fiddes's Theology of the Eucharist in a Perichoretical Key

The first element of the framework of Fiddes's theology of the Eucharist is that of a synthesis between creation and redemption, that has its focus in the sacraments of the church, as reminders of the action of God to redeem the fallen creation.[1] This redemptive action, a process that has a past, a present and a future, has as its central focus the cross of Christ, an "enabling event" not only for God's victory but also for the human "response to the forgiving love of God."[2] The Eucharist is in this context, for the Christian community, a celebration of the "three tenses of salvation." In Fiddes's words, "There is remembrance of God's redemptive act in the past, an encounter with the crucified and risen Christ who shares table-fellowship with his disciples in the present, and a longing for the final coming of the kingdom of God, expressed in the words of institution that the celebration is to continue 'until he comes.'"[3]

The second element of the framework of Fiddes's theology of the Eucharist is its connection with the idea of communion and sacrificial living. He connects it with the communion meal eaten "in front of God" in Exodus 24:11

---

1. Fiddes, *Past Event*, 27.
2. Fiddes, 29.
3. Fiddes, 30.

that seems to become the model for the primitive Christian communities' celebration of the Eucharist, "The followers of Jesus eat and drink in the presence of their risen Lord, and as the bond of the new covenant, the Eucharist focuses the nature of all of life as a costly but joyful fellowship with God and other people."[4] The model for this desired reality in the life of God's people and communities is the sacrifice of Christ that "enables and creates our gift-offerings and communion-offerings."[5]

The third element of the framework of Fiddes's theology of the Eucharist is that of the transformative victory of Christ on the cross, a costly victory,[6] a decisive victory over satan and his power,[7] and a transformative victory.[8] This victory is transformative because Christ's victory "*creates* victory" in believers "making possible their response in faith."[9] If faith in the heart is the internal result of Christ's victory, the gathering of these people of faith in the "community of the crucified" is the external result, as this community is the community in which Christ's victory is actualized and repeated.[10] This identification with the crucified and risen Lord is not only the way in which we participate in his death, dying to sin, and his resurrection, living as new humanity (Romans 6:7–9), but also the deeper fulfillment in the Eucharist of the command "do this in *remembrance* of me" (Luke 22:19, emphasis added).

The fourth element of Fiddes's framework of the Eucharist is Christ's transformative presence. Christ is present in the church "in word and

---

4. Fiddes, 78. In connecting the Eucharist with sacrificial living for Christ he is close to Stăniloae who, as we have seen above, connected the real presence of the body and blood of Christ in the Eucharist, and of human sacrifice of submission and surrender to God. See also, Max Thurian, "The Eucharistic Memorial, Sacrifice of Praise, and Supplication," in *Ecumenical Perspectives on Baptism, Eucharist and Ministry*, ed. Max Thurian, Faith and Order Papers (Geneva: World Council of Churches, 1983), 96.

5. Fiddes, *Past Event*, 79. See also, J. M. R. Tillard, "The Eucharist, Gift of God," in *Ecumenical Perspectives on Baptism, Eucharist and Ministry*, ed. Max Thurian, Faith and Order Papers (Geneva: World Council of Churches, 1983). He argues that Eucharist is "gift of God to the Church . . . a gift received in thanksgiving," (Tillard, "Eucharist," 104, 115).

6. Fiddes, *Past Event*, 125.

7. Fiddes, 129.

8. Fiddes, 135.

9. Fiddes, 136.

10. Fiddes, 137. Again here is a meeting point of Fiddes with Stăniloae in keeping the vital connection between the cross of Christ and the resurrection of Christ, in the memorial of Eucharist.

example"[11] in the outpouring of love from God to believers, in the fact that the "dwelling of Christ is poured in our souls," as Abelard taught. Christ is also present in a corporate way in the community of believers (Schleiermacher), and in "the form" of the church in the world, hidden in a humble way in the believers whose condition is that they are redeemed persons yet still sinners (Bonhoeffer).[12]

8.2. The Heart and Dimensions of Fiddes's Theology of the Eucharist

For Fiddes the Trinity with the perichoretical relationships between the Father, Son and Holy Spirit, is the model for the life of the church. Fiddes writes, "The metaphor of body begins with the Son, as the church is identified with Christ. The image of temple directs our attention first to the Spirit, indwelling the church. The image of the people of God begins from a relationship to God the Father, Father now not of one nation alone but of all humankind."[13] He considers that the development of the theology of perichoretical relationships between the Father, Son and Holy Spirit is a synthesis of the thought of the church fathers in concordance with the New Testament. As such any discussion about the Trinity is not to be done in "a language of observation," for this is not proper to the thought of the fathers, rather it is to be done in "a language of participation" with a direct correspondence with the "activity of the triune God through the church," namely, the activity of "economic Trinity."[14] Moreover, the economic Trinity cannot be separated from immanent Trinity, or action cannot be separated from being, because being is action and action is in being.[15]

---

11. See also, Simon Chan, *Liturgical Theology: The Church as Worshiping Community* (Downers Grove, IL: InterVarsity Press, 2006), 63. He says that the Reformers' understanding of the church was that "the church is constituted by Word and Sacrament," (Chan, *Liturgical Theology*, 63).

12. Fiddes, *Past Event*, 161–164.

13. Fiddes, *Tracks and Traces*, 70.

14. Fiddes, 71.

15. Fiddes, 72. The unity between immanent and economic Trinity embraced by Fiddes is another meeting point with Stăniloae and also with Rahner, both arguing in a similar manner this unity. It is a sample of how Trinitarian theology could be a great resource for providing meeting points between theologians from different traditions, as in this case Stăniloae, an Orthodox, Rahner, a Roman Catholic and Fiddes, a Baptist meet in agreement.

Mirroring this triune reality, the church's being is in action and her action is in being, but the action and being of the church are not invented by it, rather are of God:

> The church which acts as body, temple and priestly people in practical ways in the world has the power to serve, to focus the presence of the Spirit and to mediate blessing only because it is caught up in the life of the triune God. It does not have its own mission, but shares in the mission of God towards the world, God's ecstatic movement of love which draws the creation into fellowship with God's own self.[16]

One of the important subjects in which Trinitarian thought brings an important corrective, is that of authority. By saying that the theology of the Trinity is a potential corrective for the "domination of the One," Fiddes explores the process that led to this state of affairs, praising the way the early fathers resisted the idea of what is called "the theological monarchianism," and expresses his sadness that they were not so consistent in resisting "the ecclesiastical monarchianism" based on a "theology of subordination," and leading to "a hierarchy of submission."[17] The corrective for this is, in Fiddes's opinion, the theology of participation, mirroring the divine *perichoresis* as the essence for "relations which are not absorbed," and "a Fatherhood which does not oppress."[18] Fiddes also identifies three areas of domination: of the state, in the church, and of gender discrimination,[19] and affirms that the "engagement in God," brings "the discovery of the power of suffering to change events," and "the experience of *participation* in the making of freedom."[20]

Fiddes continues to show how the participatory perichoretical theological idea, could inform the practice of our prayers. There are three ideas that Fiddes evaluates critically through the lens of our engagement in God. First, is the idea of prayer as a means to obtain what is prepared by God for us, and second is the idea of prayer as a means for our internal transformation,[21] the

---

16. Fiddes, *Tracks and Traces*, 73.
17. Fiddes, *Participation in God*, 65–67.
18. Fiddes, 71–89.
19. Fiddes, 96–101.
20. Fiddes, 97–98. Also, Wright, *Free Church, Free State*, 234–249.
21. Fiddes, *Participation in God*, 121–125.

latter bringing, in Fiddes's opinion, some important insights. The third idea under scrutiny in Fiddes's critique is that of prayer as a means to make God pay special attention to a certain situation or person.[22] Eventually, Fiddes proposes a concept of prayer that he thinks harmonizes the best with the concept of the perichoretical movement of the Trinity in creation, namely, the concept of prayer as an entrance into the partnership of God's love and suffering, influence and persuasion in the world. He says:

> Like God's own presence in the world, there is a "mediated immediacy" of our presence to others. Intercession becomes the enfolding of someone in the interweaving currents of the love of God, and encouraging them to find the movements of health and healing that are already there . . . Our prayer is not needed to get God started, after which we can stand back; God always draws near to people with persuasive love, with or without us, and God's grace will be the major factor in transforming human life; but our intercessions still make a difference to what God achieves, though we be the minor partner.[23]

Fiddes continues by considering the world as the body of God and the church as the living sacrament of God in the world, affirming that sacraments are "doors into the dance of *perichoresis* in God." The incarnation of Christ is, for Fiddes, the paradigm, the lens, and the key, for a complete understanding of the world as the body of God. Church as sacrament in its practical ministry, circumscribed by the synthesis between being and doing, is a doorway to and embodiment of the triune life, as well as an encounter place[24] with the movements of the divine life. The church does this always mirroring the way the triune God acts for and in the world, "being there," understanding from within, and "touching deeply."[25] Fiddes concludes:

> The sacramental life is one that is open to the presence of God, and can open a door for others into eternal movements of love and justice that are there ahead of us, before us, and embracing

---

22. Fiddes, 129.
23. Fiddes, 137–138.
24. Fiddes, 280–296.
25. Fiddes, 296–297.

us. This openness can be felt as an invitation to a dance, but sometimes as the raw edges of a wound. This is participation in God. This is theology.[26]

This is why the Eucharist should not be seen as a static reality, focused on the substantiation of God's presence, rather it should be focused on the uninterrupted movement of God's presence that the church should see and reveal in the midst of the broken and needy world.[27] Only as such is the church a eucharistic community, and this is the subject of the next section where we discuss the dimensions of Fiddes's eucharistic theology.

The first dimension that Fiddes underlines is that of the Eucharist as constitutive for the life of the church.[28] This conception is based on the biblical text of Matthew's Gospel chapter 18 verse 20: "For where two or three gather in my name, there am I with them." For Baptists, says Fiddes, Christ is present in his authority exercised through the three offices, priest, prophet and king, as well as present in the Eucharist, in the material elements of it, as well as in the church as a body.[29] Baptists in their history, argues Fiddes, embraced a synthesis of the thought of Calvin and Zwingli, considering that the presence of Christ in the Eucharist is a spiritual one, as the resurrected body of Christ is in heaven, and cannot be present at the same time on earth. This spiritual presence was, for Baptists in the past says Fiddes, made possible through the Holy Spirit. For Baptists from the seventeenth century to today the spiritual nourishment that the Eucharist represents is along with the eating of the elements of bread and wine, and for some eating in faith opens the possibility for this spiritual nourishment.[30]

Further developments on these lines led Baptists, in the past, to speak of the sharing of the Eucharist as a means to grow, as the sacrament is a call for a closer fellowship with Christ[31] and with each other in the unity of one

---

26. Fiddes, 302.

27. Fiddes, *Participation in God*, 182–183.

28. Fiddes, *Tracks and Traces*, 157. Again here Fiddes is close to Stăniloae's view of the Eucharist as being constitutive for the church, and with Zizioulas's view that the Eucharist "is a foundational act of the church, the act that makes the church." (Fiddes, 157). See this in Karkkainen, *Introduction*, 96.

29. Fiddes, *Tracks and Traces*, 158.

30. Fiddes, 159–164.

31. Fiddes, 165.

body.³² Fiddes understands that there are differences of emphasis between different groups of Baptists, ones that will agree more with an insistence on the elements of the Eucharist and others that will insist more on the spiritual reality that they describe and lead to.

However, it is clear, says Fiddes, that for both accents the elements of both bread and wine are connected with the spiritual nourishment of believers by Christ through the Holy Spirit. A radicalization for a looser connection of the presence of Christ in the Eucharist is connected, as Fiddes argues, with a revival of a sacramentalist view in the Protestant and Catholic traditions of the nineteenth century, a radicalization that led even to an equation of the preached word with the Lord's Supper in regard to the presence of Christ. This viewpoint soon opens the way for the conception of the Lord's Supper as being a symbol of Christ's presence.³³

The second dimension of Fiddes's understanding of eucharistic theology is that of the Eucharist as a door for a deepening of God's presence in his community and a more profound transformation of the community as "the body of Christ broken for the life of the world." This is so because Baptists keep together the vertical and horizontal dimension of the communion, as communion with Christ is always vitally connected with communion with

---

32. Fiddes, 165–166.
33. Fiddes, 166–167. *Sunday School Chronicle*, 17 February 1882, "Spurgeon's Scrapbooks, Numbered Volumes," vol. 6, page 8. Spurgeon argued that "there is no sermon like the Lord's Supper" (*Sunday School Chronicle*, 8). See also Peter Morden, "The Spirituality of C.H. Spurgeon: II Maintaining Communion: The Lord's Supper," *Baptistic Theologies* 4, no.1 (Spring 2012): 49–50. Morden concludes his analysis of Spurgeon's theology of the Eucharist:

> Spurgeon believed that the Lord's Supper should be celebrated often. He stressed the importance of frequent celebration because he believed the Supper was central to the Christian life, a belief which was based, in significant degree, on his experience at the Table. Spurgeon also believed the Supper should be celebrated simply and with other Christian Approaches which detracted from this simplicity or the corporate nature of the Lord's Supper. . . . Several of Spurgeon's central emphases concerning the Lord's Supper are present in this extract. The Supper as an accessible, effectual means of communion with Christ is one such emphasis; the Supper as a place where Christians know fellowship with each other is another. At the Table Spurgeon believed that the walls that separated believers from other believers could be broken through and (although he did not say so explicitly in this extract) the walls that separated believers from Christ too. The Lord's Supper thus takes us to the heart of Spurgeon's spirituality. As the bread was broken and the wine poured out Spurgeon knew "communion with Christ and his people."

Morden, "Spirituality of C.H. Spurgeon," 49–50.

each other. Second, through participation in the body and the Eucharist the believers are also becoming a sacrament for the world, pointing to the presence of Christ, not only in the microcosm of the church but also in the macrocosm of the whole world, "becoming doorways into the flowing relationships that we call Father, Son and Holy Spirit, entrances into the dance of their *perichoresis* of love."[34]

Fiddes continues by arguing the fact that this double communion with Christ and with each other is also powerfully connected with the *anamnesis* of the community of believers, because it is the redemptive story of each individual with Christ and the common story of God's presence, through Christ in the Spirit that the community shares. This culminates with the sharing in the Eucharist by remembering the story of Christ's work for them and in them. In this dynamics of transformative *anamnesis*, in which Christ is present as the believers share the eucharistic bread and wine, the believers, argues Fiddes, become for Christ, and in submission to his lordship, "means of his presence in the world."[35] Fiddes says:

> Just as Christ uses the physical stuff of bread and wine as a meeting-place between himself and his disciples, so he uses their bodies as a means of encountering them through each other, and as a meeting place with those outside the church. If we understand the sacraments as doorways into the fellowship of God's triune life, then the community itself is being made an entrance, for its members and for all others.[36]

Pointing out that the concept of church as sacrament is a common belief for the Orthodox, Catholic and Protestant traditions,[37] Fiddes considers that there two reasons why this concept is proper for Baptists. First, is the way the church gathers to find the mind of Christ[38] in the knowledge of

---

34. Fiddes, *Tracks and Traces*, 168–174.
35. Fiddes, 169–170.
36. Fiddes, 170. See also Fiddes, *Participation in God*, 281–283.
37. Pericle Felici, "Lumen Gentium 1:9 and 48," in *The Documents of Vatican II*, ed. Walter M. Abbott, (Baltimore, MD: America Press, 1966). Also, Walter Kasper, *Theology & Church* (London: SCM, 1989), 111–127. He speaks of the church as "a universal sacrament of salvation" (Kasper, *Theology & Church*, 111). See also, Karl Rahner, *Theological Investigations*, vol. 4 (London: Darton, Longman & Todd, 1966), 36–73.
38. Fiddes, *Tracks and Traces*, 171.

Fiddes's Perichoretical Theology in His Thought about the Eucharist   151

Christ imparted horizontally through the decision of all believers, making their common baptism as "an ordination." Second, it is this ordination that bestows "responsibilities of active discipleship" for each baptized member to exercise their gifts and calling to find and fulfill Christ's will for their lives and mission.[39]

The openness of the Trinity, in this perichoretical dance, to the entire creation, is for Fiddes the model of the transformation of the Eucharist as an open communion within the multi-traditional Christian family. He agrees with Daniel Turner that "it is the duty of all Christian churches . . . to lay the table 'as open as possible' to the free access of ALL, who appear to love our Lord Jesus Christ in sincerity."[40] Such openness, argues Fiddes, is to be based first, on the mutual recognition of a common pattern of Christian initiation,[41] and second, on the discernment of "different ways of belonging to the 'body of Christ'" appropriate to "the different stages in the process of initiation."[42] Again for Fiddes this theological attitude of the Christian community is to be rooted in the *perichoresis* of the persons in the Trinity.

> Together in community they make up the whole body; so the life of the community, mapped onto the life in God, is not just "like" a body – it is the body of Christ. Likewise the actions of breaking of bread and the pouring of the wine can fit into the movement of self-breaking and self-outpouring within God, becoming the place where we encounter in an ever deeper way of the self-giving of Christ.[43]

The third dimension of Fiddes's eucharistic theology is that of the Eucharist as defining membership in the church. Fiddes observes that in their history even though they stressed the importance of adult baptism, Baptists did not make it mandatory for membership in the church. He shows that Particular Baptist theologians from the seventeenth century (John Bunyan, Henry Jessey), through the eighteen century (Robert Robinson), to the

---

39. Fiddes, 123.
40. Fiddes, 177. Also, Daniel Turner, *A Compendium of Social Religion* (London: John Ward, 1758), 119.
41. Fiddes, *Tracks and Traces*, 182.
42. Fiddes, 183.
43. Fiddes, 189–190.

nineteenth century (Robert Hall), accepted baptized infants for eucharistic communion, even though they regarded them as "unbaptized."[44]

Fiddes adds the fact that for Particular Baptists, open communion was acceptable for all believers from other Christian traditions, believers who showed the "marks of faith." The General Baptists on the other hand, continues Fiddes, opposed the practice of open communion on the basis of the connection they saw between adult baptism and the Eucharist, rather than to look at obedience to Christ as the Particular Baptists did.[45] However, for Fiddes, the reason for Baptist "open communion" is the need to preserve "the unity of church in the bond of love." He argues that this is based on the theology of the church as universal and on the catholic ecclesiology that led to a theological synthesis to regard the body of Christ in its double, local and universal dimensions.[46] Fiddes concludes, "The Supper, shared with all Christians, is both a way of manifesting unity now and a foretaste of the future oneness of the church. Likewise, as Spurgeon pointed out, the use of bread, wine and water in the sacrament is an anticipation of the 'lifting up' of matter in the final glorification of the whole creation."[47]

Fiddes is aware of the fact that the discussion of open communion among Baptists is a complex one. Theologians who are on both sides, for and against, have continually debated it, but he brings into attention another argument on which believers in open communion have based their thought, namely the need to respect and acknowledge the freedom of personal conscience of all believers.[48] This is so, they say, because everybody will be accountable to Christ.[49] Fiddes observes that for those who believe in open communion paedobaptism could have been acceptable enough for being considered a member of the church, without denying their deep conviction for adult baptism.[50] He concludes from here that it is clear from the argument of

---

44. Fiddes, 175.
45. Fiddes, 176.
46. Fiddes, 176–178.
47. Fiddes, 178–179. Also, Charles Haddon Spurgeon, "The Double Forget-Me-Not," in *Metropolitan Tabernacle Pulpit*, vol. 54, no. 3099 (London: Passmore and Alabaster, 1908), 315.
48. Fiddes, *Tracks and Traces*, 179.
49. Fiddes, 180.
50. Fiddes, 181.

the Baptists who favored open communion, that baptism is the formal incorporation into the body of Christ, being as such the beginning of the communion in the body of Christ.[51] In the words of Daniel Turner:

> Our Paedobaptist Brother pleads, "That he believes that he is rightly baptized-that if he is mistaken, it is an Error of his Head, not of his Heart . . . That is . . . does not affect the Institution itself, which he reveres, but only the Subject and Mode of it – That he . . . feels in his Conscience the same obligations to Holiness of Life, which are the Essentials of Baptism."[52]

From these observations and considerations Fiddes elaborates the connection of the Eucharist, and membership in the body of Christ, with the process of initiation. He starts from his idea of "mutual recognition of a 'common pattern of Christian initiation,'"[53] that will focus not on the "mode" of baptism but on the entire process of Christian initiation. This process of initiation, Fiddes argues,

> must include the prevenient grace of God working deep within the human heart, some act of blessing and welcome of infants by the church corporately (where children in the church are on the journey of faith), formation of faith, an obedient "yes" to God in Christ for oneself, immersion or sprinkling with water in the triune name, a first sharing in the Lord's Table, a moment of making covenant relationship with other Christians and the receiving of spiritual gifts for the ministry of God in the world.[54]

Fiddes continues by arguing the necessity for a theology of the body, as meaning that there are "different ways of belonging to the 'Body of Christ' that should inform the incorporation in this body." Distinguishing between the "incarnate, Eucharistic, ecclesial and secular" body of Christ will help us to see the way they relate with each other without being confused with each

---

51. Fiddes, 181–182.
52. Daniel Turner, *Charity the Bond of Perfection: A Sermon, The Substance of which was Preached at Oxford, November 16, 1780, On Occasion of the Re-establishment of a Christian Church of Protestant Dissenters in that City* (London: T. Evans, 1780), 26–27.
53. Fiddes, *Tracks and Traces*, 182–183.
54. Fiddes, 183.

other. The model taken into consideration is that of the "indwelling of the divine Logos" in the "body of Jesus, the church, the substance of bread, the body of the world."[55] However, as helpful as this model could be, it should not be considered as a static reality, for only keeping the relational dimension of it versus the dualistic would help us to avoid the error of separating the activities of Father, Son and Holy Spirit. Fiddes says:

> To speak of God as Father, Son and Spirit is to say that there are relationships in God;
>
> There are flowing movements of giving and receiving in love, like the father sending out a son on a mission of reconciliation in the world, a son responding in loving obedience to a father, and a spirit of discovery, always opening up the relations to new depths and a new future.[56]

Through this lens, of God's indwelling in us / the world and of us indwelling in God, we are able to see more clearly both "the connection, and difference, between different bodies." On the one hand, the physical body of Jesus Christ in total surrender and obedience to God corresponds totally to the "movement of responsive loves within God's dance of life." Moreover, it is in full correspondence with our participation in this movement of the "yes" of the Son to the Father, as children of God, through our call to the Father, and this space of encounter between us and God in the dynamics of this relationship which is, "Christ-shaped."[57]

On the other hand, the eucharistic actions "of breaking the bread and pouring of wine" correspond to the "movement of self-breaking and outpouring within God," and correspond also to the giving of believers in obedience in the framework of the covenant with God. Moreover, these correspondences with the movements in God could be seen also in the world in every action of sacrificial self-giving. Fiddes concludes by saying

---

55. Fiddes, 183–186.
56. Fiddes, 189.
57. Fiddes, 189. Also, Moltmann, *Church in the Power*, 260. He argues that "as a feast open to the churches, Christ's supper demonstrates the community's catholicity. As a feast open to the world it demonstrates the community's mission in the world. As a feast open to the future it demonstrates the community's universal hope. It acquires this character from the prevenient, liberating and unifying invitation of Christ." (Moltmann, 260).

that the common feature of all these correspondences in different bodies, that reflect the perichoretical movements of the Father, Son and Holy Spirit, is the unique space in which they happen: "In all of them Christ can be embodied . . . Through all of them the gracious presence of God can be experienced."[58] There are also differences between these different bodies in which Christ's body could be manifested, because "only the church . . . is a Eucharistic community," whilst the secular communities could become "occasions" of Christ's embodiment, and as such be "sacramental" communities.[59] This is because the church "is formed by the actions of the two sacraments which recall the story of Jesus,"

> The church can discover more about the meaning of its story through finding Christ embodied outside its walls; it may, for example, find out more about the meaning of salvation and healing in life as it experiences movements for social justice and liberation. But as a covenant community it has a particular witness to the story, and has an inescapable duty to go on telling it.[60]

This "telling" of the story of Christ should be done at the junction of the church's threefold call, to unity, communion and mission. The exploration of these issues, according to Fiddes's theology, is the subject of the next section.

8.3. Fiddes's Eucharistic Theology in an Ecumenical Perspective

In light of the present situation of ecumenical dialogue between different traditions of the Christian family, Fiddes regards the unity of the church in three dimensions, namely, unity from the roots, unity as full communion and unity in diversity. These are, in Fiddes's opinion, three present trends in the life of the churches in the world. First, unity from the roots means "sharing of resources for worship, witness and social action at local and regional levels." Also it means in many cases engagement in theological education,

---

58. Fiddes, *Tracks and Traces*, 190–191.
59. Fiddes, 190–191.
60. Fiddes, 191.

mission and even shared local campaigns against injustice.[61] Second, unity as full communion, means, taking into account the "variety of churches, each with their own heritage, tradition and emphases," and the acknowledgment that if each church is in communion with God, then all "*are already*" in communion with each other. Third, unity in diversity means to accept the "diversity in unity" based on the "true diversity" shown in the inner Trinitarian relationships that inform a "legitimate" or "reconciled" diversity.[62] Fiddes summarizes: "The sense of ecumenical call which is widespread at present is a calling to work from the roots, to work towards full communion, and to live with diversity, painful though it is."[63]

From the Pauline text in Ephesians 4, Fiddes continues by extracting three theological ideas that he explores regarding the above discussion, namely, the idea of one body, one fellowship, and one covenant. First, the idea that the body of Christ is one, says Fiddes, is an idea that is central for Paul in 1 Corinthians 12. Fiddes connects the idea of the church as the visible body of Christ with the visibility of Christ as testified by John in 1 John 1:1–4, and in the context of this connection, it is about the universal church as attested in the connection of the church with the cosmic Christ in Ephesians 1:22–23. This is supported, says Fiddes, by the use of the word "all" by Paul as he writes in 1 Corinthians 12:13.[64]

Next to the visibility of the church universal in the church local, Fiddes argues for the manifestation of the church universal in the local church. For Fiddes this freedom of God to make Christ the head of the church universal that is made visible in diverse forms within local churches, should lead to a hermeneutics of humility in regard to one's tendency to connect the church with "territorial jurisdiction." The visibility of Christ, implicit in the visibility of the church, argues Fiddes, is to be found in the exercise of the *charismata* of all members of the church towards the fulfillment of "God's ministry of reconciliation,"[65] and through a continuous cultivation

---

61. Fiddes, 193–194.
62. Fiddes, 195–196, emphasis in original.
63. Fiddes, 197.
64. Fiddes, 197–198.
65. Fiddes, 198–210.

of an exercise of hearing the word of God through the ears of one different from one's own tradition.

The second theological idea that Fiddes explores is that of the call to one fellowship. The fellowship concept, or *koinonia*, meaning "sharing, participation and communion" is a reality "existent before us," (the church), and it is a reality of God's inner Trinitarian life and of his relationship with the created world, "as broken as the world is."[66] With the model of the Father's *koinonia* with the Son and the Spirit, and of the Father's fellowship with the world through the Son in the Spirit, mirrored in her theology, the church "is the foretaste of *koinonia*" only if she will "embody it."[67] This embodiment should be seen in the unity of addressing the exclusion of different Christian groups from the Christian family, on the basis of a negative nationalism rather than mirroring the image of the Trinity.[68] Fiddes expresses the way the perichoretical relationships of triune fellowship should be mirrored in the fellowship of the church and churches, "Fellowship is a rich harmony of stories, a mutual indwelling of stories, a weaving together of the stories of one's own life, church and nation into a greater story. This common story is the drama of God's creative and redemptive acts in the universe."[69] From here comes naturally the third theological idea that Fiddes explores, namely that of one covenant. Fiddes considers that there are two dimensions of the concept of covenant, the dimension of walking together and the dimension of watching over each other.[70] Fiddes's covenantal theology and the way it roots his view of spirituality will be explored in chapter 9 of the present project.

---

66. Fiddes, 214–215.

67. Fiddes, 215. Also, Colin E. Gunton, "The Church on Earth: The Roots of Community," in *On Being the Church: Essays on the Christian Community*, eds. Colin E. Gunton and Daniel W. Hardy (Edinburgh: T & T Clark, 1989), 78. Gunton argues that "the being of the Church should echo the interrelation between the three persons who together constitute the deity. The Church is called to be the kind of reality at a finite level that God is in eternity." (Gunton, "Church on Earth," 78).

68. Fiddes, *Tracks and Traces*, 215–216.

69. Fiddes, 216.

70. Fiddes, 221.

8.4. Summary of Chapter 8

I aimed in this chapter to explore the way the thought of Paul Fiddes on the Eucharist reflects his understanding of *perichoresis*. I started the exploration by arguing that there is a framework of Fiddes's theology of the Eucharist in a perichoretical key. This framework, we observed, has four elements, namely, synthesis between creation and redemption, the idea of communion and sacrificial living, the transformative victory of Christ on the cross, and Christ's transformative presence.

From the framework of Fiddes's theology of the Eucharist, with its four elements I continued by exploring the heart of Fiddes's theology of the Eucharist, namely the Trinitarian perichoretical relationships, as a model for the life of the church, a reality that centers the three dimensions of Fiddes's theology of the Eucharist. These three dimensions are: the Eucharist as constitutive for the life of the church, the Eucharist as a door for a deepening of God's presence in his community, and the Eucharist as defining membership in the church.

The exploration ended with Fiddes's theology of the Eucharist in an ecumenical perspective. We observed that for Fiddes there are three dimensions of church unity, namely, unity from the roots, unity as full communion and unity in diversity, as three present trends in the life of the churches in the world.

In this context we observed that Fiddes connects the idea of the church as the visible body of Christ with the visibility of Christ. This visibility of Christ implicit in the visibility of the church, argues Fiddes, is to be found in the exercise of the *charismata* of all members of the church towards the fulfillment of God's ministry of reconciliation, and through a continuous cultivation of an exercise of hearing the word of God through the ears of one different from one's own tradition. The second theological idea that Fiddes explores is that of the call to one fellowship. With the model of the Father's *koinonia* with the Son and the Spirit, and of the Father's fellowship with the world through the Son in the Spirit, mirrored in her theology, the church is the foretaste of *koinonia* only if she will embody it. From here comes the third theological idea that we observed, namely that of one covenant. However, Fiddes's covenantal theology and the way it roots his view of spirituality will be explored in chapter 9 of the present project.

CHAPTER 9

Fiddes's Covenantal Theology in His Thought about Spirituality

9.1. The Concept of Covenant as a Framework for Fiddes's Theology of Spirituality

The first dimension of covenant as a framework for Fiddes's theology of spirituality is that covenant is a reality of covenanting pilgrims, a pilgrimage that involves a bi-dimensional dynamic. Fiddes starts his argument about covenant with the distinction between two of the Old Testament types of covenants. First is the "Davidic type," in which "the covenant is made between God and a representative leader of the community," and second, the "Sinaitic type," made with the entire community who constitute the people of God.[1] The latter, is in Fiddes's view, a model appropriated by Baptists with its emphasis on "personal faith and obedience," translated practically in "dependence upon God." This dependence on God is to be expressed first, in a permanent awareness of the will of God materialized in "God's new acts with his people" and second, a continuous "pilgrimage to discover what it means to be called into relationship with God."[2] Fiddes says, "To be a covenant people is to be a pilgrim people. At the heart of this is the

---

1. Paul S. Fiddes, "Covenant: Old and New," in *Bound to Love: The Covenant Basis of Baptist Life and Mission*, eds. Paul Fiddes, R. Hayden, R. Kidd, K. Clements, and B. Haymes (London: Baptist Union, 1985), 13.
2. Fiddes, "Covenant," 15–16.

faithfulness of the God of promise, for the people of Israel had to learn through the ages that God was free to fulfill his promises in unexpected ways."[3]

The second dimension of covenant as framework for Fiddes's theology of spirituality is that of the climax of the theology of covenants in the newness of the new covenant, the reality of Jesus Christ. He is, says Fiddes, the fulfillment "of the hopes of Israel for a new covenant,"[4] "the primary sign of hope"[5] for the people of God in the world of God. Christ is also the person who is the model of how a relationship with God should be, "living in the spirit of Christ."[6] In Fiddes's view, Christ is not only the model of how the spiritual life of the people of God should be, but also, how the life of God is lived in relationship with humanity. Christ's sacrifice is the ratification of the covenant, and it is the demonstration of God's own pilgrimage of suffering for fallen humanity, as well as the deepest expression of the loving mutuality of such a covenant whose newness culminates in its cosmic addressability that needs to be embraced in the thought, life and message of the church.[7]

The third dimension of covenant as a framework for Fiddes's theology of spirituality is that of covenant's horizontal coordinates vitally connected with its vertical coordinates. Fiddes shows that this connection of the vertical and

---

3. Fiddes, 17.
4. Fiddes, 18.
5. Paul S. Fiddes, "The Signs of Hope," in *A call To Mind: Baptist Essays Towards a Theology of Commitment*, Paul S. Fiddes, Keith Clements, Roger Hayden, Brian Haymes, and Richard Kidd (London: Baptist Union, 1987), 37.
6. Fiddes, "Covenant," 18–19.
7. Fiddes, 19–23. Fiddes says that
    While the covenant is not mutual in the sense of an equal status of members, it is mutual and reciprocal in that each member is affected by the other. A relationship of love cannot be otherwise. To love another is to suffer with him and for him. So, as the prophets reflect upon the disaster which Israel has brought upon herself through the breaking of the covenant, they also affirm the agony of God's heart as he feels for his people suffering the consequences of their actions . . . (Fiddes, "Covenant," 20).
    "Through his supreme servant, Jesus, God brings salvation to all nations: nor do they need to keep the laws of the covenant which Israel had received from Moses . . . the purposes of God reach even beyond all mankind to the whole universe . . . all creation will be transformed as mankind responds to God in trust and obedience." (Fiddes, 22). "to take our place in God's covenant community is to take responsibility for our world, to look for ways in which God's kingship can be extended in all society" (Fiddes, 23).

horizontal coordinates of the covenant, expresses the share of the "covenant fellowship of local Christians . . . in the covenant fellowship of God's own life."[8] Also, he shows that the concept of the covenant offers a solution to the dilemma of the connection "between divine action and human freewill," by keeping together "human responsibility" and "divine initiative."[9] Further, the horizontal dimension of the covenant is conditioned by the vertical dimension, which defines the journey of covenanting pilgrims,[10] being the recollection, envisage and renewal of the vertical dimension of the covenant without changing it.[11]

For Fiddes, the horizontal dimension of the covenant as conditioned by its vertical dimension is embodied in two domains of human existence. First, is the familial domain, with the promotion of a non-hierarchical partnership between husband and wife, expressed in what was called "submission of equality,"[12] as opposed to "a hierarchy of submission,"[13] and the second is the ecclesial one, with the promotion of a non-hierarchical partnership between members of the Christian community.[14] The key expressions of such mutual partnership are baptism and the Lord's Supper, being "the base for making the new community, the body of Christ which is the church."[15] The inter-conditionality of the two domains in which is expressed the bi-dimensionality of the covenant is argued by Fiddes in the perennial principle of wholeness,[16] of the entire reality. This principle is to be embodied

---

8. Fiddes, *Tracks and Traces*, 18.
9. Fiddes, 19.
10. Fiddes, 29.
11. Fiddes, 34.
12. Paul S. Fiddes, "Woman's Head Is Man," *Baptist Quarterly* 31, no. 8 (1986): 373. Also, C. K. Barnett, *A Commentary of the First Epistle to the Corinthians* (London: Black, 1968), 250.
13. Paul S. Fiddes, "The Theology of the Charismatic Movement," in *Strange Gifts? A Guide to Charismatic Renewal*, eds. David Martin and Peter Mullen (Oxford: Blackwell, 1984), 36.
14. Fiddes, *Tracks and Traces*, 49–52.
15. Fiddes, 53.
16. Paul S. Fiddes, "Old Testament Principles of Wholeness," in *Iosif Ton: Orizonturi noi in Spiritualitate si slujire*, eds. Sorin Sabou and Dorothy Ghitea (Oradea: Cartea Creștină, 2004), 46. Fiddes says: "Old Testament ideas of wholeness by the individual personality extending not only through the immediate family . . . but into the entire covenant community . . . If people are to be made whole they must share in the making of the

as humanity is called to participate in the journey towards wholeness, in a hermeneutic of love that will root a cosmology of love,[17] expressed in the superlative in the inner Trinitarian life imagined by Fiddes as a conversation:

> The voices that weave together in the to-and-fro of human speech need not be imposing themselves on each other; they can be responding in a sensitive way, aware of difference of the other and his or her particular contribution to the whole. When this happens they are sharing in the life and the love of God . . . The "persons" in God, three movements of self–giving love, are utterly different from each other, emptying themselves out for the sake of each other, yet at the same time one in creative purpose. We catch the echoes of their "conversation," movements of love which are like a father speaking to a son and the son responding with a glad "yes."[18]

9.2. The Story of Christ as the Centre for Fiddes's Theology of Spirituality

Fiddes considers stories as being formative for human spiritual experiences and as being a "path to maturity," and to the desired wholeness in life.[19] For Fiddes the story of Christ is "in itself a form of culture," that gives coherence to the Christian story that embraces "history and the cosmos,"[20]

---

wholeness, becoming self-creative, otherwise even the gift of freedom will be experienced as something imposed upon" (Fiddes, "Old Testament Principles," 46).

17. Paul S. Fiddes, "The Root of Religious Freedom: Interpreting Some Muslim and Christian Sacred Texts," *Oxford Journal of Law and Religion* 1, no. 1 (2012): 176–177.

18. Paul S. Fiddes, "When Text Becomes Voice: You've Got Mail," in *Flickering Images: Theology and Film in Dialogue*, Paul S. Fiddes and Anthony J. Clarke (Oxford: Regent's Park College; Macon, GA: Smyth & Helwys, 2005), 108.

19. Paul S. Fiddes, "Introduction: The Novel and the Spiritual Journey Today," in *The Novel, Spirituality and Modern Culture: Eight Novelists Write about their Craft and their Context*, ed. Paul S. Fiddes (Cardiff: University of Wales Press, 2000), 3.

20. Paul S. Fiddes, "The Story and the Stories: Revelation and the Challenge of Postmodern Culture," in *Faith in the Centre: Christianity and Culture*, edited by Paul S. Fiddes (Oxford: Regent's Park College; Macon, GA: Smyth & Helwys, 2001), 80–81. Fiddes defines culture as being "the stories that people tell about themselves in order to understand where they have come from, where they are, and where they are going." (Fiddes, "Story and the Stories," 80).

shapes the life of Christian community, that is called to represent Christ through "action (praxis)" based on reflection, and to "*redescribe* reality."[21] The Christian story, that has the revelation of God in Christ as its center,[22] is for Fiddes the judge "of the predominant spirit" of idolatry in society, through revealing "the healing reality" of God's permanent presence, who opens "God's own self to human hearts and they respond in questions, protests, and prophetic voices."[23]

Yet, the paradox of revelation, says Fiddes, is that when God reveals himself he "veils the divine self," even though God has the "freedom to be unveiled as well as veiled."[24] The consequence of such a paradox is that humanity is permanently called to transformation from merely *observer* of God to *participant* in God,[25] participation through which we are invited into "this interweaving or perichoresis of relationships," a "story of a Father who sends out a Son in a Spirit of love," a story in which we are called "to incorporate our own stories."[26] This call to participation is illustrated by Fiddes, with the story in John 20, when appearing to the disciples after resurrection "the risen Christ invites his disciples to participate in his own story of relationship to the Father."[27]

The fact that revelation is "an invitation to participate in the story of the triune God,"[28] has as a consequence not only that "we may envisage new possibilities . . . emerging from the interaction between creator and the created," but also an awareness of "what happens when a reader engages with a text," in "the dialogue with the story of the scripture."[29] This engagement

---

21. Paul S. Fiddes, "Story and Possibility: Reflections on the Last Scenes of The Fourth Gospel and Shakespeare's *The Tempest*," in *Revelation and Story: Narrative Theology and the Centrality of the Story*, eds. Gerhart Sauter and John Barton (Aldershot: Ashgate, 2000), 33, 38.

22. Nigel Wright, "Spirituality as Discipleship: the Anabaptist Heritage," in *Under the Rule of Christ: Dimensions of Baptist Spirituality*, ed. Paul S. Fiddes (Oxford: Regent's Park College; Macon, GA: Smyth & Helwys, 2008), 82.

23. Fiddes, "Story and the Stories," 84.

24. Fiddes, "Story and Possibility," 43.

25. Paul S. Fiddes, "Concept, Image and Story in Systematic Theology," *International Journal of Systematic Theology* 11, no. 1 (January 2009): 23.

26. Fiddes, "Story and Possibility," 44.

27. Fiddes, 44–45.

28. Fiddes, 45.

29. Fiddes, 45–46.

is to be done or promoted in such a way as to avoid the danger of being trapped "in the world of the text" with the consequence that the relevance of the text to today is shadowed as the connection of the world of the written text with the actual world of the readers not visible.[30]

Fiddes looks at the text in 2 Corinthians 3:6 as an example from Paul's rhetoric of how the divorce from the world of the written text and the actual world of the readers, can be avoided. If Paul's concern was to provide for his audience an acknowledgment for the necessity to transcend the literal meaning towards the spiritual meaning, Fiddes acknowledges the shift from "the letter kills but the spirit gives life," proper to the Jewish way of interpretation, to "spirit kills and the letter makes alive," proper, to postmodernity.[31] He says, "The letter 'kills,' when a legalistic principle which merely protects the self is applied within a network of signs, whether a religious text or the life of a community uses age-old images and symbols."[32]

Fiddes admits the fact that narrative theology, meaning "telling the story of God," or metaphorical theology is attractive, providing the framework for the vital connection between biblical truths, contained in the images and the stories of the Bible, and "the life and practices of the Christian community." Yet he considers that if should be crystal clear that the Scripture is the primary witness to God's revelation but that does not exclude other avenues for God's revelation.[33] He suggests that there is place for the integration of extra-biblical narratives that could be considered means of God's revelation, and this for two reasons. First, says Fiddes, doctrines are anyway "a second-order language," and second, there is need for such dialogical integration because of such differences. For example as that between literature and doctrine, namely the different tendency in regard to the meaning of the former towards openness and of the latter towards closeness. However, he is realistic in acknowledging the danger of reconstructing meaning in

---

30. Fiddes, "When Text becomes Voice," 100.

31. Fiddes, 103. Also, Fiddes, "Concept, Image and Story," here Fiddes argues the promise of narrative or metaphorical theology that "aims to be more biblical elaborating, enlarging, interpreting and connecting together the images and stories contained in Scripture as a framework for the life and practices of the Christian community," (Fiddes, "Concept, Image and Story," 7).

32. Fiddes, "When Text becomes Voice," 104.

33. Fiddes, "Concept, Image and Story," 6–8.

accordance with a certain ideology,[34] and in that, as Francesca Murphy has said, there is an intrinsic danger that "a narrative theology without a metaphysic simply dissolves God into the story."[35] Fiddes's argument is that in the light of the dangers, we have to look for "a mutual influence between literature and theology" which is without separation and without confusion, even though keeping the distinctions in roles of the two, literature's to inform the doctrinal formulations and theology's to "provide a perspective for the critique of the literary texts."[36] He distillates this mutuality:

> In poetry, drama and novel the imagination reaches out towards mystery, towards a reality for which we feel an ultimate concern, but which eludes empirical investigation . . . There is then, a universal revelation giving rise to a knowledge of God which is non-conceptual, and non-objective; Rahner identifies this as "transcendental" revelation . . . of God which happens in the human orientation towards mystery. By contrast, there are also moments when the self-giving of God takes form in historic events and gives rise to deliberate concepts (what Rahner calls "categorical" revelation). Some events "stand out" as decisive moments of disclosure, insisting that they be noticed and calling for a whole reorientation of life from the participant . . . The movement of the human spirit towards self-transcendence is bound to overlap with the theological understanding of the human spirit as being grasped by transcended reality.[37]

9.3. The Poles and the Coordinates of the Embodiment of Christian Spirituality

Fiddes considers that one of the first important developments in the life of faith, a life under the rule of Christ over the entire life, is that of attentiveness

---

34. Fiddes, 8–9.
35. Fiddes, 10. Also, Francesca Ann Murphy, *God Is Not a Story: Realism Revisited* (Oxford: University Press, 2007), 10–16.
36. Fiddes, "Concept, Image and Story," 11.
37. Fiddes, 12–13.

in its vertical dimension, namely the awareness of God,[38] that roots its horizontal dimension, that is awareness of Christ and the ones who are in Christ,[39] as well as an awareness of God's self-revelation in created order[40] and human culture.[41] This attention that is central for spiritual life assures not only the dynamics in the process of harmonization of one's life with that of Christ's,[42] but also the ability to see "the traces" of God in his hiddenness in the world.[43] If Christian spirituality is "cultivating attentiveness,"[44] or "attentiveness to the infinitely Other," Fiddes considers that there are two images that best express this reality, namely, stillness and journey, being the "two modes of giving attention to the other, this be finite others or the infinitely Other."[45]

The first image is that of stillness,[46] and for Fiddes, in accordance with Christian tradition, stillness is the framework for contemplation of God as well as for "seeing" the signs of God's presence in others and the created order. The second image is that of journey and for Fiddes it is also essential for any discussion of the subject of spirituality in the Christian tradition. Moreover, for Fiddes it is in accordance with the Christian traditional understanding of the "the two forms of spirituality, as interconnected, one leading to the other and vice versa."[47]

Fiddes acknowledges the merit of the mystical tradition in providing the directions of the spiritual journey in the framework of stillness, namely the journey "into the depths of the soul" and "upwards" towards the presence of God where there is the experience of "the silence of the spirit and the

---

38. Paul S. Fiddes, "Spirituality as Attentiveness: Stillness and Journey," in *Under the Rule of Christ: Dimensions of Baptist Spirituality*, ed. Paul S. Fiddes (Oxford: Regent's Park College; Macon, GA: Smyth & Helwys, 2008), 25.

39. Fiddes, "Spirituality as Attentiveness," 26.

40. Fiddes, "When Text Becomes Voice," 104.

41. Fiddes, "Concept, Image and Story," 16.

42. Fiddes, "Spirituality as Attentiveness," 26.

43. Fiddes, 27.

44. Fiddes, "Introduction," 11.

45. Fiddes, "Spirituality as Attentiveness," 29, 30.

46. The idea of stillness is proper to Hesychasm, and so Fiddes comes close to Stăniloae and Palamas in this regard. See, Stăniloae, *Viața și Învățătura Sfântului Grigorie Palama*, 32–33. See also, Meyendorff, *Study of Gregory Palamas*, 134. He says that Hesychasm "had become a technical term to designate the state of inner rest and silence which victory over the passions gained for a monk and so allowed him to proceed to contemplation" (Meyendorff, 134).

47. Fiddes, "Spirituality as Attentiveness," 29–30.

end of all images and words." Also, he considers that the mystical tradition provides the proper vocabulary for spirituality, "the seeing" of the divine light "experienced by the eyes of the soul as the deepest darkness," as well as the relation between darkness, stillness, and vision of God, and "the journey to the centre of the self." Moreover, if attentiveness is essential for spirituality, it implies not only a journey inward or upwards but also, to the self of others, being a journey of "forgiveness," "empathy," "moral transformation," and "mission."[48]

From these two poles of spirituality, stillness and journey, Fiddes continues with the coordinates on which spirituality is embodied. The first is the practice of praying, "free prayer" or "from the heart," a prayer that requires "purity of heart," is shaped by scripture, and is a "representative prayer," as it is acted in the interdependency of the members of the Christian community encompassed by their dependence on God.[49] Such a prayer is, in Fiddes's interpretation, more connected with the concept of journey than with that of stillness, as through prayer,

> we are drawn into the person's journey of experience, the person's journey into the world as he or she leads us in intercession for others who are encountered in daily work or social life. It may be his or her journey through the text of scripture. It may even be a journey deep into the heart of the self in confession or up to the heights of Mount of Transfiguration in praise, and so we may find that the journey leads us finally into the silence of encounter with God.[50]

The second coordinate of spirituality is that of witness as part of Baptist worship. For Fiddes witness is an invitation for the recipient, be it an individual or a community, "to give attention" to the person who witnesses and to the way the person embodies the rule of Christ in their life. Also witness is an invitation for the recipient "to share" and "to follow" the story of Christ at work in the life of the one who witnesses, "showing" the way one could come from recipient of a witness to one who in his turn is a witness.

---

48. Fiddes, 30–33.
49. Fiddes, 34–37.
50. Fiddes, 37.

Witness is a way of "seeing Christ" by participation not by observation, both for the one who witnesses and the recipient, and as such is a synthesis between journey and stillness.[51]

The third coordinate of spirituality is that of singing, as a way of "being attuned to the movements of love and relationship in the life of the triune God," as well as "giving attention to each other," listening to each other, in the search of harmony as the community tries to sing together.[52] For Fiddes singing situates the community and its members at the intersection of journey and stillness, as he says that,

> In worship we find that Christ is our new social space . . . This space offers moments of stillness; we live before the many faces which are internalized in our hearts, but we only worship the face of Christ who can be trusted to relate all other faces. Worship is an inclusive, yet uncrowded, space to be, as singing takes up the whole body into the rhythm and movement of the divine song. Yet this is inseparable from journeying . . . singing opens up the borders between ourselves and other human beings.[53]

The fourth coordinate of spirituality is that of eucharistic communion, as the "sacramental encounter with God in the gathering of disciples of Christ." The concept of journey is valued as communion involves a voyage "of remembrance into the past," and a voyage "into the self in self-examination." The concept of stillness, in its connection with that of journey, is also visible, through "attention to the elements of bread and wine," as expressions of Christ's real and spiritual presence, in the gathering of the community.[54]

The fifth coordinate of spirituality is that of reading the Bible that is central for spirituality from a Baptist perspective, having authority over the lives of the ones constituting the community. The reading of the Bible in worship, says Fiddes, first, "enables" participation in the biblical story, and

---

51. Fiddes, 38–42.
52. Fiddes, 43–44.
53. Fiddes, 45–46.
54. Fiddes, 46–49.

the exposition of the Bible "calls" to a journey into God's mission that needs to be appropriated by the community in society.[55]

The synthesis of the two elements of journey and stillness are underlined by the practices of public reading, exposition and preaching, as well as by the private reading of the scripture as a framework for the community' s role in judging the preaching in the community, in order "to gain a common mind of the meaning of scripture."[56] Fiddes concludes the discussion of the interconnection between journey and stillness as key features of spirituality:

> The still point must always be part of a journey . . . It is a sense of being held within God who is on journey, always voyaging out of God's self into the desolation of the world . . . The stillness comes . . . not by escape from time but by our working with God in taking up the past, present and future into the wholeness which does not cancel time but heals it. This is only possible by attention to God and to others, measuring all things by the rule of Christ.[57]

9.4. Summary of Chapter 9

I aimed in this chapter to explore Fiddes's covenantal theology in his thought about spirituality. I observed that the concept of covenant constitutes the framework of Fiddes's theology of spirituality. There are three dimensions of covenant that Fiddes underlines: covenant as a reality of covenanting pilgrims, the climax of the theology of covenants in the newness of the new covenant, covenant's horizontal coordinates vitally connected with its vertical coordinates, embodied in two domains of human existence, the familial domain, and the ecclesial.

From the concept of covenant as a framework for Fiddes's theology of spirituality, I continued by exploring the center of Fiddes's theology of spirituality, namely, the story of Christ. We observed that in Fiddes's argument the story of Christ is in itself a form of culture, that gives coherence to the

---

55. Fiddes, 49–50.
56. Fiddes, 51.
57. Fiddes, 53.

Christian story, that in its turn is the judge of the predominant spirit of idolatry in society.

The last step in my exploration was that of observing the poles and coordinates of the embodiment of Christian spirituality. We have seen that for Fiddes spirituality is cultivating attentiveness, and that for him there are two images that express this reality, and constitute the poles of Fiddes's theology of spirituality, namely, stillness and journey. We also observed that for Fiddes there are five coordinates on which spirituality is embodied: the practice of praying, witness, singing, eucharistic communion, and reading the Bible.

Part 3

Conclusions

CHAPTER 10

The Dialogical Dimension of the Spiritual Journey: Results of the Conversation

10.1. Theology of Participation and the Spiritual Journey

The first thing to be noted is that both thinkers, Stăniloae and Fiddes, are systematic Trinitarian thinkers, trying to develop a theology of participation desired to be the foundation for the Christian life and for the church. The way they are doing this reflects their faithfulness to their own traditions. However, noticeable is the way the pre-eminence of tradition, with few exceptions, roots Stăniloae's use of Scriptures. In the case of Fiddes, noticeable is the way that, different from the traditional baptistic insistence solely on Scripture, he shows an ability to understand the value of patristic theology that brings the necessary balance in the interpretation of Scriptures.

From looking at both of them, one could detect as a common feature the understanding of the interpretive key role of the fathers for a contemporary understanding of Scripture. This is one of the most necessary acknowledgments in the contemporary Romanian theological arena. First is the necessary reminder for many in the Orthodox tradition, that the fathers were profoundly biblical in their formulations.

The second common feature is that they were able to interact with the philosophy and culture of their times without being enslaved by secular patterns of thought. A third feature is that for them Scripture was the controlling element of the veracity of any theological formulation.[1] On the other hand, for many in the Baptist tradition, a necessary reminder should be that even though the Scriptures are normative for the Christian life, their interpretation should always be developed in the light of what has always been believed, thought and confessed.[2]

Second, even though Stăniloae and Fiddes frame their theology of participation differently, they have in common the premise of the centrality of the doctrine of the Trinity. For both of them the saying of what Catherine Mowry LaCugna states is true: "The doctrine of the Trinity is ultimately a practical doctrine with radical consequences for the Christian life."[3]

Stăniloae's framework starts from the being of God with its super-essential, spiritual attributes and inner Trinitarian relations. Fiddes, in his turn, starts from the concept of *perichoresis* reflected in the three dynamics of what he calls the interplay of grace and faith, the interplay of spirit and water, and the interplay of Christ's body and church. However, both theologians are thinking in a way in which they try to demonstrate that the perichoretical relationships between Father, Son and Holy Spirit, inform the relationship of God with humanity and the relationships within the church. This truth of correspondence between the Trinity and the church, which Stăniloae and Fiddes agree on, is well expressed by Nigel Wright: "As the people of God the church is called together by the Father; as the body of Christ the church exists in, for and through the Son who is its head; as the temple of the Holy Spirit the church is indwelt by the Spirit of God who gives life to all."[4]

---

1. St. Athanasius, "On The Incarnation of the Word," in *Nicene and Post-Nicene Fathers*, series 2, vol. 4, edited by Philip Schaff (Peabody, MA: Henrickson, 1999). As a constant feature of Athanasius's way of theologizing is his constant return to Scripture for validation of theological argument. See also, "Defence against the Arians," in *Nicene and Post-Nicene Fathers*, series 2, vol. 4, edited by Philip Schaff (Peabody, MA: Hendrickson, 1999). And also, Basil of Caesarea, "The Hexameron," in *Nicene and Post-Nicene Fathers*, series 2, vol. 8, edited by Philip Schaff and Henry Wace (Peabody, MA: Hendrickson, 1995), 51–107.

2. Pelikan, *Christian Tradition*, 1. Defining doctrine as "what the church believes, teaches and confesses on the basis of the word of God," Pelikan continues "the form which Christian doctrine, so defined, has taken place in history is tradition . . . Thus tradition means the handing down of Christian teaching during the course of history of the church, but it also means that which is handed down," Pelikan, *Christian Tradition*, 6–7.

3. Catherine Mowry LaCugna, *God For Us: The Trinity and Christian Life* (San Francisco, CA: HarperSanFrancisco, 1993), 1.

4. Wright, *Free Church, Free State*, 4.

From the exploration of the previous chapters I understand that both theologians seem to be in agreement that baptism is an important stage in the process of Christian initiation. Both of them agree also on the importance of faith in the act of baptism, of the person baptized or of the persons who present him or her for baptism. While Stăniloae insists on the importance of infant baptism for its role in the annihilation of ancestral sin, Fiddes speaks about both forms of baptism, infant and adult, without forgetting the importance of personal or corporate faith.

Stăniloae, even though insisting on baptism as the beginning of this process, considers also that baptism together with chrismation is the moment when Christ gives faith and the gift of the Spirit to the baptized. He creates space for the conception of process in regard to baptism when he speaks time after time about the actualization of baptismal power in later life, through active faith and obedience. Fiddes in his turn, insists on the precedence of faith over the act of baptism, and speaks about the role of the church's faith in keeping the candidate in the actualization and confession of faith.

Moreover, first, in the case of Fiddes, it is clear that he regards baptism as a process, yet his view is not dependent on process theology, even though he interacts with it. Rather his influences come from the biblical theology of participation in Christ's death and resurrection and its consequences for the entire Christian life,[5] and he also seems to be aware of the fact that there are patristic resources that sustain such a concept. A sample of such a patristic resource that Fiddes acknowledges is expressed by Gordon S. Mikoski in his analysis of the thought of Gregory of Nyssa on baptism who says: "Baptism for Gregory was not merely a one-time event. It forms the architectonic pattern for the entirety of the life of the church and those who are members of it."[6]

---

5. Corneliu Constantineanu, *The Social Significance of Reconciliation in Paul's Theology: Narrative Readings in Romans* (London: T & T Clark, 2010). Constantineanu argues that "through baptism, the believers are incorporated 'in Christ' and so in their new life they are animated by the same life of obedience to God manifested through a renunciation of their own desires and a concern for the needs of others . . . life which is totally defined and shaped by their union with Christ, in the power of the Spirit," Constantineanu, *Social Significance*, 136.

6. Gordon S. Mikoski, "Baptism, Trinity, and Ecclesial Pedagogy in the Thought of Gregory of Nyssa," *Scottish Journaal of Theology* 59, no. 2 (2006): 177.

Second, in the case of Stăniloae, the fact is clear that he is characterized by conservatism in his view of the way other traditions see and practice baptism, a conservatism that characterizes his entire ecclesiology, that make some to charge him of spiritual reductionism[7] and clericalism.[8] However, one would agree that this conservatism is not only proper to Stăniloae, it being a feature of the contemporary situation in the Romanian Orthodox Church. Yet, in spite of his conservatism Stăniloae seems to be aware of the complexity of the discussion in the theological arena of the larger Christian family.

Another meeting point between Stăniloae and Fiddes is their sacramental view of baptism. For Stăniloae saving grace is already present in the baptismal water that was transformed in a salvific medium through the touch of the Holy Spirit. For Fiddes, the baptismal water is the place of encounter with the grace of God. Stăniloae considers that the grace of God produces the faith that is bestowed on the baptized in the act of baptism. He also considers that grace is strengthened by the act of chrismation as a continuation of baptism, and is maintained and actualized by the Eucharist.

Fiddes speaks about the prevenient grace of God's initiative that matches the corporate faith of the church, and/or the vicarious faith of parents or godparents, in the case of infant baptism or of children raised in the church. The prevenient grace is continued by the transformative grace that permits the growth of vicarious faith into the owned faith of the believer who is baptized or commits to conscious faithful obedience. The equilibrium between the grace of God's initiative and the response of faith of the believer/believers seems to be kept, or at least declared by both, Stăniloae and Fiddes, this necessary complementarity between the initiative of grace of God and the

---

7. Emil Bartoș, *Deification*, 335; and, Emil Bartoș, *Conceptul îndumnezeirii în Teologia lui Dumitru Stăniloae* [The concept of Deification in Dumitru Stăniloae's theology] (Oradea: Cartea Creștină, 2002), 437.

8. Mănăstireanu, *PM*, 283.

answer of the believers' faithful obedience[9] and trust,[10] in a lifelong process that confirms the past cleansing in his life.[11] Moreover, Stăniloae and Fiddes both are rightly saying that faith is a gift from God. Yet, God gives the gift of faith, not automatically from the church, pneumatized as she is, to the person,[12] but rather through the hearing of the word of Christ, through a pneumatized proclamation.[13]

Stăniloae sees the "water" in John 3 as being the baptismal water transformed by the pneumatized Christ,[14] whilst Fiddes considers that the water

---

9. Edwin A. Blum, "2 Peter," in *The Expositor's Bible Commentary: New Testament*, abridged ed., ed. Kenneth L. N. Barker and John R. Kohlenberger, III (Grand Rapids, MI: Zondervan, 1994). Also, Craig S. Keener, *The IVP Bible Background Commentary: New Testament* (Downers Grove, IL: InterVarsity Press, 1993), 726. J. C. Beker, "Second Letter of Peter," in *The Interpreter's Dictionary of the Bible*, ed. George Arthur Buttrick (Nashville, TN: Abingdon, 1962), 769.

10. Ben Witherington, III, *Paul's Narrative Thought World: The Tapestry of Tragedy and Triumph* (Louisville, KY: Westminster John Knox, 1994), 265.

11. The Petrine text speaks of the necessary complementarity between God's actions and the believer's response:
> His divine power has given us everything we need for a godly life through our knowledge of him, who called us by his own glory and goodness. Through these he has given us his very great and precious promises, so that through them you may participate in the divine nature, having escaped the corruption in the world caused by evil desires. For this very reason, make every effort to add to your faith goodness; and to goodness, knowledge; and to knowledge, self-control; and to self-control, perseverance; and to perseverance, godliness; and to godliness, mutual affection; and to mutual affection, love. For if you possess these qualities in increasing measure, they will keep you from being ineffective and unproductive in your knowledge of our Lord Jesus Christ. But whoever does not have them is nearsighted and blind, forgetting that they have been cleansed from their past sins. (2 Pet 1:3–9).

12. C. H. Dodd, *The Epistle of Paul to the Romans* (London: Hodder & Stoughton, 1932), 16. Also, John Ziesler, *Paul's Letter to the Romans* (London: SCM, 1989), 69. See also David Wenham, *Paul: Follower of Jesus or Founder of Christianity?* (Grand Rapids, MI: Eerdmans, 1995), he says that according to Paul "faith is not something for which we deserve any credit," 68.

13. Markus Barth, *Ephesians: Introduction, Translation, and Commentary on Chapters 1-3* (New York: Doubleday, 1974). He says: "the saving grace itself opens a wide field of 'good works' as 'our way of life' (Eph 2: 5, 8, 10)," 249. And the Pauline text:
> That is the message concerning faith that we proclaim: If you declare with your mouth "Jesus is Lord," and believe in your heart that God raised him from the dead, you will be saved . . . how can they believe in the one of whom they have not heard? And how can they hear without someone preaching to them? . . . Consequently, faith comes from hearing the message, and the message is heard through the word about Christ. (Rom 10:8–9, 14, 17).

14. See also, Alexander Schmemann, *Din Apă și din Duh: Studiu Liturgic al Botezului* [Of water and the spirit], (București: Symbol, 1992), 38.

is "a place of encounter with God for renewal of life."[15] We have also noticed that Stăniloae considers that Christ is leading the process of salvation through the Spirit, from and in the temple of our being. Fiddes on the other hand, speaks of different comings of the Spirit, appropriate to various stages of the process of initiation. For Stăniloae baptism is vital for the annihilation of and cleansing from ancestral sin, and for Fiddes it is a symbol of spiritual cleansing, as he considers that "Paul speaks of sin as if it has a kind of objective existence 'reigning' in our bodies, making us slaves."[16]

Conclusions

We have tried in this section to reflect on the common features of Stăniloae's and Fiddes's understandings of baptism as the beginning of the process of Christian initiation. Even though they represent two traditions that differ significantly in their way of regarding baptism, we found many meeting points between Stăniloae and Fiddes that could be valuable for the dialogue between Orthodox and Baptists in Romania. In our analysis we understood that both of them regard baptism as a dynamic reality being simultaneously an act and a process through which a person becomes part of the people of God, is integrated with the body of Christ and is transformed as the temple of the Spirit. How these Trinitarian features of baptism, detected in the thought of Stăniloae and Fiddes, could inform a theology of baptism as a way of life and how the dimensions of baptism as a way of living could be used to articulate a transformative way of regarding baptism in the Romanian Christian communities will be argued in the first part of chapter 11.

---

15. For a different view see F. F. Bruce, *The Gospel of John* (Grand Rapids, MI: Eerdmans, 1983), 84. Also, Bruce Milne, *The Message of John: Here is Your King* (Leicester: Inter-Varsity Press, 1993), 76. Scott M. Lewis, *The Gospel According to John and the Johannine Letters* (Collegeville, MI: Liturgical Press, 2005). He says that the expression "water and spirit" could refer to natural birth (water) and rebirth (spirit) even though a reference to baptism could not be excluded, (Lewis, *Gospel According to John*, 20). For a view of the baptismal water as a signifier and birth from above as the reality signified, see Lesslie Newbigin, *The Light Has Come: An Exposition of the Fourth Gospel* (Grand Rapids, MI: Eerdmans, 1982), 39. In the same line see, Merril C. Tenney, "John," in *The Expositor's Bible Commentary, New Testament*, eds. Kenneth L. N. Barker and John R. Kohlenberger, III (Grand Rapids, MI: Zondervan, 1994), 304.

16. Fiddes, *Past Event*, 115.

10.2. Perichoretical Theology and Spiritual Journey

The first thing to be remarked in comparing Stăniloae and Fiddes in their thinking about the Eucharist is that both of them argue from the perspective of the entire Christ event, keeping together the incarnation, crucifixion and resurrection. If one of the reasons for Stăniloae's insistence on the resurrection in regard to the Eucharist is rooted in his disagreement with the insistence of Protestantism on the cross of Christ, the other could be that in the Scriptures eucharistic theology is argued from the perspective of the resurrection of Christ. For Fiddes, on the other hand, keeping together the elements of the Christ event is rooted in his understanding of the redemptive story of the Scripture, from creation to eternity. The direct consequence of the intrinsic complementarity between incarnation, life, death and resurrection of Christ is that it helps maintain the necessary horizontal dimension of the Eucharist, as an occasion to celebrate, in the togetherness of the spiritual community, the uniqueness of the God of love embodied in Christ and to make this celebration a meaningful resource to imitate his example in concrete social mission and ministry.

Moreover, a common feature of Stăniloae and Fiddes is that they do argue from the perspective of the three aspects of redemptive actions of God that are celebrated in the Eucharist. First, in regard to the remembrance of God's past redemptive acts, the incarnation is underlined. Second, both of them acknowledge the significance of the Eucharist in the present for the edification of the church, and third, they acknowledge the eschatological significance of the Eucharist. Stăniloae speaks of the Eucharist as a feeding for the eternal life and Fiddes speaks of the eucharistic communion as a sign of the covenant with God, through Christ, in the Holy Spirit, that not only operates here and now in the life of believer, but is a reflection of the future eucharistic feast of God's Kingdom towards which Jesus himself pointed in his eucharistic discourse in the upper room.

This common view of the two theologians, in regard to the unity of the Christ event (incarnation, death and resurrection), is very important for the theological conversation between theologians of the two traditions they represent. Even if their emphases are different, they are not contradictory, but rather complementary. The Orthodox could be enriched, in their important insistence on resurrection, by the Baptist's insistence on the cross because the entire Christian family constantly needs a profound theology of the cross as a lens through which the real difficulties and hardness of life can be regarded in the hope of resurrection. Stăniloae is profoundly concerned with the imprint of the cross on all realities of life, as we will have seen in chapter 5. At the same time Baptists in Romania with their, important, insistence on the cross can be enriched by the Orthodox insistence on resurrection as a vital reminder that the suffering of the cross in Christian life is always followed by the joy of resurrection.

For both, Orthodox and Baptists, it could be an important reminder that as there is no cross for Christ without the incarnation of Christ, and there is no resurrection without the cross. The three should be kept together even though the writers of the New Testament, not without acknowledgment of this continuum, emphasize one or another depending on the needs of their communities. When it was necessary to balance a theology of the cross with a theology of glory, in order to promote courage in hard times, the writers emphasized the resurrection, as for example in the community addressed by the Gospel of Mark,[17] whilst when it was necessary to balance a theology of glory with a theology of the cross, they emphasized the crucifixion, as for example the community addressed by Paul's letter to the Corinthians.[18]

One of the other areas of agreement between Stăniloae and Fiddes is that of the centrality of Christ's presence in the Eucharist. Both of them see the Eucharist as the reality where Christ's presence is a real presence, a transformative spiritual presence, as part of the process of transformation in which believers are being conformed with the image of Christ.[19]

This is an important reminder of the vital importance for the life of believers of the real, pneumatic, sanctifying communion with Christ, mediated by the Word. On the other hand for both, Romanian Orthodox and Baptists, it could be an important reminder that the eucharistic communion should

---

17. Robert H. Gundry, *Mark: A Commentary on His Apology for the Cross* (Grand Rapids, MI: Eerdmans, 1993). He says, "Mark corrects the theology of glory with the theology of cross," (Gundry, *Mark*, 2).

18. Gordon Fee, *The First Epistle to the Corinthians* (Grand Rapids, MI: Eerdmans, 1987), he speaks of the problematic Corinthians "who have an exaltation Christology that avoided the cross," (Fee, *First Epistle*, 58).

19. Seyoon Kim, *Paul and the New Perspective: Second Thoughts on the Origin of Paul's Gospel* (Grand Rapids, MI: Eerdmans, 2002), 172–173.

be encompassed by a daily appropriation of Christ's life, in a eucharistic way of living, led by the complementary work of the Spirit of God and the word of God. Third, as such for both Orthodox and Baptists, there is a necessary reminder that the Eucharist is to be seen as the "climax of the table fellowship, which Jesus had had with publicans and sinners,"[20] a "new covenant-making event,"[21] a "constant renewal of the covenant between God and the church,"[22] and "a kingdom-anticipating, kingdom-producing event."[23]

Moreover, for both Orthodox and Baptists in Romania, the above comparative considerations underline an important reminder in regard to the word of God, as a form of God's revelation. This is the need for the continual balance between the normative role of the word of God as a form of God's revelation, whilst it is also important to regard carefully the interpretative role of tradition, for the life of the church. This practice was vital for the fathers of the church in the first centuries of church history, whose vigilance provided the possibility to answer heresies and consequently to promote and preserve a healthy spirituality for the life of the church, as a necessary foundation for a meaningful mission of the church.[24]

It was considered in previous studies that one of the major problems of Stăniloae's theology is that connected with his view of the nature of sin. In this regard Bartoş argues that the "aspect of sin as a violation of God's standards is secondary in Stăniloae's approach, with clear effects on his view on the doctrine of redemption and justification . . . an authentic and holistic

---

20. R. S. Wallace, "Lord's Supper," in *Evangelical Dictionary of Theology*, ed. Walter A. Elwell (Grand Rapids, MI: Baker Books, 1984), 652. See also, Peter Toon, "Lord's Supper," in *Baker Theological Dictionary of the Bible*, ed. Walter A. Elwell (Grand Rapids, MI: Baker Books, 1996), 492.

21. David Wenham, "How Jesus Understood the Last Supper: A Parable in Action," *Churchman* 105, no. 3 (1991): 254.

22. M. E. Osterhaven, "Views of the Lord's Supper," in *Evangelical Dictionary of Theology*, ed. Walter A. Elwell (Grand Rapids, MI: Baker Books, 1984), 653.

23. Wenham, "How Jesus understood," 255.

24. In this regard Ivana Noble argues that "the renewed emphases, one on a living personal relationship with God, instead of on a set of rules, and the other on the interdependence between the two material authorities, Scriptures and tradition, though the supremacy of the Scriptures remained, opened up new ecumenical possibilities," see, Noble, *Tracking God*, 118.

understanding of deification must deal with the objective reality of guilt and not merely with the subjective experience of feelings of guilt."[25]

Yet we need to remember, as we argued in chapter 4, that Stăniloae distinguishes between ancestral sin, a reality that is annihilated by Christ in baptism, and sins after baptism that are annihilated, as we have seen in chapter 5, through faith that becomes fear of God, a fear to sin, a fear that leads to repentance. In the same chapter we have seen also that Stăniloae argues for permanent repentance, directed to our vices and sins, in the process of purification. Moreover, Stăniloae prefers to speak of shame consequent to sin, shame being a spiritual instinct of the soul in regard to past sins and a help in avoiding the future sins.

The permanency of repentance in the spiritual journey of life, is underlined even in the Eastern Orthodox tradition, by the prayer of the heart: "Lord Jesus have mercy on me, a sinner!" However, Stăniloae's consideration that the efficiency of the penances depends on the degree the believer practices the recommendations of the priest in his own spiritual life,[26] could be something hard to accept for Baptists in Romania. They will insist on the personal dimension of confession and repentance. Yet, the emphasis on obedience in the Orthodox tradition, which is a concretization of obedience to God, as seen in Stăniloae's view of sin and repentance, could constitute an important reminder about the need to speak and promote repentance that is embodied in obedience to a concrete and sinful person and community, that is the church.

Moreover, Stăniloae discusses the idea of confession in front of the priest. First, he discusses the text in James 5:14, and his perspective could be an important reminder for Baptists in Romania about the often forgotten and not very much promoted dimension of confession, to another person. Many Baptists in Romania would agree that this is necessary, especially in the case of repeated sins, the spiritual assistance of a fellow believer is of paramount importance, in overcoming sin as a way of living. A close reading of the text from James could reveal that it is concerned with the pastoral work of

---

25. Bartoş, *Deification*, 317.
26. Stăniloae, *TDO*, 3, 95.

believers to each other too. They will agree also with Fiddes in his argument about corporal oversight of the believers.[27]

The second text that Stăniloae uses in order to support his affirmations about the confession of sins is the text about the case of Ananias and Sapphira (Acts 5:3). Stăniloae uses this text to prove the practice of confessing sins in front of the apostles. From here it would also be appropriate to consider that Luke is concerned with the comparison between two ways of practicing charity. One, a practice of charity that is transparent and not rooted in the need and desire to impress but rather to help, represented by Barnabas (Acts 4:36–37). The other, under the direct confrontation of the apostle Peter, is that based on wrong motivations as proved by the liars, Ananias and Sapphira (Acts 5:1–11). The result of this public confrontation is a good sample of the primitive church's preoccupation with genuine service for Christ and his church. This is a very important dimension of the ecclesial life that should constitute a perennial preoccupation for the churches from both traditions in Romania.

In regard to repentance in connection with the Eucharist, Stăniloae does not discuss the Pauline corrective for the practice of the Eucharist in the Corinthian Church in which Paul exhorts the believers in Corinth to participate in the Eucharist but to do that examining themselves and distinguishing the body of Christ (1 Cor 11:27). This is relevant, for it could be plausible that the corrective is directed to those who stop themselves and others from sharing in the Eucharist.[28] What is clear from the entire message of the New

---

27. One of the examples is the exhortation of the author of Hebrews: "See to it, brothers and sisters, that none of you has a sinful, unbelieving heart that turns away from the living God. But encourage one another daily, as long as it is called 'Today,' so that none of you may be hardened by sin's deceitfulness" (Heb 3:12–13). "[Let us] not giving up meeting together, as some are in the habit of doing, but encouraging one another" (Heb 10:25). "See that no one is sexually immoral, or is godless like Esau, who for a single meal sold his inheritance rights as the oldest son" (Heb 12:16). These texts show that there is a corporate responsibility for encouragement, confrontation and help that is to be assumed by all believers. This reality is assisted by God, his Spirit and word and through his Son: "For the word of God is alive and active. Sharper than any double-edged sword, it penetrates even to dividing soul and spirit, joints and marrow; it judges the thoughts and attitudes of the heart" (Heb 4:12).

28. Moltmann says:
> The Lord's Supper is not the place to practice church discipline . . . Christ's original feast of joy is then unfortunately transformed into a meal of repentance where people beat their breasts and gnash their teeth. This moral legalism spoils the evangelical character of the meal just as much as dogmatic legalism . . .

Testament, and this is a common feature of the thought of Stăniloae and Fiddes, is that repentance is not once for all or is not something that the believers should do only regarding the Eucharist, rather, repentance should be a permanent reality, a once and always practice. This reality of permanent sinfulness in the mirror of God's character is the reason a believer should be in a permanent state of repentance. Another important acknowledgment and reminder for the ecclesial communities from the Orthodox and Baptist traditions in Romania is, in this context, the discussion about the internal work of the Holy Spirit in revealing personal sin and in conviction about sin, promoting the confession of it, as the Gospel of John underlines.

Fiddes's concept of repentance is not connected with the Eucharist. He connects it with the requirement of God's justice which is not asking for "payment but repentance." The Father, says Fiddes, "is finally 'satisfied' not by any penalty but by the change of heart to which a penalty is intended to lead."[29] Fiddes continues his argument in a way that is a deeper reflection of *perichoresis*, naming the cross of Christ "the great confessional" where through the penitence of Christ on our behalf, he "wins us to repentance."[30] In fact, Fiddes continues, the repentance of believers is "a share in the penitence of Christ" under "the influence of the penitential spirit of the crucified Jesus."[31] Baptists in Romania, will interpret the Scripture as arguing that it is the prerogative of the Holy Spirit to reveal the sinfulness of human beings, according to the sayings of Jesus to his disciples about the coming and the work of the Holy Spirit.[32]

Embraced in this complementary work of the Spirit and the Word, the believer is then reminded that "nothing . . . is hidden from God's sight . . . to whom we must give account"[33] and that eventually sins are correctly dealt

---

The acknowledgment of a "special ministry" obscures Christ's giving of himself "for all" and the fellowship of brothers and sisters into which all are to enter. Hierarchical legalism spoils the evangelical character of the Lord's Supper just as much as dogmatic and moral legalism.
Moltmann, *Church in the Power*, 245–246.

29. Fiddes, *Past Event*, 104.

30. Fiddes, 105. He quotes P. T. Forsyth, *The Work of Christ: Lectures to Young Ministers* (London: Independent Press, 1938), 150.

31. Fiddes, *Past Event*, 106.

32. John 16:8 and Hebrews 4:12–13.

33. Hebrews 4:13.

in the framework of our intimation with the merciful high priest, Christ, the base on which we can "approach God's throne of grace with confidence so that we may receive mercy and find grace to help us in our time of need."[34] Fiddes speaks of the double meaning of *koinonia* or communion that Fiddes considers is attested by the Johannine theology when the apostle John writes that the love for God that believers confess should be proved in their sacrificial love for each other which should mirror the love that God showed us in Christ, making us his children.[35] This overlapping action of the two realities is for John the way the church could avoid a practice of a spirituality that is not a mirror of God's love, namely, to "love with words or speech" rather than "with actions and in truth."[36]

Conclusions

I have aimed in this section to explore the way the concept of *perichoresis*, expressing the reality of Trinitarian persons to be mutually indwelt by each other, without confusion, contradiction or separation is reflected in the thought of Stăniloae and Fiddes. I have seen that the first area in which the reflection of *perichoresis* constitutes a common feature of both theologians is that of the unity of the Christ event. We can conclude that will be instructive for the conversation between Baptists and Orthodox in Romania, this common feature of the two theologians' thought, as keeping together the incarnation, life, death on the cross and resurrection is an important constitutive dimension for a balanced christology that will root a holistic ecclesiology.

We have also seen that the second area in which the reflection of *perichoresis* constitutes a common feature of both theologians is that of Christ's real presence in the Eucharist. Here we observed that Fiddes's move from a symbolic view of Christ's presence, towards a more sacramentalist view of this presence, situates him close to the Eastern view represented with fidelity by Stăniloae. This observation points to a necessary clarification

---

34. Hebrews 4:15–16. The same reality is described in the Johannine theology of repentance:
> If we confess our sins, he is faithful and just and will forgive us our sins and purify us from all unrighteousness . . . if anybody does sin, we have an advocate with the Father – Jesus Christ, the Righteous One. He is the atoning sacrifice for our sins, and not only for ours but also for the sins of the whole world. (1 John 1:9–2:2).

35. 1 John 4:20.
36. 1 John 3:18.

for Baptists in Romania, as in their majority they regard the presence of Christ in the Eucharist as being symbolic. It is also interesting that Fiddes is close to Stăniloae's view only regarding the mode of Christ's presence in the Eucharist.

When it comes to the centrality of the priest for confession before the Eucharist and the vital role of priest in administering the Eucharist, Fiddes remains in the mainstream of the Baptist view just as Stăniloae does this in regard to the Eastern view. We can conclude that the understanding of Stăniloae's view, as well as of Fiddes's view, of Christ's presence in the Eucharist will be beneficial for Baptist communities in Romania, and a good platform for a necessary redefinition of the spiritual role of the Eucharist in the life of Baptist communities in Romania.

Also, Stăniloae's insistence and Fiddes's resistance for the centrality of the ministerial priesthood in the Eucharist could constitute a good reminder that this is one of the important differences between the two traditions in Romania. The consistency of Fiddes's view on the general priesthood of all believers could constitute a good example for Baptists in Romania, especially because one can detect a subtle tendency towards a hierarchical view of the structure of the church that could be considered contradictory with a healthy emphasis on the general priesthood that imparts the responsibility for ministry and mission on each believer in the body of Christ.

As an overall conclusion, we can affirm that regardless of the meeting points between Stăniloae and Fiddes in their view of the Eucharist, there are still huge differences of accent and conception between the two views of the Eucharist. We believe that by detecting the common features of the reflection of *perichoresis*, namely, the unity of the Christ event, the real presence of Christ and the role of the Eucharist in the life of the church for enhancing spiritual life, we have shown a path which could open the way towards discovering reasons for open communion between the two churches in Romania. A proposal for a possible further direction in developing the platform for this communion will be the subject of one of the sections of chapter 11.

10.3. Trinitarian Theology and the Spiritual Journey

The first thing to be noted after the comparison of Stăniloae's and Fiddes's thought on spirituality, is the fact that they meet on the common ground of their Trinitarian thinking. When Stăniloae considers that the Holy Trinity is the foundation for Christian spirituality he develops his thought in three directions. First, he argues the spiritual life of the Trinity in the communion of the plurality of three divine persons. Second, divine spirituality shared by the three persons is the model for the spirituality of Christian communities, and third, the model of Christian spirituality that is divine spirituality is infused through divine uncreated energies, love being one of them. Moreover, Stăniloae argues elsewhere that the uncreated energies are inseparable from the Spirit, as the Spirit is the vehicle for the uncreated energies.[37]

For Fiddes the foundational importance of the model of Trinity for Christian spirituality is expressed in the call of such a model for a transformation from observer to participant in the spiritual mission of the Father, through the Son in the Spirit, a mission in the world and for the world. The aim of such a participative journey with God is that of transforming the fractured realities of the world through a wholeness that is proper to the divine life. The way this journey towards wholeness in the image and likeness of Holy Trinity is developed by Fiddes on the coordinates of covenant and communion with God, with its vertical and horizontal dimensions, is what could be called a Baptist way, *theosis*, meaning not being like God but "sharing to the most intimate degree in the fellowship of the divine life."[38]

Fiddes and Stăniloae meet in agreement, when arguing from the perspective of the *perichoresis* concept that speaks of no confusion, no contradiction and no separation, as both of them consider that participation in the divine life is not alteration of the "I" of the believer[39] or confusing God with created order, the participation of the believers being always fractured in the present life.

---

37. Stăniloae, *Rugăciunea lui Iisus și experienta Duhului Sfânt*, 112.
38. Fiddes, *Track and Traces*, 18, 19.
39. Stăniloae, *Spiritualitate Ortodoxă*, 23.

These Trinitarian-framing and Spirit-based common features of the two theologians views of spirituality is an important reminder and an important reflective theme for Baptists in Romania, where there is a necessary reformulation of a theology of the Spirit that will keep in their vital connection not only the three persons of the Trinity, but also the person, work, fruit and gifts of the Spirit.

The second important thing to be noted in a comparison of Stăniloae's and Fiddes's thought is that of Christ's centrality for Christian spirituality. If for Stăniloae, the centrality of Christ is translated in the cross of Christ that is present in all realities of life and the world, for Fiddes the centrality of Christ is the foundation for the hope of the new people of God in the actual world of God. Stăniloae sees the imprint of the cross, in the world, the relationships between human beings, and the pleasures of the body. For him the growth and development of Christian spirituality is conditioned by the adoption of a Christlike attitude to the cross, in accepting it. For Fiddes Christ and his life are the starting points of authentic spirituality. Christ is also the model of how the relationship with God should be, as well as the demonstration of God's own covenantal pilgrimage of suffering for fallen humanity.

Stăniloae continues from the vertical dimension of Christ's centrality for Christian spirituality to the horizontal dimension that is translated in the believers' responsibility for the creation in general and for other persons in the world in particular. He affirms the importance of these responsibilities in order to address a possible misunderstanding of Christian spirituality, that of withdrawal from the world into a state of indifference. Rather he affirms that the authenticity of the vertical dimension of Christian spirituality is proved in spiritual living as participation in the work of divinity in preserving and sustaining the created order. Such participation is for Stăniloae the way of releasing the spiritual potencies that God in his initial design imprinted on human beings.

Moreover, Stăniloae argues that this identification with Christ is materialized in ascetical efforts that aim at the mortification of the vices, reflecting identification with Christ's death, and in replacing the vices with virtues, reflecting the identification with Christ's resurrection. This process

The Dialogical Dimension of the Spiritual Journey 189

of identification started at Baptism and continues with the Eucharist, both being forms of Christ's presence and assistance in our ascent towards God.

This presence, says Stăniloae, is embodied through the work of the Spirit in the space of communion with Christ, namely, the church. Besides the important role of Baptism and the Eucharist for the ascent journey, both of them being sacraments that are ecclesially bounded, Stăniloae seems to promote an innovative personalism in line with the prevalent personalism of twentieth-century Orthodox theology, as a reaction to "the reductionist challenge of modernity, with its different expressions of nihilism and atheism, liberal individualism and totalitarian Marxist collectivism."[40]

For Fiddes's theology of spirituality, the horizontal dimension is vitally connected with its vertical dimension. But different from Stăniloae, he brings into view the concept of covenant that expresses the intimate connection between God's initiative and actions as well as human responsibility and response. For Fiddes, all these are embodied in familial life and ecclesial life. Both domains, again, different from Stăniloae, are in Fiddes's view conditioned by the model of divine life as reflected in a non-hierarchical partnership between husband and wife, expressed in what was called "submission of equality,"[41] as opposed to "a hierarchy of submission."[42] He tries to base his line of thought on a close reading of New Testament Scriptures, as for example the Pauline concept of wholeness of the entire reality that overlaps the divine, the familial and ecclesial realities, the vertical and horizontal dimensions of spirituality and the divine and human participation in the macrocosm of the ecclesial community as well as in the microcosm of ecclesial reality that is family, in the necessary journey towards what Fiddes calls the "cosmology of love."[43]

Another meeting point for Stăniloae and Fiddes in their reflection on Christian spirituality is the fact that both of them affirm the centrality of Christ for the revelation of God and for union with God. In Stăniloae's argument this is seen in the threefold meaning of the cross' imprint on human

---

40. Rogobete, *O ontologie a iubirii*, 22.
41. Fiddes, "Woman's Head Is Man," 373. Also, Barnett, *Commentary of the First Epistle*, 250.
42. Fiddes, "Theology of the Charismatic Movement," 36.
43. Fiddes, "Root of Religious Freedom," 176–177.

existence, namely, the revelation of God's transcendence over the gifts that he offers to the world and humanity, the revelation of God's sovereignty that provides an understanding of God's uniqueness, and the revelation of the true love for God as person, despite the presence or absence of his gifts. One of the things to be noted is that Stăniloae roots his reflections on the three meanings for the imprint of the cross on human existence on a profound scriptural reflection of the book of Job.

Fiddes in his turn considers that the revelation of God in Christ is central for the Christian story and as such roots the prophetic ministry of the Christian community in the world against the idolatry in society. The power of this revelation, in Fiddes's opinion, is not in the fact that God forces himself over humanity, rather this power consists in the endurance with which God invites humanity to participate in "this interweaving or *perichoresis* of relationships," a "story of a Father who sends out a Son in a Spirit of love," a story in which we are called "to incorporate our own stories."[44] Moreover, in Stăniloae's thought, the centrality of Christ is seen in his affirmations about union with God through identification with Christ. This identification is not the replacement of the believers' self with that of Christ, rather Christ's life becomes the power by which a believer lives.

For Fiddes, Christ's centrality for the union with God through identification with Christ is seen in his argument about the rule of Christ over the life of the community. This rule is to be translated into awareness of Christ, expressed in two modes: stillness that will enable the contemplation of God and journey in ascent towards God. Fiddes's argument about the complementarity of the two is very close to that of Stăniloae, when arguing the two dimensions of the journey, namely, the inward one, into the depths of the soul, and the upward one, in the silence of the spirit.

At this point in his discussion about the body, heart soul and spirit, Stăniloae has a threefold contribution. First, in the discussion of the difference of *soma – sarx*, when arguing that vices are irrational deformations that have connections with the body and the soul, he provides some important corrections for ascetical practices oriented towards the body without the vital connection with spiritual education and disciplining of mind and will.

---

44. Fiddes, "Story and Possibility," 44.

Second, he discusses the difference between sublimation and abolition when speaking of bodily affects that need to be kept under control not extinguished. His third contribution is important in clarifying the theological vocabulary for the concepts of soul, heart, mind, etc., in conversation with modern psychology.

Another common thing to be noted is that for both Stăniloae and Fiddes, spirituality is a dynamic reality that develops on the trajectory of the ascent towards God. Stăniloae speaks of stages or phases of the ascent journey, from purification from vices that are replaced by virtues, through illumination by the light of the Spirit, to union with God in love. Fiddes on the other hand speaks of this journey in the terms of embodiment of attentiveness to God and to the others who are in Christ, namely, between two poles, stillness and journey.

Stăniloae argues the pneumatic unity of the ascent through all the stages in the life of a believer and he sees distinctions between the power of the Spirit and the light of the Spirit consequent to the movement from purification towards union, through illumination. Fiddes also seems to be close to a integrative conception of the work of the Spirit in the life of believers in the necessary continuum of the individual and communal dimensions, when he argues the interdependence of the coordinates of embodiment of spirituality, namely, prayer, witness, singing, eucharistic communion, and reading of the Bible, all those expressing the unifying role of the Spirit in the life of community.

Another difference to be noted is that even if both theologians seem to agree about the vital role of faith in the ascent of spirituality the apparent mechanicism of the process of purification seems to be overcome by Stăniloae's consideration of the importance of grace as God's empowering initiative with the conclusion that faith is simultaneously the gift of God and an answer to human obedience and permanent repentance. Stăniloae argues admirably that faith has the role of strengthening reason and is to become a life style and a fear of God, yet he sadly does not show the way in which the actualization of faith reality in the life of the believer and community is to happen.

Complementarily, Fiddes understands the importance of the word of God and of fellowship in prayer, worship and eucharistic communion in a community context for the strengthening of faith towards more and more spiritually mature participation in mediation of "seeing Christ" through a necessary move from being witnessed to, towards being a witness to Christ. This is for Fiddes a way to participate in God's mission in the world. Stăniloae too speaks of "seeing" differently the meaning of your existence, of the created order and the spiritual meaning of Scriptures. This different seeing is done through the work of the Spirit in illumination, on the coordinates of pure prayer. Here Fiddes adds another vital element for the spiritual journey that of a pure heart as a vital ingredient for true prayer shaped by scripture and encompassed by the *koinonia* of community.

Conclusions

Overall, in regard to the dynamics of the trajectory of the ascent in spirituality, we can conclude that for both theologians a preoccupation with stating the unity in the work of the Spirit in different aspects of the journey, and in keeping the necessary balance between the individual and the communal aspects of spirituality in their interdependence, is evident. This could be a salutary corrective for the excessive individualism proper to many baptistic communities in Romania in regard to spirituality, as well as an important example for the way the Trinitarian theology of participation could and should inform spiritual life and its interpretation in baptistic communities in Romania.

Moreover, first, the way Stăniloae sees the dynamics of ascent in spirituality – though following a Hesychastic path and through the complementarity of ascetic and mystique mirroring of the christological-pneumatological convergence – brings a fresh perspective that could be a useful corrective for the two possible extremes in regard to spirituality, in contemporary Orthodox communities in Romania. These are that of mechanical ascetics without any spiritual content and significance, and that of excessive mystical orientation without any connection with the necessary mission in the real life of society.[45]

---

45. See also, Ion Bria, *Romania: Orthodox Identity at a Crossroad of Europe* (Geneva: WCC Publications, 1995), 43. He argues against the movement
    calling for a return to the spirituality of the so-called "Eastern Mysticism," which promotes detachment from historical events and isolation of the people from civic affairs . . . the task of the church is precisely to help the society to shape a new economic system, to promote alternative structures that will enhance social and economic justice and lead to a genuine community of democracy.
Bria, *Romania*, 43.

Second, Fiddes's engagement with mystical theology is a model of the necessary theological engagement of Baptist theology with theologies from other Christian traditions within the Romanian Christian family. Also, the Hesychastic elements in the thought of both theologians are an important reminder for believers from both traditions that the Christian life is a shared journey, assisted by God in Christ through the Spirit. Also it is a reminder that the shared journey of Christian life means growth into the likeness of Christ, and that activism should always be balanced by contemplation, action by understanding, and ministry by spirituality. The theme of Christian life as a shared journey will be explored in the last section of chapter 11 in this project.

CHAPTER 11

The Transformative Dimension of the Spiritual Journey: Lessons from the Conversation

11.1. Baptism as a Way of Living

In chapter 10, of this work we understood that Stăniloae and Fiddes are in agreement and bring into full attention the importance of the Holy Trinity for our participative progress towards God, as "the foundation, infinite reservoir, power and model of our growing eternal communion,"[1] and as the foundation of Christian spirituality,[2] and having the concept of *perichoresis* as the best way to express the theology of participation.[3] I also argued that the two theologians meet in agreement, on the fertile terrain of a dynamic view of baptism, having faith as the essential element not only for baptism as a starting place but also for the "continuation and actualization of baptism,"[4] a process of a "life-long growth into Christ,"[5] led by Christ,[6] and empowered by the Holy Spirit.[7]

---

1. Stăniloae, *Revelation and Knowledge*, 247.
2. Stăniloae, *Spiritualitatea Ortodoxă*, 29.
3. Fiddes, *Participating in the Trinity*, 385.
4. Stăniloae, *Spiritualitatea Ortodoxă*, 44.
5. Fiddes, "Baptism and the Process of Christian Initiation," 56.
6. Stăniloae, *Spiritualitatea Ortodoxă*, 43.
7. Stăniloae, *TDO*, 3, 25. Also, Fiddes, "Baptism and the Process of Christian Initiation," 61.

There are a few important possible developments from the conversation of the two theologians' thoughts about Trinitarian participation that are of real significance for the model of the church as a community that mirrors the divine *perichoresis*, which we explore in the following section. As already observed in the analysis of Stăniloae's and Fiddes's views of the economic Trinity, Christ is the meeting place of the Father and the Spirit, and the meeting place of divinity and humanity. The direct consequence of these realities is the reality of Christ as the meeting place of believers with each other as the people of God, having Christ in the center, as in Christ we meet the Father in the Spirit. Therefore progress in understanding baptism not only as a static reality of immersion in water, but also towards a dynamic lifelong reality of immersion in the divine *perichoresis*, is possible only when Christ is the center.

Based on this important finding in the exploration of chapters 3 and 7, we aim to argue the way those findings could be applied in a possible reformulation of the theology of baptism for baptistic communities in Romania. This is necessary because in Romania one of the major disagreements between the Orthodox and Baptists is in their view of baptism. Yet, as we have seen in chapter 10 in the comparison of Stăniloae's and Fiddes's views on baptism, there are areas where the two traditions could be in agreement. Those intersections of agreement I aim to reveal in the present section of chapter 11.

Thus, in the present section I want to explore, first the constitutive dimension of baptism for being the people of God, second, the confessional dimension of baptism for becoming the body of Christ and third, the missional dimension of baptism in the ordination of the church as the temple of the Spirit. In light of the conversation between Stăniloae and Fiddes we will argue that being the people of God is based on Christ's person, work and status, being the body of Christ requires our participation, and being the temple of the Spirit means to be immersed in God's mission in the world through the Son in the Holy Spirit. This concentric character of the church's mission is expressed in the *kerygmatic* dimension of Christian discipleship, the *koinonial* character of Christian prayer, and the kenotic embodiment of Christian *diakonia*.[8]

---

8. Lesslie Newbigin, *The Gospel in a Pluralistic Society* (London: SPCK, 1992), 131. He says:
> The missionary movement at the present time suffers from the running battle between those who make this emphasis on the primacy of evangelism, of the

The Constitutive Dimension of Baptism: Being the People of God

The constitutive dimension of baptism could be seen in the fact that being the people of God is possible only if Christ is in the center as the premise for our participation in the movement of the Father towards the Son in the Spirit, and of the Spirit towards the Father through the Son. To participate in this reality means to be embraced by the Father, as he embraces the Son, and to be embraced by the Spirit as he embraces the Father through the Son. This participation that is centered in Christ is fundamental for a dynamic encounter with one another as the people of God.[9] Human persons centered in Christ cannot remain captive in the privacy of their individuality, for if they are immersed in the divine persons' movements towards each other, the human persons "meet" with each other as they share in the center that is Christ, share the embrace of the Father in Christ, and share the embrace of the Spirit in Christ. It is a *perichoresis* of movements that has Christ as the center, a *perichoresis* that mirrors the divine *perichoresis* in which each divine person makes the other the center, being fulfilled by the other without being dissolved in the other, fulfils the other without confusion with the other, and centers the other without being separated from the other.[10]

---

declaratory function of the Church, and those who insist that the first priority must be given to action for challenging injustice, prejudice, and oppression, action for justice and peace . . . If we turn to the Gospels we are bound to note the indissoluble nexus between deeds and words.
Newbigin, *Gospel in a Pluralistic Society*, 131.

9. Lesslie Newbigin, *The Household of God: Lectures on the Nature of the Church* (London: SCM, 1964), 25. He says, "The Church is the pilgrim people of God . . . Therefore the nature of the Church is never to be finally defined in static terms, but only in terms of that to which it is going" (Newbigin, *Household of God*, 25).

10. Stăniloae, *Holy Trinity*, 23, 27. Speaking about the centrality of the other for each person in the Trinity as an open experience for us, Stăniloae argues:

the Father does not want to miss out on experiencing the Son's love for Him, as He unites His feelings as Father toward the Son with the experience of the Son's love for Him, without thereby confusing Himself with the Son. The Father experiences the Son's feelings toward Him as a subject, without becoming confused with the Son. We see the unconfused unity of the Father with the Son in this relationship . . . We experience this fact even in our relationships among each other. (Stăniloae, *Holy Trinity*, 23).

"We too live this phenomenon in part, but we are limited, dependent, created beings, and we cannot fully appreciate infinity . . ." (Stăniloae, 24). "The mode in which the Holy Trinity is united is thus the origin and the eternal helper in creating unity between conscious things" (Stăniloae, 27). See also, Ben Witherington, III, and Laura M. Ice, *The Shadow of*

Therefore, the unifying center of the *perichoretical* church, in its vertical and horizontal dimensions, is the Christ, meaning to put Christ in the center, as the Father put him in his plan. In fact the Son himself, in his person and work, mirrors the character of the Father and fulfils the Father's plan. On the other hand, to put Christ in the center should mirror the way the Spirit put him in his work, a reality shown in the fact the Spirit himself in his person and work mirrors the Son's character and reveals the Son's work.[11] This is the constitutive dimension of the church as the people of God, constituted by God through the Son in the Spirit.[12] This is a participation that starts in water baptism and continues in baptism as a way of life, namely the immersion of the life of the church in the perichoretical movements of the Trinity, on the coordinates of God's will and mission, promoted in Christ and after the model of Christ's appropriation of God's will and of the Holy Spirit's work,[13] an immersion that imprints the model and the likeness of Christ in the people of God.

Christ first has to be in the center, because, Christ is the one who redefines the people of God in his person, becoming, in his incarnation and life, not only the second Adam,[14] but also the New Israel.[15] He is, in the argument

---

the Almighty: Father, Son, and Spirit in Biblical Perspective (Grand Rapids, MI: Eerdmans, 2002), 63–64. Witherington argues the centrality of the Son for the Father is the thought of the New Testament writers: "the relationship of early Christians with God made possible by Jesus and enabled by the Holy Spirit. The Father is seen through the eyes of the Son and on the basis of the teaching." (Witherington and Ice, *Shadow of the Almighty*, 63–64).

11. Daniel G. Oprean, *Comuniune și participare: Reflecții teologice cu privire la dimensiunea spirituală a existenței* [Communion and participation: Theological reflections on the spiritual dimension of existence] (Timișoara: Excelsior Art, 2011), 95.

12. We have noticed in the previous chapters that Stăniloae and Fiddes are in agreement with the fact of the double constitution of the church, in a christological-pneumatological synthesis. In this chapter we want to explore further how this synthesis could inform a sketch of a theology of baptism as way of living.

13. Bulgakov, *Orthodox Church*, 1, says "The Church of Christ is not an institution; it is a new life with Christ, and in Christ, guided by the Holy Spirit." See also, James J. Stamoolis, *Eastern Orthodox Mission Theology Today* (Maryknoll, NY: Orbis Books, 1986), 123.

14. Norval Geldenhuys, *The Gospel of Luke* (Grand Rapids, MI: Eerdmans, 1977); Michael Wilcock, *The Message of Luke: The Saviour of the World* (Downers Grove, IL: InterVarsity Press, 1979), 60.

15. N. T. Wright, *The New Testament and the People of God* (London: SPCK, 1992), 408. See also, N. T. Wright, *Jesus and the Victory of God* (London: SPCK, 1996), 481.

of the Synoptic Gospels, the true Israel,[16] and the one who "reinstates" the true people of God.[17] Christ fulfils the will of God as the representative of the people of God, a direct critique of the failure of Israel to fulfill the mission of God as his representatives in and for the world. Therefore, Christ's exemplary life is the model of the true people of God, who continue to embody in an obedient and faithful lifestyle, the reality of which water baptism is a sign, picture, and representation,[18] a reality of a continual immersion in the reality of the triune life, will and mission.

The people of God are thus constituted in this dynamic encounter with the obedient Son who glorifies the loving Father, living in the Holy Spirit. The encounter with the loving movement of the Father towards the Son in the sanctifying transparency of the Spirit, and of the obedient movement of the Son towards the Father through faithfulness produced by the Spirit, is the atmosphere to be breathed by the people of God, is the reality that the people of God should embody, and is the dynamic in which the people of God should live as a perichoretical church.

Christ has to be in the center, second, because Christ is also the one who forms the people of God through his work, through which he reforms the people of God, in the formation of his body. The people of God, as Christ's body are not formed on the national and ethnic specificity of Israel as a nation,[19] rather they are a multiethnic, multinational people, as Paul understood it, the mystery of God revealed in the gospel,[20] by the revealer who is the Holy Spirit.

Christ has to be in the center, third, because, he is the one who is the head of the people of God by his status. Christ is the Son of God,[21] "very

---

16. R. Alan Cole, *The Gospel According to Mark* (Leicester: Inter-Varsity Press, 1989), 110. See also, Donald English, *The Message of Mark: The Mystery of Faith* (Downers Grove, IL: InterVarsity Press, 1992), 44; and, R. T. France, *The Gospel According to Matthew* (Grand Rapids, MI: Eerdmans, 1985), 97.

17. Wright, *New Testament and the People*, 320. Also, George Eldon Ladd, *The Presence of the Future: The Eschatology of Biblical Realism* (Grand Rapids, MI: Eerdmans, 1974), 252.

18. Wright, *New Testament and the People*, 14.

19. Gordon D. Fee, *Paul, the Spirit and the People of God* (Peabody, MA: Hendricksen, 1996), 64.

20. Charles Hodge, *A Commentary on the Epistle to the Ephesians* (London: Banner of Truth, 1964), 162.

21. Stanley Hauerwas, *Matthew* (Ada, MI: Brazos Press, 2006), 20.

God of very God."[22] Christ is also king, prophet, and high priest.[23] He is first the king whose reign should be not only declared but also recognized. The resurrection of Christ is proof that in the eternal plan of the Father, the kingdom was inaugurated. The truth of Christ's reign is echoed in the first proclamation of Peter in Jerusalem after Pentecost: "God has made this Jesus, whom you crucified, both Lord and Messiah" (Acts 2:36). Paul also understood and developed the concept of Christ's reign inaugurated in his resurrection (Eph 1:18–23), a reign rooted in his sacrifice and acknowledged in his ascension (Phil 2:6–11).

Christ is, second, the prophet of God,[24] a prophet whose message should be acknowledged. The Synoptics acknowledge this truth that was testified by the Father to the disciples in the experience of Christ's transfiguration (Matt 17:2, Luke 9:29) when the Prophets and the Law (represented by the appearance Moses and Elijah) where fulfilled in Christ's office as Prophet and Message. This is declared by the Father himself: "This is my Son, whom I love; with him I am well pleased. Listen to him!" (Matt 17:5, Luke 9:35). Christ is also the prophet whose message should be obeyed. The Synoptics picture this truth in the story of Christ's triumphal entry into Jerusalem (Matt 21:11–13, Mark 11:15–17, Luke 19:45–48). After his resurrection, Christ proves that he is the prophet whose message must be acknowledged and obeyed because it is true (Luke 24:19–27).

Christ is, third, the high priest whose sacrifice should be understood in its uniqueness and definitiveness and baptism is "a living and expressive representation of Christ's high-priestly death and resurrection."[25] He is a unique high priest[26] because he is not like the other high priests of the Old Covenant priesthood. Christ is not characterized by the same weaknesses that the other high priests shared with the people they served, and consequently

---

22. Grudem, *Systematic Theology*, 1169.

23. Calvin, *Institutes*, 1, 494–503. Also, Dumitru Stăniloae, *The Experience of God, Orthodox Dogmatic Theology 3: The Person of Jesus Christ as God and Savior* (Brookline, MA: Holy Cross Orthodox Press, 2011), 85–155 (referred to as *Person of Jesus Christ*, hereafter).

24. Oscar Cullmann, *The Christology of the New Testament* (Philadelphia, PA: Westminster, 1963), 44. He says that "The authority of Jesus was . . . that . . . of the 'final Prophet.'" (Cullmann, *Christology*, 44).

25. Karl Barth, *The Teaching of the Church Regarding Baptism* (Eugene, OR: Wipf & Stock, 2005), 18.

26. Wright, *New Testament and the People*, 410.

in need of offering substitutionary sacrifices for themselves (Heb 5:2–3). Instead, his sinless life became an offering to the Father (Heb 5:7), thus he is also the sacrifice for the salvation of humanity.

To sum up, the constitutive dimension of baptism for the people of God can be understood with Christ in the center as the one who is consubstantial with the Father through his divinity and also consubstantial with us through his humanity. He is the necessary center because Christ assures the Trinity's participation in humanity and humanity's participation in God. He is the necessary center because he redefines, reforms and leads the people of God.

In his person Christ is the recapitulation of Israel, being at once the true, obedient and faithful Israel and also the foundational model for the new people of God. In his work Christ is the one who forms the new people of God, as a multinational, multiethnic, multiracial[27] reality, over which he is the head and is all in all (Col 3:11). In his status Christ is the King of kings and the Lord of lords, being also the embodiment of the kingdom. He is the prophet who recapitulates the message of God's prophets being the final prophecy of God, and is the unique high priest of God who replaces the human high priest's office, being also the once for all sacrifice.[28]

The Confessional Dimension of Baptism: Becoming the Body of Christ

The confession of the Christian communities is first, a threefold confession. First, it contains the declaration that there is a unique God in three persons, Father, Son and Holy Spirit. Second, it contains the declaration that the true church is of those called to a personal, real and live relationship with the Father, Son and Holy Spirit. The third dimension of this confession is the declaration that Christian communities do not exist separately from each other, but they exist in communion with each other, united in the

---

27. John R. W. Stott, *The Message of Acts: To the Ends of the Earth* (Leicester: Inter-Varsity Press, 1990), 40–44.

28. Ivana Noble, "How to Avoid Grand Narratives in Christology: A Challenge of Postmodern Hermeneutics," *Milltown Studies* 65 (2010). Ivana Noble warns rightly about the danger of transforming Christology into ideology. She also says that one of the ways to avoid this danger is to never separate what Christ is from what Christ does, Christology from soteriology. This is what we tried to do in the following. also what we have learned from the thought of Stăniloae and Fiddes that, keeping Christology in its vital connection with Pneumatology and especially with the doctrine of the Trinity is of similar importance.

same Spirit, under the lordship of the same Lord, and in the embrace of the same Father, the one who is the Father of all, the one who is over all, and works in all.

The confession of the Christian communities is second, a permanent confession based on the threefold declaration in Christ's baptism; that is his profound and unique identification with humanity. In Christ's own baptism are three declarations. The first declaration in Christ's baptism is that of the Son, in regard to the fact that his identification with humanity is real. His identification with humanity was neither merely apparent, nor superficial, but a real one in that he was made sin for us.[29] The Son of God as Christ had to travel the entire journey of fallen humanity, being exposed to sin, standing in front of sin, being tempted to sin, assuming the sins of humanity, yet without sin every moment of his life. As such he was made the promoter of our salvation[30] that is rooted above all in Christ's identification with us. He embraced our fallen humanity cleansing it, redeeming it and sanctifying it from inside out in his life.

Through incarnation Christ brings a revolution in the understanding of salvation and of sanctification, for his holiness was not one of separation from people, things, and realities, but an internal holiness based on his unique love for his Father, on his unique understanding of the heart of the Father, and on his participation in the Father's *pathos* for fallen humanity. Christ took the cross from the Father's heart and made it his own. He walked on the Father's *Via Dolorosa*, making it his own path from the Father to the Father, from incarnation to resurrection.[31]

The second declaration is that of the Spirit that the identification of the Son with humanity is total (Matt 3:16 and 1 John 5:6). There is no domain of our humanity that his identification does not immerse (Heb 2:14, 17

---

29. Stăniloae, *Chipul evanghelic*, 31. He says that Christ's "solidarity with us was not only juridical but also real, for He appropriated not only our passions and death because of sin, and also of the repentance as man, for our sin" (Stăniloae, 31). See also, Willmer, "Jesus Christ the Forgiven," 26–27.

30. Raymond Brown, *The Message of Hebrews: Christ Above All* (Leicester: Inter-Varsity Press, 1982), 101.

31. Dumitru Stăniloae, *Iisus Hristos sau Restaurarean Omului* (Craiova: Omniscop, 1993), 256. Commenting on the communion of suffering in the life of the Father and the Son in the Spirit, Stăniloae says: "Love, sacrifice, communion are all together. One is in the other as are Father, Son and Holy Spirit." (Stăniloae, *Iisus Hristos sau Restaurarean Omului*, 256).

and Rom 8:3). There is no sin to which in his identification with humanity he would not be tempted, therefore there is no sin that is not forgiven potentially in his sacrifice and reality in our repentance. This is the reason salvation in Christ is an offer for all people as potential, yet it is to be appropriated personally in our identification with Christ.

The third declaration in Christ's baptism is that of the Father, that the Son's identification with humanity is admissible. Only the Son could have saved us. Only one who is like the Father, only someone who comes from the Father, someone who is the form of the Father, the one who is the image of the Father,[32] only the one who comes from the perfect communion and love of the Father, could have saved us.[33] This admission came on the path of the Son's *kenosis*, in order to become like man, and was permanently actualized in his humble obedience (Phil 2:8) becoming "the author" of our salvation (Heb 2:10), "the source of eternal salvation, for all who obey Him" (Heb 5:8–9).

Christian baptism should be a continuous mirroring of this identification through the confession of him in a threefold testimony. First is the testimony of the Spirit, which is the internal declaration of life, connected with the work of the Spirit, that is inclusion in Christ[34] which testifies to the metamorphosis, through the word of Christ that became reality in our lives in the work of the Spirit (Rom 6). This transformation about which the Spirit testifies is that produced by the immersion of our lives in the life of Christ. But this is only the beginning not the end of a process. The declaration of the Spirit, in regard to the internal, unseen transformation,

---

32. N. T. Wright, *Colossians and Philemon* (Leicester: Inter-Varsity Press, 1986), 68. Commenting on the concept of the image of God in Col 1:15, Wright argues that "Paul uses the present tense ('is') to refer to him as having taken the place of world sovereignty marked out of humanity ('the image of God') from the beginning (*cf.* Eph 1:20-23)." (Wright, *Colossians and Philemon*, 68).

33. Witherington, III, and Ice, *Shadow of the Almighty*, 85. He says: "the language is covenantal, denoting a special relationship between God and His Son, The word agapatos literally means 'beloved' but it can connote 'unique' or 'special' on occasion . . . What we see here is the confirmation given to Jesus of who he is in relationship to the heavenly Father." (Witherington, III, and Ice, 85).

34. Newbigin, *Household of God*. His answer to the question of "what is the manner of our ingrafting in Christ?" is threefold: first "we are incorporated in Christ by hearing and believing the Gospel," second, "we are incorporated by sacramental participation in the life of the historically continuous Church," and third, "we are incorporated by receiving and abiding in the Holy Spirit," (Newbigin, 30).

called generically, being born again, is not only in regard to a change of direction in life, it is not a static reality. It starts with an analysis operated by the Spirit over an entire life with all its domains, and continues with the dynamics of walking towards God. Therefore, repentance is one stop on the road of walking from God, a turn, and the start of walking towards God, with Christ in the Spirit.

Second is the testimony of the water (baptism), that is the external declaration of life, that is not only the moment of water baptism, rather is walking in the reality of baptism, walking in and with the Lord of baptism (Rom 10:6–13, 1 Pet 3:21–22). Third, is the testimony of blood (the agent of cleansing in the new covenant) that is the permanent declaration of life, that of cleansing in the blood of Christ, a reality of sanctification, of a life covered with the blood of Christ (1 John 1:9), a repentant confession that is not once for all, rather is once and always. Authentic Christian life, is lived in the expiration of sins and inspiration of the Spirit. Arno C. Gaebelein is right when affirming:

> Faith and repentance are not successive stages on the road of life, they are not independent guides to direct the pilgrim's path; they are not separate acts to be successively accomplished by the sinner as a condition of his salvation. But, in different phases of it, they represent the same Godward attitude of the soul, which the truth of God *believed* produces . . . Jordan is always in the Word a type of death . . . The people came, confessed their sins, seeing then their true position, what they were and what they deserved . . . They heard, they believed, they confessed and witnessed to it outwardly . . . Christian baptism is unto Christ's death, who has taken our place and died for us.[35]

Yet, the question could be how all these concentric confessional and declarative realities find their expression in the communal thought and life of the church? The church's identification with the death of Christ should find expression in "the taking off the old clothes of the old Adam." The church first needs to take off, paradoxically, the "cloth" of her pride of being the

---

35. Arno C. Gaebelein, *The Gospel of Matthew: An Exposition* (Neptune, NJ: Loizeaux Brothers, 1961), 65, 67, 68.

people of God. That will mean real identification with Christ in his death. As for Christ, renouncing himself was a permanent reality beautifully expressed in the Pauline christological hymn in Philippians 2, from incarnation to ascension, so the church should follow Christ, denying herself and daily taking up the cross in a "hermeneutics of humility,"[36] in regard to her life and her mission. The church would do that by being ready to acknowledge and deal with her idols of power and influence which mirror the secular ideologies of the day, rather than the perennial example of servanthood expressed in the superlative in the thought, life and work of her Master. For this church needs to return to a theology of permanent repentance that means turning again and again, from secular ways of thinking to the mind of Christ.

Only such repentance will reveal the second "cloth" that the church needs to put off, namely, the pride of being saved that leads many times to categorizations of people into "saved" and "lost." The salvation that the church's people experience would be genuine only if such an experience would lead to thankfulness to God, in the acknowledgment that salvation is entirely God's work, in his Son, through the Spirit. Thankfulness rooted in the recognition of our dependency on God would then be translated not in "professing a great faith while living by small concepts,"[37] but in a life that would mirror the reality of faith.

The third "cloth" the church needs to put off in her authentic identification with the death of Christ is that of the pride of being spiritual. Spirituality of the church should be the product of her theology that comes from the interaction of the word and of the Spirit. Yet, such spirituality is not something to be proud of in such a way that will lead to isolation from other people who are not spiritual. This was the way the Pharisees developed their spirituality that became pathological and was disapproved by Christ, for it led to a "holiness" of separation, based on a sterile *external conformation* to a set of rules not rooted in an *internal transformation* as a

---

36. Kevin J. Vanhoozer, *Is There A Meaning in This Text?* (Grand Rapids, MI: Zondervan, 1998), 463.

37. William M. Pickard, *Rather Die Than Live – Jonah* (New York: Education and Cultivation Division Board of Global Ministry, 1974), 39.

lifelong process.[38] Christ's own spirituality was a powerful corrective to their pathological spirituality:

> For Christ holiness was not only external but internal, grounded in his relationship with God. For Jesus separation is a "separation to rather than separation from." Jesus is holy not because he isolated himself from either people or the world, nor because of some elaborate system of ritual purification. He is holy because he is consumed with passion for both God and the world. Because the love of God is burning in his heart, Jesus is holy. And because he is holy, the entire world has become clean to him.[39]

Christ's spirituality was one of humbleness, rooted in a "theology of the towel" (John 13),[40] and accordingly, the spirituality of the church that means the taking off of pride to be spiritual and be in "full identification with Jesus,"[41] a spirituality of discipleship,[42] that produces Christlike,

---

38. Daniel G. Oprean, "When Salt Loses its Saltiness: Causes of Spiritual Abuse within the Church," (unpublished paper, Osijek, 2003).

39. Ridell Michael, *Threshold of the Future: Reforming the Church in the Post- Christian West* (London: SPCK, 1998), 80.

40. Daniel G. Oprean, "Reconciliation in Church and Society: Church's Ministry as God's Reconciliation Agency," in *Reconciliation: The Way of Healing and Growth*, eds. Janez Juhant, Bojan Zalec (Zürich: Lit Verlag, 2012), 179–187.

41. Miroslav Volf, *Exclusion and Embrace: A Theological Exploration of Identity, Otherness, and Reconciliation* (Nashville, TN: Abingdon, 1996), 92. He describes the mechanism of the identification with Christ:
> The Spirit enters the citadel of the self, de-centers the self by fashioning it in the image of the self-giving Christ, and frees its will so it can resist the power of exclusion in the power of the Spirit of embrace. It is in the citadel of the fragile self that the new world of embrace is first created (2 Corinthians 5:17). It is by this seemingly powerless power of the Spirit – the Spirit who blows even outside the walls of the church – that selves are freed from powerlessness in order to fight the system of exclusion everywhere – in the structures, in the culture, and in the self.

Volf, *Exclusion and Embrace*, 92.

42. Myron Augsburger, *The Robe of God: Reconciliation, the Believers Essential* (Scottsdale, PA: Herald Press, 2000) 136. First, it "is based on a personal relationship with the Lord Jesus Christ," (Augsburger, *Robe of God*, 140). Second, a spirituality of discipleship requires the indwelling of the Holy Spirit, (Augsburger, 142). Third it identifies us with Christ, spirituality as seen in incarnation that is not withdrawal from the material; instead it makes all of life sacred, (Augsburger, 144). Fourth, a spirituality of discipleship places priority on the kingdom of Christ. It is a life style, (Augsburger, 145). Fifth, it is expressed by involvement in the community of Christ, (Augsburger, 146). He concludes: "In fact we do unbelievers the most good by maintaining our integrity and living out the love of Christ," (Agusburger, 148).

kenotic and pneumatic communities. Only as such can the church live as Christ lived on the earth "full of grace and truth." Living the truth not in proudness but in humbleness, a *kenotic* spirit being the framework of every action of the church in the world.[43] The things that the church should put on in her identification with the resurrection of Christ will be explored in the next section.

The Missional Dimension of Baptism: Ordained as the Temple of the Spirit

As Christ's baptism was his ordination for ministry, from the Father, through the Spirit, so Christian baptism should be regarded as the ordination of believers for Christian ministry. In fact Christian ministry as well should be regarded as participation of believers in God's mission, through the Son, in the Spirit, a mission of God *in* the world and *for* the world. In this section we will explore some of the dimensions of the life of the church as the temple of the Spirit and also some coordinates of a Christlike pneumatic ministry of the church in the world.

The dimensions of the life of the church as the temple of the Spirit will be explored in the framework of the church's "putting on" the character of Christ imprinted in the life of the church through the Spirit. The first new "cloth" that the Spirit needs to put on in the life of the church is the humbleness of continual transformation through a fresh understanding of her way of living in the society, expressed in the Pauline concept of the circumcision of the heart, a recurrent theme in regard to the people of God.

---

43. Paul Tillich, *Love, Power, and Justice* (London: Oxford University Press, 1954), 121. He says: "Spiritual power through words or thought, through what he is and what he does, or through the surrender of them or through the sacrifice of himself. This is the power which elevates the holy community above the ambiguities of power." (Tillich, *Love, Power*, 121). See also, Karl Barth, *Against the Stream: Shorter Post-War Writings, 1946-52* (London: SCM, 1954). He says:
>How extraordinary the Church's preaching, teaching, ministry, theology, political guardianship and missions would be, how it would convict itself of unbelief, in what it says, if it did not proclaim to all men that God is not against man but for man. It need not concern itself with the "No" that must be said to human presumption and human sloth. This "No" will be quite audible enough when as the real Church it concerns itself with the washing of feet and nothing else. This is the obedience which it owes to its Lord in this world.

Barth, *Against the Stream*, 73.

The second new "cloth" that the Spirit needs to put on in the life of the church is the reality of *koinonial* discipleship. The first dimension of *koinonia* in the life of the church as the temple of the Spirit is *kerygma*, considered traditionally as "the proclamation of the saving act of God in Christ," and also "the phenomenon of the call which goes out and makes a claim upon the hearers."⁴⁴ The church has to aim this highest performance of its proclamation to facilitate for the hearers not only the intellectual understanding of the Gospel, but also the event of the Word.⁴⁵ Because Christ "continues to teach His Church (as Prophet),"⁴⁶ the Word comes alive for the listener.⁴⁷ It becomes the space of meeting God in the power of the Holy Spirit.

The second dimension of *koinonia* in the life of the church as the temple of the Spirit is prayer, an important practice of the primitive church (Acts 2:42). Prayer should be a Christlike practice following the model of his life and office as the high priest. Christ the high priest is "at the same time the one who brings the sacrifice and the sacrifice itself," being the model and basis for our sacrifice.⁴⁸

That leads to the third dimension of *koinonia* that constitutes also the third "cloth" that the Spirit needs to put on in the life of the church, namely, the humbleness of a *kenotic diakonia* in the world. For as Christ became the

---

44. C. Brown, "Proclamation, Preach, Kerygma," in *Dictionary of New Testament Theology*, vol. 3, ed. Collin Brown (Grand Rapids, MI: Zondervan, 1978), 53. Also, J. S. Baird, "Preaching," in *Evangelical Dictionary of Theology* ed. Walter A. Elwell (Grand Rapids, MI: Baker Books, 1984), 869.

45. Karl Barth, *God Here and Now: Religious Perspectives* (New York: Harper & Row, 1964).

> The essence of the Church is the event in which God's Word and revelation in Jesus Christ, and the office of Jesus as God's ordained Prophet, Priest and King, is accomplished to the extent that it becomes a Word which is directed toward, reaches, and touches certain men. The essence of the Church is the event in which the Holy Scriptures as the prophetic-apostolic witness to Jesus Christ carries through the "demonstration of the Spirit and power" for particular men, so that these men receive the freedom to know themselves as men enlightened and overcome by this witness, by Him to whom this witness points.

Barth, *God Here and Now*, 63–64.

46. Stăniloae, *TDO*, 2, 231. Also, Dănuț Mănăstireanu, "Dumitru Stăniloae's Theology of Ministry," in *Dumitru Stăniloae, Tradition and Modernity in Theology*, ed. Lucian Turcescu (Iasi: Center for Romanian Studies, 2002), 133.

47. Karl Barth, *Church Dogmatics*, vol. 1.2 (Peabody: Hendrikson Publishers, 2010), 752. "Jesus Christ in the power of His resurrection is present wherever men speak really of God." (Barth, *Church Dogmatics*, vol. 1.2, 752).

48. Stăniloae, *TDO*, 2, 232–233. Also, Mănăstireanu, "Dumitru Stăniloae's," 133.

temple of God, a reality of mediation between God and humanity, so the church as the temple of the Spirit is called to be the reality of mediation between God and the world. *Diakonia* of the church is rooted "in the person of Jesus Christ and His example."

Christ's *diakonia* was his way of fulfilling his office as King. Christ's *diakonia* was not a theoretical concept, or an administrative one, but a participative one. His *diakonia* was God's *diakonia*[49] in the entire history of humankind. Accordingly, the church as the agent of God's reconciliation for the world, as the body of Christ for the world, and as the temple of the Spirit for the world, has to follow the pattern Christ's *diakonia* showed forth in his entire ministry. Therefore *diakonia* of the church in the world means first a presence of faith.

The aim of the church's presence in the world should be the promotion, mediation, cultivation and strengthening of faith in the lives of the people of this world. The presence of the church in the world does not mean only to facilitate the "hearing" of the gospel, as important as this should be, but also the kind of presence that embodies the gospel. Moreover, if the *diakonia* of the church first, means the presence of the church in the world, second it means actions of love in the name of Christ embodied in the church's relationships to the world.

The action of the church is possible only when the theology of the church is a holistic one. This means that the church has to regard as valuable in human beings not only the soul but also the whole body-spirit. Although Christians no longer live under the tyranny of *sarx*, for them *soma* is still important. Once the church is clear in its theology concerning its social role it will be able to see the needs. When it sees the needs it can start to elaborate strategies for social assistance. Especially in the Majority World countries,[50] the Christian gospel should mean actions rather than merely words, food in soup-kitchens not merely prayers, shelters for the homeless not merely sermons, social programs for development not merely evangelistic strategies. All of these would be true expressions of Christian love.

---

49. K. Hess, "Serve, Deacon, Worship," in *Dictionary of New Testament Theology*, vol. 3, ed. Colin Brown (Exeter: Paternoster, 1971), 547.

50. Ronald J. Sider, *Rich Christians in an Age of Hunger: A Biblical Study* (Downers Grove, IL: InterVarsity Press, 1977), 33.

When the church has the conviction that doing the things needed for the poor, oppressed, homeless, sick, is all for Christ, then truly the church is the embodiment of God's Kingdom. These considerations lead to the third ministry of the church in the world, her prophetic ministry, as a sign of hope.

The church as the presence and embodiment of the values of the kingdom of God is a sign of hope for and in the world. Yet besides its presence the church is to point to the one in whom all things are possible. Pointing to God and what he has done in Christ means bringing hope in the midst of world despair.[51] The prophetic ministry of the church is based in the all-encompassing work of Christ to reconcile humankind to God. This hope is to be offered to the people of the world by bringing acknowledgment of God's love and his deep interest in human beings into the public arena. The prophetic ministry of the church means therefore for the church to be that community illuminating this truth of the gospel to the world. This is the universal hope (contained in the prophetic ministry of the church) that in regard to our sinfulness and slavery to sin, God does not leave us alone. He offers Christ as the one who is the victor. This is enough for the church and for the world.

Summary

The aim of this section was to explore three dimensions of baptism as a way of life in a perichoretic church, namely, the constitutive dimension of baptism, the confessional dimension of baptism, and the missional dimension of baptism. Corresponding to the three dimensions, we argued, are three coordinates in which the divine Trinitarian life embraces and participates in the life of the church, namely, the church's being the people of God, the church's becoming the body of Christ and the church's ordination as the temple of the Spirit, all these overlapping realities being mediated from the center who is Christ.

In regard to the constitutive dimension of baptism of the church as the people of God, we argued that Christ redefines the people of God in his person, forms the people of God through his work, and is the head of the

---

51. Noble, *Tracking God*, 9. She argues that "the Scriptures depict hope as a still deeper insight into God's promise, an insight that does not necessarily come up with coherent solutions, but functions as medicine for a wounded life without a future" (Noble, 9).

The Transformative Dimension of the Spiritual Journey

people of God by his status. Christ is the king whose reign should be declared and recognized, He is the prophet of God, whose message should be acknowledged and obeyed, and he is the high priest whose sacrifice should be understood in its uniqueness and definitiveness.

In regard to the confessional dimension of baptism for the church as the body of Christ, we argued that the confession of the Christian communities is first a threefold confession, containing a declaration of a unique God, in three persons, Father, Son and Holy Spirit. A declaration that the true church is of those called to a personal, real and live relationship with the Father, Son and Holy Spirit, and a declaration that Christian communities do not exist separately from each other but exist in communion with each other, united in the same Spirit, under the lordship of the same Lord, and in the embrace of the same Father.

Second, we argued that the confession of the Christian communities is a permanent confession based on the threefold declaration in Christ's baptism, first of himself that his identification with humanity is real, second the declaration of the Spirit that the identification of the Son with humanity is total, and third the declaration of the Father that the Son's identification with humanity is admissible. Then this threefold declaration in Christ's baptism should be continually mirrored in Christian baptism, in the testimony of the Spirit, which is the internal declaration of life, the testimony of the water (baptism), that is the external declaration of life, and the testimony of continual cleansing through the blood of Christ that is the permanent declaration of life.

We continued by arguing that all these concentric confessional and declarative realities have to find their expression in the communal thought and life of the church. First, the church's identification with the death of Christ should find expression in "the taking off the old clothes of the old Adam." The church needs to take off the "cloth" of her pride of being the people of God, second, the church needs to put off the pride of being saved, and third, the church needs to put off the pride of being spiritual.

The missional dimension of baptism for the church as the temple of the Spirit was argued from the perspective of the church's "putting on" the character of Christ imprinted in the life of the church through the Spirit. The Spirit needs to "put on" in the life of the church the humbleness of continual transformation through a fresh understanding of her way of living in the society, second, the Spirit needs to put on in the life of the church the reality of *koinonial* discipleship, and third the Spirit needs to put on in the life of the church, the humbleness of a *kenotic diakonia* in the world. These actions will make the church a presence of faith that will act in love being a sign of hope.

11.2. The Eucharist as a Perichoretical Reflection

In chapter 10 of the present project we saw that Stăniloae and Fiddes are in agreement in regard to Christ's presence in the Eucharist, as a real, transformative, spiritual presence. We also saw that their dynamic view on the Eucharist would be important for the conversation between Orthodox and Baptists in Romania, as an important reminder of the importance, in the journey of life, of a real, spiritual, sanctifying communion with Christ, mediated by the word. Also, we have argued that this fact could be an important reminder that eucharistic communion should be encompassed by a daily appropriation of Christ's life, in an eucharistic way of living, led by the complementary work of the spirit of God and of the word of God.

In the present chapter we will try to explore three key dimensions that overlap what God has done in Christ, through the Spirit, and what we are, do, and promote, in Christ through the Spirit. This will be a way to show how the centrality of Christ's presence should be reflected in the status and relationships of Christian communities. We hope that the exploration of this chapter will move attention away from issues in regard to the Eucharist that build walls against mutual communion (as for example what happens with the elements and worthiness to attend communion) towards an understanding that will give pre-eminence to the real subject of the Eucharist, Christ and what he does for us in the journey of Christian life.

The first dimension that can be acknowledged as valid by both traditions, Orthodox and Baptists in Romania, is that of remembering Christ's sharing in us, in our humanity, in our sinfulness and in our spiritual redemption, and the fact that he initiated a new covenant that is eternal and definitive. The second dimension, that can also be considered valid for the two traditions, is that of discerning our sharing in him, in his death, resurrection and life. The third dimension, which can also be considered common for the two traditions, is that of proclaiming God's share, in Christ through the Spirit in the suffering and life of the world.

The Covenantal Dimension of the Eucharist: Remembering Christ's Sharing in Us

The institution of the Eucharist by Christ was his last act before the crucifixion, an act that points further to the culmination of the salvific embrace in Christ of our humanity by God in order to redeem it. In this regard Karl Barth says that Jesus Christ, "let himself be taken prisoner in the power of the god of this world, and in doing so strikes him down and dispatches him once for all. But that which was accomplished in God's Son Jesus Christ in our nature was done in our place and therefore for us . . . Everything else is a repetition of this first thing."[52] The crucifixion, to which the Eucharist then and there was a pointer, is also the culmination of Christ's identification with us that opens the possibility of our identification with him, in the context of the cosmic salvation that Christ accomplished in his person, life and work.[53] Christ's identification with humanity comes by way of the consubstantiality of his divine and human nature, mirroring the consubstantiality between him and the Father.[54] In the union between his divine and human nature Christ experienced humanity from within:

> . . . by assuming an Adamic "sinful humanity," the Son did not quarantine himself from our sinful and suffering plight, but instead immersed himself within it . . . the human experiences of the Son were neither anaesthetized by his divinity nor desensitized by some generic or pedigreed humanity which differed from our own. Rather, this fallen humanity was united immediately and intimately to the Son as he exists personally in

---

52. Barth, *God Here and Now*, 15–16.
53. Barth, 30, 32. Barth says that "coming into the depths of the human existence in Jesus Christ, God wanted to 'make it like Himself'" and doing this to be "the guarantor of the future of man and His universe . . . In the incarnation of the Word of God, in the cross and resurrection of Jesus Christ, was universally decided, in the middle of human history, that we men are not given over and left to ourselves, to our misery, even to our own inclinations" (Barth, 32). See also, Lossky, *Mystical Theology*, 137. Lossky says: "On the cross He unites paradise, the dwelling place of the first men before the fall, with the terrestrial reality where the fallen descendants of the first Adam now dwell" (Lossky, 137).
54. Lossky, *Mystical Theology*, 143.

as God . . . The Son of God, within the unmediated immediacy of his own human "I," experienced the totality of suffering entailed in being affiliated with the fallen race of Adam.[55]

Moreover, in the redemptive act, in his Son incarnate, God himself demonstrates "the closest possible proximity,"[56] entering and sharing the human condition.[57] Through his righteous life Christ represented humanity in her fidelity to God and through his sacrifice Christ overcame "the triple barrier which separates us from God – death, sin and nature,"[58] transforming, in himself, human nature:

> The work accomplished by Christ is related to our nature, it is no longer separated from Christ by our fault. It is a new nature, a restored creature which appears in the world. It is a new body, pure from all taint of sin, free from all external necessity, separated from our iniquity and from every alien will by the precious blood of Christ. It is the pure and incorruptible realm of the Church where one attains union with God.[59]

In the eucharistic celebration then and there, with his disciples, in the sadness and the suffering of the very close rejection, mocking and crucifixion that he needed to face, Christ states the coordinates of the new covenant that has the relationship with him as the center, his life infused in the life of

---

55. Thomas G. Weinandy, *Does God Suffer?*, 212.

56. Stăniloae, *EG*, 181.

57. Bonhoeffer, *Ethics*, 10. He says: "He Himself enters into the life of man as man and takes upon Himself and carries in the flesh the nature, the character, and the guilt and suffering of man. Out of love for man God becomes man. He does not seek out the most perfect man in order to unite Himself with him, but he takes human character upon Himself as it is." (Bonhoeffer, *Ethics*, 10). Also, Thomas G. Weinandy, *In the Likeness of Sinful Flesh: An Essay on the Humanity of Christ* (Edinburgh: T & T Clark, 1993); and, Willmer, "Jesus Christ the Forgiven," 17–18.

58. Lossky, *Mystical Theology*, 136.

59. Lossky, 155. Here Lossky's overrealized eschatology is expressed in undermining the fact that even if in Christ the believer is a new creation, the old has gone and the new has come (2 Cor 5:17), the tense of the verb speaks of a continual process of transformation towards union with God, rather than a past transformation, whether circumscribed by baptism or the ecclesial hypostasis. Moreover, this necessary continual transformation is worked by the Holy Spirit, in the likeness of Christ (Rom 8:29), not without human cooperation (2 Pet 1:3–4). Consequently, the final transfiguration will take place, according to the Johannine report, when we will see him (1 John 3:2).

The Transformative Dimension of the Spiritual Journey

the church as the atmosphere in which the church breathes and his sacrifice as the base for the church's redemption and sanctification. This reality of infusion from him to us mirrors the interpenetration of the Father's life with the Son's life and of the Son's activity with the Father's activity. It should be mirrored in the interpenetration of the Son's life with the church's life and of the church's activity with the Son's activity, the one that implicitly energizes both realities being the Holy Spirit.

All these truths constitute the foundation for the celebration of the Eucharist here and now, a celebration first of the permanent embrace of us by the Father through the Son in the Spirit, an embrace that is proclaimed "through 'memorial' and 'remembrance,'"[60] realized by the Spirit through the Word. The celebration is the communal expression of the shared experience of God's transforming presence, the spiritual inhabitation of obedient believers by the Father, Son and Spirit. The Eucharist here and now is the celebration of God with us,[61] a presence that is the medication for the loneliness of humanity.[62] Or in the words of James William McClendon, Jr:

> By presence is meant quite simple the quality of being there for and with the other . . . We remember that God's presence with us is one of the great gifts of the gospel, associated with the incarnation of the Word, the giving of the Spirit and the return of the Lord; we recall that in Christian history his presence is

---

60. Toon, "Lord's Supper," 492.

61. Barth, *CD*, 1.1, 2nd ed., 319. He says:
But just because Immanuel had been unconditionally fulfilled in Jesus, the crucifixion of Jesus was bound to mean something different from the stoning of even the greatest prophets, namely, the end of history of Israel as the special people of revelation, the destruction of the house of stone as the dwelling of the name of the Lord, the free proclamation, not of a new Gospel but of the one ancient Gospel to both Jews and Gentiles . . . Christ the telos of the Law (Ro. 10: 4). We see here the theme of the great battle which Paul above all others fought at the rise of the Church. It was not a battle against the Old Testament, but was like the battle of Jesus Christ Himself, to whom he simply wishes to testify, it was a battle for the Old Testament, i.e., for the one eternal covenant of God with men sealed in time, for acknowledgment of the perfect self-unveiling of God.
Barth, *CD*, 1.1, 2nd ed., 319.

62. We have observed in chapter 5 that Stăniloae argues that the Eucharist is medication for eternity. Yet we argue here that the presence of God in Christ through the Spirit provides the necessary foundation for a healing view for the entire humanity through the eucharistic community.

celebrated in every eucharistic meal, invoked at every baptism, and claimed anew at every gathering of disciples.[63]

In the Eucharist here and now we celebrate second, the sacrifice of God for us, in Christ through the Spirit that made possible the new covenant of God with us. The broken bread is "a picture of His taking common flesh . . . and allowing it to be 'broken' for humankind," and the sharing of the wine "stands for the shed *blood* of Jesus."[64] This was possible because of Christ's salvific assuming of the disfiguration of God's image in human beings.[65]

To sum up, these are the elements of the new covenant of God with humanity. First, the permanency of God's presence with us, through Christ in the Spirit. Second, the permanency of God's being for us through Christ's sacrifice that provides the forgiveness of sins. Third, the permanency of God's transforming work in us through the Spirit in the likeness of Christ. Therefore the new covenant is the recapitulation and fulfillment of all the covenants that were initiated by God for enhancing communion with humanity. All covenants are coordinates of a trajectorial development for God's revelatory actions,[66] and are occasions for the revelation of some aspects of God's revelatory character.[67] From the beginning God's will was that human persons would participate in "the divine covenant of grace."[68]

---

63. James W. McClendon, Jr, *Systematic Theology*, vol. 1, *Ethics* (Nashville, TN: Abingdon, 1986), 106.

64. Cole, *Gospel According to Mark*, 292–293.

65. What happened with the image of God in human beings after the Fall is another matter of disagreement between different Christian traditions. Yet even in the context of this unsolved disagreement, all Christian traditions would agree with the fact that Christ is the one who restores God's image in humanity, being at once the second Adam and a human being as it should be in relationship with God. The dynamics of transformation after the likeness of Christ is analysed in part 3, chapter 12 of this book.

66. Gerhard von Rad, *Old Testament Theology*, vol. 1, *The Theology of Israel's Historical Traditions* (London: SCM, 1975), 129. He says "The most striking decisive moments of this kind are the making of covenants by Yahweh" (von Rad, *Old Testament Theology*, 129). Also, William Dyrness, *Themes in Old Testament Theology* (London: Paternoster, 1998), 85. He says that a covenant is "the core of the Hebrew understanding of their relationship with God." (Dyrness, *Themes in Old Testament*).

67. Walther Eichrodt, *Theology of the Old Testament*, vol. 1 (Philadelphia, PA: Westminster, 1961), 37.

68. Karl Barth, *Church Dogmatics*, vol. 3, part 3, *Doctrine of Creation* (Edinburgh: T & T Clark, 1966), 80 (referred to as *CD*, 3.3, hereafter). Also, Fiddes, *Tracks and Traces*. For Fiddes there are two dimensions of the covenant that mirror and are in a vital connection with the eternal covenant of grace that God made with humankind. The first dimension of

The uniqueness of the new covenant in the Christ event is that God himself in his Son embraced humanity from within, by becoming a man. The incarnation of the Son of God is the revelation of the climax of God's revelatory activity. From then on, God knows humanity from inside, opening through the Holy Spirit the possibility for man to know God from within. The *shalom* of creation is in this way restored through the koinonial dimension of the relationship of God with man that encompasses human beings as well as the entire creation.

The *Koinonial* Dimension of the Eucharist: Discerning Our Share in Christ

The second important dimension of the Eucharist is that of discerning our share in Christ as members in the body of Christ.[69] In this context the Eucharist is the representation and revelation of the church as the body of Christ,[70] and this is so because the corporeal dimension of Christian life, grounded in the individual's status of being in Christ, is important. Christ

---

covenant is that of walking together, He says: "In this drama of the 'solemn covenant of the church,' the members are not just recalling that they have been included in God's eternal covenant, but envisage themselves as somehow entering it at that very moment" (Fiddes, *Tracks and Traces*, 34). The second dimension is that of watching over each other expressed in the three dimensions of the *episkope*: personal, collegial and communal, the communal oversight being the responsibility of the entire community, the personal oversight being the responsibility of persons with special commissions, and the collegial oversight being the responsibility of a team of persons with special commissions (Fiddes, 221). This three-dimensional view of *episkope* is an important reminder for the complex reality of oversight and of direct relevance for the Romanian baptistic communities where personal oversight is the only dimension represented. It has been observed that, unfortunately, the lack of the other two dimensions of *episkope* lead to a more and more present separation between "clergy" and "laity," that is in dissonance with most of the confessions of faith in the baptistic communities that affirm the priesthood of all believers and reject any idea of clericalism.

69. Zizioulas, *Being as Communion*, 53, affirms that if through birth the human being enters biological existence, he becomes a person through ecclesial existence, which he enters through baptism. The human being transcends biological existence towards the status of person by becoming an ecclesial hypostasis, a member of the church, where through the Eucharist communion between being and truth receives its maximal expression. See also, Karl Barth, *Church Dogmatics*, vol. 1, part 1, *Doctrine of the Word of God* (Edinburgh: T & T Clark, 1936), 40 (referred to as *Doctrine of the Word*, hereafter). He speaks of "believing existence," an expression that seems to be more adequate as a description of the believer's status in Christ and in the church. This is important in the context of Zizioulas's theological construct that has been criticized as not having space for faith at all, (Volf, *After Our Likeness*, 95).

70. Lucian Turcescu, "Eucharistic Ecclesiology or Open Sobornicity?," in *Dumitru Stăniloae, Tradition and Modernity in Theology*, ed. Lucian Turcescu (Iasi: Center for Romanian Studies, 2002), 92.

himself guarantees the balance between the individual and corporeal dimensions of being in Christ.

Furthermore, the unity of the church as the body of Christ is circumscribed by the experience of identification with Christ (in his death, resurrection and suffering), that even if it is experienced as personal transformation should be followed by the integration in the community of those who have also experienced the same transforming identification with Christ.[71] Therefore, being in Christ cannot mean at all to remain in the individuality of this experience, rather it is completed by integration in the body of Christ. In regard to that McClendon says, "In such a context, the ideas to which we are naturally led are those of group solidarity, of an identity that includes rather than excludes, that inclusion being the incorporation of the lives of the gathered disciples not only into their crucified and risen Lord, but also into one another."[72] Moreover, the manifestation of the body of Christ is the proclamation of Christ's lordship upon individuals, and as Ernst Kasemann puts it: "the Body of Christ is the real concretion before the *Parousia* of the universal sovereignty of Christ."[73] It is this very practice of the Eucharist in the church with its intrinsic message, precisely, that emphasizes the corporeality of being in Christ. No individual could alone share in the Eucharist, it being always a corporate action.

Yet, there is another important dimension connected with the Eucharist, namely, the fact that the Eucharist is the communal expression of individual participation in the death of Christ. In the remembering of Christ's sacrifice and the giving of his body, we also remember our identification with him in his death. Moreover, if identification with Christ's sufferings, for the individual was by the way of a *kenotic* attitude,[74] this seems to be the case

---

71. John Ziesler, *Pauline Christianity* (Oxford: Oxford University Press, 1990), 58.

72. McClendon, *Systematic Theology: Ethics*, 216.

73. Ernst Kasemann, *Essays on New Testament Themes* (Philadelphia, PA: Fortress, 1982), 68. Also, W. G. Kummel, *The Theology of the New Testament: According to Its Major Witnesses Jesus–Paul–John* (London: SCM, 1974), 210.

74. Speaking about the kenotic attitude of the Christian community as a mirroring of Christ's kenosis, we need to understand what kenosis means for Christ. We agree with those who favour a relational understanding of kenosis opposed to a substantial understanding of it. In this regard see, Vanessa Herrick and Ivan Mann, *Jesus Wept: Reflections on Vulnerability in Leadership* (London: Darton, Longman, and Todd, 1998), 13–14. The authors compare the kenoticists' substantial view of kenosis in Christ, that allows an understanding of human

also in the horizontal interpersonal relationships in the body of Christ, the church and with the larger society. This leads to another important dimension of the Eucharist that points to the future.

The Social Dimension of the Eucharist: Proclaiming Christ's Sharing in the World

In the previous sections we argued that the Eucharist as an all-encompassing reality, because the life of the church has a covenantal dimension that should be always acknowledged on the coordinates of remembering the salvific activity of Christ in the synthesis of what he did then and there and what church is here and now. Second, we have seen that in the *koinonial* dimension, the Eucharist pictures the reality of the present through discernment of the church's call as community, and a call to participate in Christ's death, resurrection and suffering. Third, as will be argued in the next section, the Eucharist has a social dimension,[75] being the church's proclamation of the future of humanity. Furthermore, the proposal in this section is that the church's eucharistic proclamation is one that mirrors Christ's brokenness, in self-denial, character and integrity.

The first domain in which the church's eucharistic proclamation mirrors Christ's brokenness is a personal one, through acceptance of the brokenness in Christlike self-denial. That means to respond in fear of the Lord, to God's giving in Christ through the Spirit in daily care and in the infusion of Christ's life in us. These are the coordinates of spiritual medication for the fear of tomorrow, which is denial of God's care, the fear of men, which

---

nature and divine nature as being in contradiction, with the Barthian view that is relational. See also, Barth, *CD*, 4.1, 180, he says that "the kenosis consists in a renunciation of his being in the form of God alone."

75. Zizioulas, *Being as Communion*, 152, says that in the early church the Eucharist was a public work, for all the Christians from a city. Also, Barth, *God Here and Now*, 65–66, says:
> The essence of the Church is the event in which these many men, as often as they have all received the bread and the cup of the Lord's Supper, anticipating the power and joy of the future revelation, share already here and now in the "feast of the Lamb" . . . This community must be open to the world in order to make visible, with its proclamation of the kingdom of God, the clear, but also severe limits of all human movement and effort, progress and regress, ascents and descents. The Church does not exist by pondering, studying, discussing, and preparing itself for this relationship to the world. The Church exists in actually accomplishing this relationship in each time with the appropriate sense of security, realism, and necessity.

is denial of God's lordship, and the fear of death, which is denial of God's life through Christ.

There is a second domain in which the church through her eucharistic proclamation can mirror Christ's brokenness, in what could be called a togetherness of faith. In the words of Christ, the Eucharist is participation in the new covenant, sealed with the blood of Christ.

The third domain in which the church's eucharistic proclamation mirrors Christ's brokenness is the familial one, through the promotion of brokenness in Christlike integrity, expressed in the development of familial relationships that reflect Christ's relationship with his church.[76]

This familial reflection of the relationship between Christ and the church is meant to extend from the relationship between partners in marriage, to relationships between children and parents, and between masters and slaves (in that cultural context in which many times the slaves were considered part of the family).[77]

The eucharistic proclamation of the church should be always at the intersection of what we are at the personal level, do at the community level and promote at the familial level. The church should always ask how much all these elements of our proclamation mirror the giving of the Christ who we remember when we break the eucharistic bread. The new creation in Christ whose first fruits are the believers who form the body of Christ is, in the world, a presence that brings a new alternative way of living. This new alternative illustrates the two kinds of people of society in the world, belonging to two ways of living, in "bondage and liberation, guilt and justification, estrangement and reconciliation, deformity and transformation."[78]

---

76. Herman Ridderbos, *Paul: An Outline of His Theology* (Grand Rapids, MI: Eerdmans, 1975), 308. "On the one hand the unity of Christ and the church therefore receives its explanation from the mysterious unity of husband and wife in marriage . . . conversely, the unity of Christ and the church throws light on the true experience of the unity of marriage" (Ridderbos, *Paul*, 308). Also, John Piper, *Desiring God: Meditations of a Christian Hedonist* (Portland, OR: Multnomah Press, 1986), 181. Amazingly, Nikolai Berdiaev considers that the New Testament denies the family, an institution that is a worldly establishment, see Nikolai Berdiaev, *Sensul Creatiei: Încercare de îndreptățire a omului* (București: Humanitas, 1992), 196, 198.

77. Derek Tidball, *The Social Context of the New Testament* (Grand Rapids, MI: Zondervan, 1983), 81.

78. Wayne A. Meeks, *The First Urban Christians: The Social World of the Apostle Paul* (New Haven, CT: Yale University Press, 1983), 184.

Summary

What we have tried to argue in this chapter is in light of one of the necessary changes in the life of baptistic communities in Romania which would be in regard to the Eucharist. Based on the comparison between Stăniloae's and Fiddes's view of the Eucharist and following what they have in common in their views, namely, the centrality of Christ's presence, we proceeded to sketch a possible way of understanding the Eucharist rooted in the centrality of Christ, and as reflection of the reality of *perichoresis*.

This we considered as necessary for the baptistic communities in Romania, for it was observed that many times the eucharistic communion is an occasion of excluding other believers rather than including them into the fellowship of the church. One of the reasons could be an inappropriate understanding of the Eucharist as being rather centered in what the believers are and do than in what Christ is, has done and does, as premises for what the believers are, do and should become. Therefore, we aimed to bring to attention some key dimensions that the centrality of Christ in the Eucharist communion features and which the church in her life should reflect.

First, we argued the covenantal dimension of the Eucharist through remembering Christ's share in us, in our humanity and in our lives as members of the people of God. We have observed that the new covenant instituted by Christ in the eucharistic meal with his disciples on his last night with them is the conclusion and culmination of all the covenants of God with humanity.

We have also observed in a perichoretical key that this new covenant contains a threefold reality, the permanent presence of God with us through Christ in the Spirit, the permanence of God's being for us through Christ's sacrifice that provides the forgiveness of sins, and the permanence of God's transforming work in us through the Spirit in the likeness of Christ.

Second, we argued the *koinonial* dimension of the Eucharist in discerning our share in Christ that pictures the reality of the present through discernment of the church's call to be a community and to participate in Christ's death, resurrection and suffering. We have seen that this discerning has to do with two realities, the reality of his body broken on the cross and the reality of his body that we are, at the corporate level through our identification with him on the personal level. The Eucharist therefore shows the corporeality of being in Christ. We have also argued that this corporeal participation in Christ has to be experienced in a *kenotic* attitude in the interpersonal relationships in the body of Christ, as a reflection of Christ's own *kenosis*.

Third, we argued the social dimension of the Eucharist, being the church's proclamation of the future of humanity, a proclamation that mirrors Christ's brokenness, in self-denial, character and integrity. We have also argued that the eucharistic proclamation of the church should be always at the intersection of what believers are on the personal level, do at the community level and promote at the familial level. The church should always ask how much all these elements of our proclamation mirror the giving of Christ who we remember when we break the eucharistic bread.

11.3. Spirituality as a Shared Pilgrimage

We have seen in chapter 5 that Stăniloae's view of spirituality is an actualized reflection of the christological-pneumatological convergence. Also, we have seen in chapter 9, how Fiddes's view of spirituality is framed by the concept of covenant, is centered in the story of Christ, and should be embodied in the lifelong spiritual journey of the believers.

In chapter 10, we concluded that the Trinitarian-framing, christologically-centered and pneumatologically-based common features of the two theologians' view of spirituality is an important reminder and an important reflective theme for Baptists in Romania where there is a necessary reformulation of a theology of the Spirit that will keep in their vital connection not only the three persons of the Trinity, but also the person, work, fruit and gifts of the Spirit.

Based on the conclusions of chapter 10, the aim of the present chapter is that of reflecting on the theme of the Christian spiritual life as an expression of participating in the indissoluble togetherness of the work of the Father, through the Son. That will hopefully show the importance of Trinitarian christological-pneumatology for the necessary theological reformulation of dimensions of spiritual life in the baptistic communities of the Romanian third millennium, a spirituality that will mirror the life of the Trinity, and will embody the loving embrace of the Father in the Son through the Spirit.

Accordingly, in the following section of this chapter we will argue the dimension of spiritual life as a shared journey that is restoration of the *imago Dei*, a journey from an existence characterized by the absence of God, to

The Transformative Dimension of the Spiritual Journey 223

a living *with* and *for* God. The second section will focus on the dimension of spiritual life as a shared journey that is transformation into the likeness of Christ, a journey from being in Adam to being in Christ. The last section will focus on the dimension of a spiritual life as a shared journey from emptiness of the human condition to the fullness of the Spirit, a journey in which the Spirit infuses the character of the Father, in the fruit of the Spirit, that is revealed in the life of Christ, and imprints the life of Christ, that reflects the character of the Father, in the Spirit's gifts, manifested in him.

Spiritual Life as a Shared Journey from a Life without God To a Life with and for God, Restoration of *Imago Dei*

If the spiritual life is a lifelong journey of believers, it is first a journey of restoration of the *imago Dei* in human beings. In fact says Miroslav Volf "the triune God stands at the beginning and at the end of the Christian pilgrimage,"[79] therefore this restoration means a move from a living without God into a more and more profound life with and for God. All human beings start their lives on the earth being inheritors of "an empty way of life," a life without God, a life of "a suffocating loneliness,"[80] a life from which human beings need to be redeemed.[81] Miroslav Volf describes this life in this way, "a way of life characterized by the lack of knowledge of God and by misguided desires . . . the transitoriness of the present world in which all human efforts ultimately end in death . . . the meaningless of sin and hopelessness of death."[82]

---

79. Miroslav Volf, "Being as God Is: Trinity and Generosity," in *God's life in Trinity*, eds. Miroslav Volf and Michael Welker (Minneapolis, MN: Fortress, 2006), 3. Henri J. M. Nouwen, *Reaching Out: The Three Movements of the Spiritual Life* (New York: Doubleday, 1966), 14.

80. Volf, "Being as God Is."

81. 1 Peter 1:18–19. See Peter H. Davids, *The First Epistle of Peter* (Grand Rapids, MI: Eerdmans, 1990), 71. He says: "This 'way of life' which included not just their religious but also their ethical values and actions . . . by which Peter means that it was worthless, futile and empty of hope and value when viewed in the light of the gospel." (Davids, *First Epistle*, 71). See also, Edmund Clowney, *The Message of 1 Peter: The Way of the Cross* (Leicester: Inter-Varsity Press, 1988), 69. He argues that "the way in which Peter speaks of our redemption here shows how central it was to the apostolic gospel" (Clowney, *Message of 1 Peter*, 69). Also, I. Howard Marshall, *1 Peter* (Leicester: Inter-Varsity Press, 1991), 55. He argues that "the way in which Peter frames the thought makes it clear that the reminder is not so much of the redemption itself but rather of the cost of the redemption" (Marshall, *1 Peter*, 55).

82. Miroslav Volf, *Captive to the Word of God: Engaging the Scriptures for Contemporary Theological Reflection* (Grand Rapids, MI: Eerdmans, 2010), 71–72. See also, Karen H. Jobes,

One of the metaphors used in the New Testament by Paul to describe life without God is that of darkness. Paul speaks of a darkened understanding,[83] of being darkness, of producing fruitless deeds of darkness,[84] and being under the "dominion of darkness."[85] This is the reason *metanoia* is crucial in order that the new life from God replaces the old life without God. The new creation in Christ implies a new understanding of self,[86] others, and of Christ, a spiritual understanding that replaces the darkened understanding.

But what is the model for this new relationship with God that human beings enter through the sacrifice of Christ? A possible answer is that the life of the Trinity is the model of how redemption should be embodied authentically. Therefore, looking at the way the relationship of the Father, Son and the Spirit promote and fulfill the work of redemption in their journey of togetherness to, with and for humanity, we could find a meaningful model

---

1 Peter (Grand Rapids, MI: Baker Academic, 2005), 117. She says that Peter wants to remind the Christians that "Christ's redemption has delivered them from the bondage of the sin that characterized their former way of life and that continues to be practiced all around them in pagan society" (Jobes, *1 Peter*, 117).

83. Ephesians 4:18. Also, Markus Barth, *Ephesians: Translation and Commentary on Chapters 4-6* (New York: Doubleday, 1974), 500. He argues that "When knowledge is identified with light and ignorance with darkness, then the previously mentioned ontological dimension of the mind's activity is made apparent. Just as knowledge means participation in life and obedience to God, so ignorance equals the inability to live, to grow, to act sensibly." (Barth, *Ephesians: 4–6*, 500).

84. Ephesians 5:8, 11, and Romans 13:12. Markus Barth, *Ephesians: 4-6*, 569–570, argues that "the fruitless deeds of darkness stand in contrast to the 'fruit of the Spirit' described in Gal 5:22-23." Also, Ziesler, *Paul's Letter to Romans*, 320. He argues that the expression "let us cast off the works of darkness and put on the armour of light . . . is the language of Christian catechesis . . . in which converts were urged to get rid of old habits, goals, and practices, and to adopt new ones appropriate for Christians." (Ziesler, 320).

85. Colossians 1:13. Markus Barth and Helmut Blanke, *Colossians: A New Translation with Introduction and Commentary* (New York: Doubleday, 1994), 188. Commenting on the structure of this verse he argues that "*Basilea* . . . means the kingly *realm* of the Messiah. Analogously, *exousia* means the *dominion* of darkness." (Barth and Blanke, *Colossians*, 188). Also, J. B. Lightfoot, *St Paul's Epistles to the Colossians and to Philemon* (London: MacMillan, 1875), 207. He explains that the verse should be understood in this way, "We were slaves in the land of darkness. God rescued us . . . He transplanted us . . . and settled us as free colonists and citizens in the kingdom of His Son, in the realms of light" (Lightfoot, *St Paul's Epistles*, 207).

86. Dietrich Von Hildebrand, *Transformation in Christ: On the Christian Attitude* (San Francisco, CA: Ignatius Press, 2001). He considers that "true self-knowledge is an important instrument of sanctification," (Hildebrand, *Transformation*, 44), "fruitful knowledge," (Hildebrand, 47) which "grows out of man's self-confrontation with God," and leads to "true self-surrender" to God, (Hildebrand, 48).

for the Christian communities in their shared journey of restoring the *imago Dei*. For Martin Lloyd-Jones the affirmation by Paul of this model "is the highest statement of Christian doctrine that one can conceive of or even imagine . . . Paul seems to me to be laying down what is after all a principle that governs everything . . . We must look at God and consider His being and nature. If I am to imitate God I must know something about Him."[87]

First, when we look at the relationship between the Father and Son in the Spirit we contemplate a unique way of self-giving that is in contrast with the inherited human tendency to self-centeredness and self-absorption.[88] Human beings, as masterpieces of creation, are created in their uniqueness[89] and autonomous from created order and other human beings, in interdependence with them, and in dependence onGod.

> To be made in the image in God's image means something like the idea that one can look in the mirror as a human being and see traces of the divine being who designed us. We resemble God in our capacity to love, to reason, to feel, to relate to other creatures, to imagine, to plan, to create, to contemplate . . . Another key aspect of the image of God has to do with a unique responsibility before God and in relation to all creatures.[90]

This reality from the beginning mirrors the way the Father and the Son work together through the Spirit, revealing not only the uniqueness of God's character but also the will of God for the functioning of everything in creation. Moreover, the way in which each divine person uniquely makes the other the center of their being is the perennial challenge for the communal life of humanity. The entire history of humankind from a spiritual perspective is a history of redemptive acts of the Father through the Son in the Spirit. This redemptive work in the interdependence of three persons is revealed by

---

87. D. M. Lloyd-Jones, *Darkness and Light: An Exposition of Ephesians 4:17-5:17* (Edinburgh: Banner of Truth, 1982), 291–292.

88. Michael L. Lindvall, *The Christian Life: A Geography of God* (Louisville, KY: Geneva Press, 2001), says that "the way home begins here, in the radical reorientation that is death to self-orientation," (Lindvall, *Christian Life*, 28).

89. Robert W. Jenson, *Systematic Theology: The Works of God*, vol. 2 (Oxford: Oxford University Press, 1999), 53.

90. David P. Gushee, *Only Human: Christian Reflections on the Journey Towards Wholeness* (San Francisco, CA: Jossey-Bass, 2005), 16–17.

the fact that the Father is the one who redeemed us from the dominion of darkness and moved us into the kingdom of the Son of his love.[91]

The Son, who is "the image of the invisible God" a concept that summarizes "the fullness of divinity that dwells bodily in the Lord Jesus,"[92] and "the first born over all creation" is not only pre-existent to created order, or the agent of all created things seen or unseen, but is the cohesive principle of all creation and of all redemption, the one who contains the entire redemption, and the one who contains the entire fullness of God.[93]

The eternal Father made the eternal Son in the eternal Spirit to be the center of his entire activity before the creation of the Universe, in creation and in history. Similarly, the eternal Son, through the eternal Spirit made the eternal Father's plan the reason of his existence,[94] being the image of the Father, the agent of the Father, and the unifying and sustaining principle of the Father's work in eternity, creation and history. Consequently, the

---

91. Colossians 1:12–13. Also, Jürgen Moltmann, *God in Creation: An Ecological Doctrine of Creation* (London: SCM, 1985), 17. He says:
all relationships which are analogous to God reflect the primal, reciprocal indwelling and mutual interpenetration of the Trinitarian *perichoresis*. God *in* the world and the world *in* God; heaven and earth *in* the kingdom of God, pervaded by his glory; soul and body united *in* the life-giving Spirit to a human whole; woman and man *in* the kingdom of unconditional and unconditioned love, freed to be true and complete human beings . . . All living things – each in its specific way – live in one another and with one another, from one another and for one another. (Moltmann, *God in Creation*, 17).
See also, Barth, *Church Dogmatics*, 1.1, 360. He says: "The divine modes of being mutually condition and permeate one another so completely that one is always in the other two in the one. Sometimes this has been grounded more in the unity of the divine essence and sometimes more in the relations of origin as such. Both approaches are right and both ultimately saying the same thing." (Barth, *CD*, 360).

92. Boris Bobrinskoy, *The Mystery of the Trinity: Trinitarian Experience and Vision in the Biblical and Patristic Tradition* (Crestwood, NY: St. Vladimir's Seminary Press, 1999), 123.

93. Colossians 1:14–23. Also, Michael P. Knowles, "Christ in You the Hope of Glory: Discipleship in Colossians," in *Patterns of Discipleship in the New Testament*, ed. Richard N. Longenecker (Grand Rapids, MI: Eerdmans, 1996). Knowles says that for Paul "Christ is the ontological, epistemological and soteriological focus of all human thought and experience. Christ is the foundation of reality itself," (Knowles, "Christ in You," 180).

94. Jürgen Moltmann, "God in the World – The World in God: Perichoresis in Trinity and Eschatology," in *The Gospel of John and Christian Theology*, eds. Richard Bauckham and Carl Mosser (Grand Rapids, MI: Eerdmans, 2008), 372–375. Speaking about the Gospel of John and the perichoretic way of thinking, and commenting on the text in John 17:21, Moltmann argues that "the perichoretical unity of the divine Persons and Spaces is so wide open that the whole world can find room and rest and the fullness of eternal life within it" (Moltmann, "God in the World," 327–375).

restoration of the *imago Dei* that is one of the important dimensions of the Christian life as a shared journey is to be embodied at the community level through imitation of God in reflecting the Son's centrality for the Father in all things in the centrality of Christ in all the Christian communities think, speak or do.

These overlapping of movements of the divine reality and ecclesial reality, have three important consequences for the life of Christian communities in their shared journey of Christian living. First, the sovereignty of Christ from eternity communicates for the Christian community the sufficiency of redemption through Christ in history, as a means for a spiritual understanding of the vital necessity of taking off what we have been in Adam and putting on what we have become in Christ. Second, the centrality of Christ in the church communicates the importance of the continuous work of Christ through the Spirit, as a means for spiritual growth of Christian communities. Third, the fullness of Christ in creation and redemption communicates the necessity of Christ's lordship over the entire reality as a means for the foundation of deep spiritual convictions in the life of Christian communities. We can speak therefore about a participative model of spiritual restoration that is aimed at re-establishing of a meaningful relationship of human beings with God. "The fellowship which God seeks and creates with the human subject through the event of revelation, the Christ event, is fellowship through participation with himself, the God who is fellowship and partnership."[95]

Spiritual Life as a Shared Journey from Adam to Christ. Transformation in the *Imago Christi*

In the last section we argued, following closely Stăniloae and Fiddes, that the model for Christian life is the life of the Trinity.[96] The three persons in their self-giving to the others and to humanity constitute the model for

---

95. Paul M. Collins, *Trinitarian Theology: West and East: Karl Barth, the Cappadocian Fathers and John Zizioulas* (Oxford: Oxford University Press, 2001), 228.

96. We have seen in chapter 6 that for Stăniloae the Holy Trinity is the foundation for Christian spirituality. See, Stăniloae, *Spiritualitate Ortodoxă: Ascetica și Mistica*, 35. Also, we have seen in chapter 6 that according to Fiddes, humanity is permanently called to transformation from merely *observer* of God to *participant* in God, participation through which we are invited into "this interweaving or perichoresis of relationships," a "story of a Father who sends out a Son in a Spirit of love," a story in which we are called "to incorporate our own stories." See in this regard, Fiddes, "Concept, Image and Story," 23 and Fiddes, "Story and Possibility," 44.

the journey of Christian communities from darkness to light, from self-absorption to self-giving. The aim of this section is to answer the question, "What is the dynamics of this threefold shared journey?"

The first coordinate of such a dynamic would be an existence centered in the fullness of Christ that involves a receiving of Christ in order to live in him, being rooted and built in him, strengthened in faith, being given the fullness of Christ. He is not only the foundation of existence but also the resistance structure of it as the receiving of Christ is authenticated and validated by the following of Christ. Also, rootedness in Christ is validated through being filled with Christ, and third, growth in Christ is realized through knowledge of Christ.[97] Paul contrasts the two ways of living which are possible for humanity, or humanity's "two possible manifestations,"[98] namely, "in Adam" and "in Christ."[99] Moreover, Adam "is . . . the type of Him who was to come. Man's essential and original nature is to be found, therefore, not in Adam but in Christ."[100]

Being "in Adam" means to live as an old self who is not crucified and therefore to live as a slave of sin, living according to the sinful nature, and being subject to death. In contrast, being "in Christ" means to live as a new self, born from the crucifixion of the old self, living according to the Spirit, and being subject to life. In this context Paul develops what has been called "the interchange in Christ."[101] The main idea in this interchange, is that "Christ became what we are in order that *in him*, we might become what he is." Therefore the profound reality of Christ's identification with humanity opens the possibility for what could be called "conformity to Christ."[102]

---

97. Colossians 2:6–10. See Ralph P. Martin, *Colossians: The Church's Lord and the Christian Liberty* (Exeter: Paternoster, 1972), 72.

98. Ziesler, *Pauline Christianity*, 57.

99. Romans 5:12–20. See also, Karl Barth, *The Epistle to the Romans* (London: Oxford University Press, 1933), 181, says "Adam is the 'old' subject, the EGO of the man in the world . . . Christ is the 'new' subject, the EGO of the coming world." Also, Mark Strom, *Reframing Paul: Conversations in Grace and Community* (Downers Grove, IL: InterVarsity Press, 2000), 92.

100. Karl Barth, *Christ and Adam: Man and Humanity in Romans 5* (New York: Harper & Brothers, 1956), 29.

101. Romans 6:6 and 8:5–6. See also, Morna D. Hooker, *From Adam to Christ: Essays on Paul* (Cambridge: Cambridge University Press, 1990), 13.

102. L. Ann Jervis, "Becoming like God through Christ: Discipleship in Romans," in *Patterns of Discipleship in the New Testament*, ed. Richard N. Longenecker (Grand Rapids,

The Transformative Dimension of the Spiritual Journey

This leads us to the second coordinate of the dynamics in the shared journey of the Christian life, that of a life embraced by the life of Christ. This embrace is an overlapping of movements in which the church is invited to participate in her mission in the world. First, the incarnation of the Son of God gives visibility to the eternal embrace for the Son of the *Via Dolorosa* of the love of Father in the history of humanity. The Son assumes the cruciform mission of the Father in history[103] making his own, assumes the suffering from the Father's heart making it his own suffering for the salvation of humanity. The Son lovingly accepted the call, through incarnation, life and death on the earth, to mirror the way God has been wearing the cross for humanity from eternity.[104]

Second, the cross of Christ is the conclusion of the Son's *Via Dolorosa* in which the church is called to participate. It is the suffering of transformation from the image of the earthly man in order that the image of the heavenly man can be imprinted. It is a cruciform journey of transformation in accordance with the will of God as opposed to conformation "to the pattern of this world."[105] Therefore, the call of the Father for the church is to mirror the Son's entire life through the power of the Holy Spirit and this is to be done in the spirit of the *Via Dolorosa* in the world.

> In a Christian theological perspective, the world and the self are really related as coexistent. Both are really related to the God who, as Love, is their beginning and their end. That God as Love affects all and is affected by all. That God, in the decisive self-manifestation of who God is in the proleptic event of Jesus Christ, also discloses who we are in our real-as-graced possibility and what the world is in its graced reality. By the emancipatory power of that revelation, the Christian faith is a risk taken in

---

MI: Eerdmans, 1996), 154. Also, Wolfhart Pannenberg, *Christian Spirituality* (Philadelphia, PA: Westminster, 1983), 104.

103. Here we recall Stăniloae's view about cruciform living as having Christ as model, that we analyzed in chapter 6.

104. Jürgen Moltmann speaks of "the pathos of God . . . in his passion and in his interest in history," in Moltmann, *Trinity and the Kingdom*, 26.

105. Romans 12:2.

the trust that, in spite of all, the self and the world are held in the always-already, not yet reality of God's redemptive love.[106]

Third, the resurrection of Christ as a result of the *Via Dolorosa* of the Spirit[107] is his declaration with power of the divine sonship of Christ.[108] The Spirit himself traveled the journey of the Son into the deepness of humanity's estrangement from God. The Spirit himself was a witness of the Son's total and perfect obedience to the Father's will, a unique obedience through which the Son is proved by the Spirit the one worthy to become "the source of eternal salvation for all who obey him."[109] The call of the testimony of the Spirit from the *Via Dolorosa* of the Son is that only the cross assumed fully and carried to the very end of existence, in obedience and in accordance with the will of the Father embodied in the Son, makes the resurrection possible in us and in the world we live in.[110]

These are the coordinates of the new creation after the likeness of Christ as revealed by the Spirit according to the plan of God for humanity. Yet there are important consequences for the life of Christian communities as they dare to travel on the *Via Dolorosa* of the Father, in the Son through the Spirit. Living in the reality of the new creation in Christ is translated first in the permanency of Christ's truth in relation to others as a consequence of the taking off of the lies in relationship with God and self.[111]

Furthermore, living in the reality of the new creation in Christ is translated in the embodiment of Christ's forgiveness in the way in which forgiveness

---

106. Tracy, *Analogical Imagination*, 438.

107. Ivana Noble speaks of the kenosis of the Spirit considering that "the kenosis of the Spirit complements the kenosis of the Son." (Ivana Noble, *Theological Interpretation*, 176–177).

108. Douglas Moo, *Romans 1-8*, The Wycliffe Exegetical Commentary (Chicago, IL: Moody, 1991), 40.

109. Peter T. O'Brien, *The Letter to the Hebrews*, Pillar New Testament Commentary (Grand Rapids, MI: Eerdmans, 2010), 201.

110. Stăniloae, *Victory of the Cross*, 2. He argues that the believer is carrying the cross with the hope of transforming resurrection and, as I mentioned in chapters 5 and 6, this is the way the theology of the cross is vitally connected with the theology of resurrection. This is an important element in keepng together in their mutual synthesis the incarnation, life, death and resurrection of Christ, with direct relevance to the way believers should see their carrying of the cross.

111. James D. C. Dunn, *The Epistles to the Colossians and to Philemon: A Commentary on the Greek Text* (Grand Rapids, MI: Eerdmans, 1996), 219–221.

is practiced in ecclesial relationships rooted in love. Moreover, living in the reality of the new creation in Christ is translated in the rule of Christ's peace and dwelling of Christ's word in the synthesis of the individual life and communal life, as well as in familial and social life.[112] In the words of Michael J, Gorman:

> To be "in Christ" is to live within a community that is shaped by his story, not merely to have a "personal relationship" with Christ. The corporate character of being in Christ corresponds to the inherently relational character of cruciformity. Cruciform faith is not complete until it issues in cruciform love for others, Cruciform love and power are ways of being for others, expressions of commitment to the weak, to a larger body, and to enemies, Even cruciform hope requires a vision of the future much broader than the fate of the self alone.[113]

Spiritual Life as a Shared Journey from Spiritual Emptiness of the Human Existence to the Fullness of the Spirit

We have seen in the first two sections of this chapter, following Stăniloae and Fiddes, that the Christian life as a shared journey starts with the restoration of the *imago Dei* materialized in the likeness of Christ[114] in the life of Christian communities in all domains of societal life. In this section we will explore a possible answer to the question, "How did the restoration of the *imago Dei* and growth into the likeness of Christ become visible in the life of Christian communities?"

If in their life the divine persons, of the Father, Son and Holy Spirit are not separated, confused or contradicted in their essence and work, the same could be affirmed about the internal reality of each divine person and work.

---

112. Dunn, *Epistles to the Colossians*, 231–244.

113. Michael J. Gorman, *Cruciformity: Paul's Narrative Spirituality of the Cross* (Grand Rapids, MI: Eerdmans, 2001), 350.

114. We have seen in chapter 6 that for Stăniloae, Christian spirituality is the process of progressing on the road of perfection in Christ and for him the *telos* of Christian spirituality is the union of a believer with God in Christ, through the work of the Spirit. See in this regard, Stăniloae, *Spiritualitate Ortodoxă*, 5; and Stăniloae, "Desăvârșirea noastră în Hristos după învățătura bisericii Ortodoxe," 76. We have also seen in chapter 6 that for Fiddes in his turn, Christ is the person who is the model of how the relationship with God should be lived in the spirit of Christ. See in this regard, Fiddes, "Covenant: Old and New," 18–19.

As the person of the Son is constituted only in relation to the Father and the Spirit, so the person of the Spirit is constituted only in relation to the Father and the Son. Consequently, the Holy Spirit is revealed as the Spirit of God the Father, being sent by him,[115] and the Spirit of Christ,[116] through the revelation of the Son,[117] who in his turn reveals the Father.

In the light of the above considerations we can reach the conclusion that not only the three persons in their essence and work are unseparated, unconfused and uncontradicted, but also in the work of each person the others are fully revealed. From here follows the fact that the person of the Holy Spirit reflects the persons of the Father and of the Son, as well as the work of the Holy Spirit reflects the work of the Father and of the Son.

The way in which the Spirit, in his person and work, reflects the persons of the Father and of the Son becomes evident in the fruit of the Spirit, as revelation of the qualities of the Father revealed in and by Christ, a fruit that is the framework validating the appropriation of the charisms of the Spirit. Therefore, the person and the work of the Spirit in their inseparability in regard to the persons and work of the Father and of the Son, constitute the center of the understanding of the manifestations (*charismata*) of the Spirit.

Accordingly, this reality of the Spirit's fullness blossoms from the work of the Spirit's fruit in us according to the model of the work of the Spirit's fruit in the life of Christ. For, all the characteristics of the Spirit's fruit are proper as well in the life of the Father as in the life of the Son and the Spirit expressing the moral attributes of divinity: kindness expressed in love, mercy, grace, long enduring patience, righteousness, truth, justice.[118] These qualities are then shown in the life of the incarnate Son: love, joy, peace, long enduring patience, kindness, faithfulness, gentleness, and self-control.[119]

This reality of the fruit of the Spirit in the life and the work of Christ needs to be reflected in the life of Christian communities through the work

---

115. John Wijngaards, *The Spirit in John* (Wilmington, DE: Michael Glazier, 1988), 38.

116. N. T. Wright, *John for Everyone*, part 2, *Chapters 11–21* (London: SPCK, 2002), 63.

117. Wright, *John for Everyone*, 86.

118. Hammond, *In Understanding*, 47. Also, Louis Berkhof, *Systematic Theology* (London: Banner of Truth, 1958), 70–73.

119. Oprean, *Comuniune și participare*, 99.

of the Spirit.[120] But the fruit of the Spirit is not an impersonal work of the Spirit, it necessitates a believer's participation through renunciation of walking in the ways of disobedience and a perseverant walk on the way of obedience of God. In the last instance, the fruit of the Spirit is the expression of the Holy Spirit's life, "a metaphor used by Paul to describe the virtues that manifest the realities of Christ's life,"[121] the reality that demonstrates "the work of the Spirit in believers,"[122] and that characterizes the way of living for the one indwelt and empowered by the Spirit.[123]

The nine features of the fruit of the Spirit even though they are representative and not exhaustive,[124] mirror the *imago Christi* in all domains of Christian life. All these representative features of the fruit of the Spirit are not only expressions of the internal life of believers they are also expressions of the relational life in the body of Christ and in society.[125] All these dimensions of the fruit of the Spirit are a rejection of the egocentric closure towards himself, and promote the altruism that opens towards the other, a truth that is foundational not only for the fruit of the Spirit but also for the manifestations (*charismata* of the Spirit).[126]

Another key dimension in regard with *charismata* is the togetherness of the Father, the Son and the Spirit in their work. This work together is seen first, in the fact that the Father is the one who gives the Spirit, *charismata* being manifestations of the Holy Spirit.[127] Second, *charismata*, or the manifestations of the Spirit, mirror the character of God expressed in his attributes

---

120. Fee, *Paul*, 112. Also, Gordon D. Fee, *God's Empowering Presence: The Holy Spirit in the Letters of Paul* (Peabody, MA: Hendrickson, 1994), 882.

121. Dockery, "Fruit of the Spirit," 316.

122. Dockery, 318.

123. F. F. Bruce, *Epistle to the Galatians*, New International Greek Testament Commentary (Grand Rapids, MI: Eerdmans, 1982), 251.

124. Fee, *God's Empowering Presence*, 444.

125. Fee, *Paul*, 115.

126. Fee, *God's Empowering Presence*, 446.

127. Robert L. Thomas, *Understanding Spiritual Gifts* (Grand Rapids, MI: Kregel, 1999), 11. He argues that the triune God is the unified source of spiritual gifts.

as spirituality, omniscience, wisdom and veracity.[128] Third, *charismata* are embodied in the Son, his life and his work on the earth.[129]

Summary

We argued in this section that the Christian life as a shared journey happens at the intersection of the work of the Father, through the Son in the Holy Spirit. The overlapping of the divine persons' movements is a reality in their work from creation to restoration, from fall to redemption and from estrangement to transformation in the life of Christian communities. As a consequence, the restoration of the *imago Dei*, the transformation after the *imago Christi* and the embodiment of the fruit of the Spirit is a perichoretical

---

128. Berkhof, *Systematic Theology*, 65–69 and Hammond, *In Understanding*, 46.

129. There are many occasions in which the manifestations of the Spirit are seen in the life and work of Christ. For example, in his answers to the questions of the teachers in the temple (Luke 2:40–52), Christ exercises the *charismata* of the message of wisdom that we meet constantly in his ministry (Matt 7:28–29). From this posture, Christ says to his disciples when he prepares them for the coming times of persecution: "For I will give you words and wisdom that none of your adversaries will be able to resist or contradict" (Luke 21:15). For the apostle Paul, Christ "has become for us [the] wisdom from God," (1 Cor 1:30) and as such he is the source of wisdom in Christian life so that you "may know the mystery of God, namely, Christ, in whom are hidden all the treasures of wisdom and knowledge" (Col 2:2–3). Then, in the meeting with the Samaritan women (John 4:17–18), Christ manifests the *charismata* of the message of knowledge (1 Cor 12:8). This manifestation of the Spirit in Christ could be detected in the meeting with the invalid at the Bethesda pool (John 5:6) and in Christ's confrontation with the teachers of the law (Mark 2:8 and Matt 9:4). Moreover, Christ himself teaches his disciples about the conditions of their mission in the world. He tells them that in the world there will be adversities and they will be interrogated but they are not to worry because they "will be given what to say, for it will not be you speaking, but the Spirit of your Father speaking through you" (Matt 10:19–20). This participatory dimension of the overlapping of God's foreknowledge poured in the words of believers' messages and knowledge is very well illustrated by the word of knowledge that Paul addressed in the desperate situation of the shipwreck on the Adriatic sea (Acts 27:22–26). The *charismata* of faith (1 Cor 12:9), also accompanies the work of Christ, as for example in the episode with the resurrection of Lazarus (John 11:41–42). The participative dimension of such a *charismata* is revealed in the episode experienced by two disciples in their ministry when they declare with conviction the healing of a crippled man in the name of Jesus Christ (Acts 3:1–6). The *charismata* of healing (1 Cor 12:9), is also a reality in the life of Jesus Christ (Matt 8:14–16), and through its manifestation the fulfillment of the Old Testament prophecies is revealed (Matt 8:17 and Isa 53:4). The *charismata* of miraculous powers (1 Cor 12:10) which means the powerful intervention of God in the natural realm (resurrection of dead persons and exorcism) is a manifestation of the Spirit present in the life of Christ (Mark 5 and John 11) and of his disciples (Acts 5:12 and 19:11). These three *charismata*, faith, gifts of healing and miraculous powers are miraculous manifestations that express the power of the Spirit, and the message of wisdom, the message of knowledge, prophecy, speaking in different kinds of tongues and the interpretation of tongues are manifestations of the inspiration of the Spirit.

reality in the synthesis of its vertical ascendant dimension and its horizontal ecclesial dimension.

The inseparability of the three divine persons is the reflection of the inseparability of each person's work understood in relationship with the others. Therefore, in the work of the restoration of *imago Dei* the Father's plan is that this restoration be done in the likeness of his Son, the one who is the image of God the Father, in the Spirit, and the one who reflects the Father's character and will. At the same time the Son's likeness is worked out according to the will of the Father, by the Spirit of the Father who is simultaneously also the Spirit of Christ. In his work to transform human beings into the likeness of the Son, the Spirit imprints the fruit of the Spirit which is nothing other than the expression of the Father's moral attributes, lived out in the person and work of his Son, through the Spirit. Moreover, the charisms of the Spirit as expressions of the Father's spiritual attributes, embodied perfectly in the person and work of Christ, are produced in human beings on the basis of the profound operation of Christ's work of transformation in their lives in accordance with the will of the Father.

CHAPTER 12

General Conclusion

We started the book with a desire to answer the question of how the existing theological resources could be used for the enhancement of the theological conversation between Orthodox and Baptists in Romania. We also started with the premise that in the contemporary society of Romania, the baptistic communities would benefit substantially if they could be provided with the understanding that being open to conversation with Orthodox theology would be enriching and would contribute to the strengthening of their own ecclesial life. Our premise is rooted in the understanding that there are valuable theological resources not only for the enhancement of theological conversation between Orthodox and Baptists in Romania, but also for the strengthening of the ecclesial life of baptistic communities in Romania.

12.1. Summary of the Study

I started the actual project with an introduction that states first, the context of Romanian Baptists and their need for a non-reductionist understanding of baptism, the Eucharist and spirituality as important elements for a holistically understood process of the spiritual journey. Also, in the introduction I stated my hypothesis that ecclesiology, via the conversation between an Orthodox theologian, Dumitru Stăniloae, and a Baptist theologian, Paul Fiddes, could contribute to that.

In part 1 of the book, I explored the dynamic of spiritual journey in Stăniloae's theology. Accordingly, in chapter 2 I focused on Stăniloae's spiritual journey, and started with a description of the spiritual and intellectual climate in Romanian Orthodoxy at the beginning of the twentieth century. Then I continued with an exploration of Stăniloae's biography, spiritual legacy and theology. In chapter 3 I focused on the way Stăniloae's theology of participation informs and roots his view of baptism as the first step in the spiritual journey of a Christian. In chapter 4, I focused on the way Stăniloae's theology of the Eucharist reflects the concept of *perichoresis* and in chapter 5, I focused on the way in Stăniloae's theology of spirituality, the christological-pneumatological convergence is actualized.

In part 2 I explored the dynamic of spiritual journey in Fiddes's theology. Accordingly, in chapter 6, I started with Fiddes's spiritual journey, and I understood his worldwide recognition as a leading theologian in the contemporary Baptist world. Following that I showed some influences that I consider being important for his spiritual and intellectual journey. In this context I explored the way his theology developed. In chapter 7, I focused on the way Fiddes's theology of participation informs his thought about baptism. In chapter 8, I focused on the way Fiddes's perichoretical theology informs his thought about the Eucharist, and in chapter 9 I focused on the way his covenantal theology informs his thought about spirituality.

In part 3, the conclusions underlined, based on the conversation between Stăniloae and Fiddes, the dialogical and the transformative dimensions of the spiritual journey. Therefore, in chapter 10, I focused on the way theology of participation, the perichoretical and Trinitarian theology are connected with the spiritual journey. In chapter 11, I focused on the subjects of baptism as a way of living, the Eucharist as a perichoretical reflection, and spirituality as a shared pilgrimage.

12.2. Conclusions

The first conclusion that I reached after the research is that of the truth of theology as a dialogical discipline. I learned, from Stăniloae and Fiddes, that when theological discourse is rooted in an interdisciplinary conversation with philosophy, history, literature and psychology the possible result is that theological formulations are relevant and productive in their aim to transform the ecclesial reality. I am pleased to conclude that both Stăniloae, as an Orthodox theologian, and Fiddes, as a Baptist theologian, proved to have the capacity for conversation with other disciplines as a common feature of their thought. This is due, in my opinion, to their permanent struggle for knowledge. We have also learned from both Stăniloae and Fiddes that conversation with other traditions from the Christian families could prove to be instrumental for strengthening one's own spiritual journey. Knowing the other, understanding the differences of the other, is a meaningful way of knowing oneself. As a respected Orthodox thinker of the twentieth century stated in the title of one of his books, "Through others to yourself!"[1] Therefore, I conclude that dialogical theology edifies Christian life.

The second conclusion that I reached from the research is that theology produced in an interdisciplinary manner and in conversation with representatives of other Christian traditions could reveal areas where the differences should be not only acknowledged but also accepted. I learned from Stăniloae and Fiddes that ecumenical encounters should not have as their purpose the changing of one's own options and practices, but with the purpose of deepening mutual understanding and when this understanding will be profound then even the critique will be adequate and informed. Therefore, I conclude that dialogical theology enriches Christian living.

The third conclusion that I have reached during the present research is that Trinitarian theology is a solid affirmation of the Christian family. Even though Christians from different traditions will interpret differently the mystery of the Holy Trinity, there is a general agreement on the formative role of this doctrine for Christian theology. Therefore, I conclude that Trinitarian theology unites the Christian family.

Overall, during the research I reached the understanding that theology done in conversation with other traditions could be an enriching experience not only for theologians but also for their communities of reference. There are the great themes of Christian theology, namely, Trinity, Christology, pneumatology, soteriology, sanctification, eschatology, ecclesiology, that wait to be treated in theological conversation in Romania. What I have tried to show in this actual research was one of the many ways in which Baptists and Orthodox in Romania should converse with each other. The only hope at the end of this research is that, even as limited as it is, this work will be a brick in the foundation for the enhancement of the conversation between Orthodox and Baptists in Romania. This can be a desired conversation of mutual understanding, respect and love, in such a way that we will be, even in the fractureness of our fallen humanity, participants in the Father's embrace of the entire world, in the Son through the Spirit.

---

1. Nicolae Steinhart, *Prin alții spre sine* (București: Eminescu, 1988).

APPENDIX A
Bibliography of Paul S. Fiddes

Books

Charismatic Renewal: A Baptist View: A Report Received by the Baptist Union Council with Commentary. London: Baptist Publications, 1980.
The Creative Suffering of God. Oxford: Clarendon, 1988.
Freedom and Limit: A Dialogue between Literature and Christian Doctrine. Basingstoke: Macmillan, 1991.
A Leading Question: The Structure and Authority of Leadership in the Local Church. London: Baptist Publications, 1986.
Participating in God: A Pastoral Doctrine of the Trinity. London: Darton, Longman, & Todd, 2000.
Past Event and Present Salvation: The Christian Idea of Atonement. London: Darton, Longman, & Todd, 1989.
The Promised End: Eschatology in Theology and Literature. Oxford: Blackwell, 2000.
Seeing the World and Knowing God: Hebrew Wisdom and Christian Doctrine in a Late-Modern Context. Oxford: Oxford University Press, 2013.
Tracks and Traces: Baptist Identity in Church and Theology. Carlisle, Cumbria: Paternoster, 2003.
The Trinity in Worship and Preaching. London: London Baptist Preachers' Association, 1991.

Chapters and Articles

"Ambiguities of the Future: Theological Hints in the Novels of Patrick White." *Pacifica* 23, no. 3 (2010): 281–298.
"Baptism and Membership of the Body of Christ: A Theological and Ecumenical Conundrum." In *Gemeinschaft der Kirchen und gesellschaftliche*

Verantwortung: die Würde des Anderen und das Recht anders zu denken: Festschrift für Professor Dr. Erich Geldbach, edited by Lena Lybæk, Erich Geldbach, Konrad Raiser, et al., 89–93. Ökumenische Studien 30. Münster: LIT Verlag, 2004.

"Baptism and the Process of Christian Initiation." In *Dimensions of Baptism: Biblical and Theological Studies*, edited by Stanley E. Porter, and Anthony R. Cross, 280–303. London: Sheffield Academic Press, 2002.

"Baptism and the Process of Christian Initiation." *The Ecumenical Review* 54, no. 1 (2002): 49–65.

"Baptist Ecclesiology." *Ecclesiology* 1, no. 3 (2005): 87–100.

"Baptism of Believers." In *Baptism Today: Understanding, Practice, Ecumenical Implications*, edited by Thomas F. Best, 73–80. Collegeville, MI: Liturgical Press, 2008.

"The Body as Site of Continuity and Change." In *New Topics in Feminist Philosophy of Religion: Contestations and Transcendence Incarnate*, edited by Pamela Sue Anderson, 261–277. New York: Springer, 2009.

"The Canon as Space and Place." In *Die Einheit der Schrift und die Vielfalt des Kanons* [The unity of Scripture and the diversity of the canon], edited by Michael Wolter, 127–149. *Beihefte zur Zeitschrift für die neutestamentliche Wissenschaft und die Kunde der älteren Kirche, Bd. 118*. Berlin: De Gruyter, 2003.

"Christianity, Culture and Education: A Baptist Perspective." In *The Scholarly Vocation and the Baptist Academy: Essays on the Future of Baptist Higher Education*, edited by Roger Ward, and David P. Gushee. Macon, GA: Mercer University Press, 2008.

"Christian Doctrine and Free Church Ecclesiology: Recent Developments among Baptists in the Southern United States." *Ecclesiology* 7, no. 2 (2011): 195–219.

"Church and Sect: Cross-currents in Early Baptist Life." In *Exploring Baptist Origins*, edited by A. R. Cross and N. J. Woods. Oxford: Regent's Park College, 2010.

"Concept, Image and Story in Systematic Theology." *International Journal of Systematic Theology* 11, no. 1 (2009): 3–23.

"Covenant: Old and New." In *Bound to Love: The Covenant Basis of Baptist Life and Mission*, edited by Keith Clements, Paul Fiddes, Roger Hayden, Brian Haymes, and Richard Kidd, 9–23. London: Baptist Union,1985.

"Creation out of Love." In *The Work of Love: Creation as Kenosis*, edited by John Polkinghorne, 167–191. Grand Rapids, MI; Cambridge: Eerdmans, 2001. Also published by SPCK, 2001.

"C.S. Lewis the Myth-maker." In *A Christian for All Christians: Essays in Honour of C.S. Lewis*, edited by Andrew Walker and James Patrick, 132–155.

London: Hodder & Stoughton, 1990. Reprinted as *Rumours of Heaven: Essays in Celebration of C.S. Lewis* (Guildford: Eagle, 1998).

"Daniel Turner and a Theology of the Church Universal." In *Pulpit and People: Studies in Eighteenth Century Baptist Life and Thought*, edited by John H. Y. Briggs, 112–127. Studies in Baptist History and Thought 28. Carlisle, Cumbria: Paternoster, 2009.

"Dual Citizenship in Athens and Jerusalem: The Place of the Christian Scholar in the Life of the Church." In *Questions of Identity: Essays in Honour of Brian Haymes*, edited by Anthony R. Cross, and Ruth M. B. Gouldbourne. Centre for Baptist History and Heritage Studies 6. Oxford: Regent's Park College, 2011.

"Ex Opere Operato: Rethinking a Historic Baptist Rejection." In *Baptist Sacramentalism 2*, edited by Anthony R. Cross, and Philip E. Thompson, 219–238. Milton Keynes: Paternoster, 2008.

"Facing the End: The Apocalyptic Experience in Some Modern Novels." In *Called to One Hope: Perspectives on the Life to Come*, edited by John Colwell, 191–209. Carlisle, Cumbria: Paternoster, 2000.

"G. M. Hopkins." In *The Blackwell Companion to the Bible in English Literature*, edited by Rebecca Lemon, Emma Mason, Jonathan Roberts, et al., 563–576. Chichester: Wiley-Blackwell, 2009.

"God and History." *Baptist Quarterly* 30, no. 2 (1983): 74–90.

"Learning from others: Baptists and Receptive Ecumenism." *Louvain Studies* 33, no. 1–2 (2008): 54–73.

"Millennium and Utopia: Images of a Fuller Presence." In *Apocalyptic in History and Tradition*, edited by Christopher Rowland and John Barton, 7–25. *Journal for the Study of the Pseudepigrapha*, Supplement Series. London: Sheffield Academic, 2002.

"On God the Incomparable: Thinking about God with John Macquarrie." In *In Search of Humanity and Deity: A Celebration of John Macquarrie's Theology*, edited by Robert Morgan, 179–199. London: SCM, 2006.

"On Theology." In *The Cambridge Companion to C. S. Lewis*, edited by Robert MacSwain and Michael Ward. Cambridge Companions to Religion. Cambridge: Cambridge University Press, 2010.

"Participating in the Trinity." *Perspectives in Religious Studies* 33, no. 3 (2006): 375–391.

"The Passion Story in Literature." In *The Oxford Handbook of English Literature and Theology*, edited by Andrew Hass, David Jasper, and Elizabeth Jay, 742–759. Oxford University Press, 2007.

"The Place of Christian Theology in the Modern University." *Baptist Quarterly* 42, no. 2 (2007): 71–88.

"Process Theology." In *The Blackwell Encyclopaedia of Modern Christian Thought*, edited by A. E. McGrath, 471–476. Oxford: Blackwell, 1993.

"The Quest for a Place Which Is 'Not-a-place': The Hiddenness of God and the Presence of God." In *Silence and the Word: Negative Theology and Incarnation*, edited by Oliver Davies, Oliver and Denys Turner, 35–60. Cambridge: Cambridge University Press, 2002.

"Salvation." In *The Oxford Handbook to Systematic Theology*, edited by John Webster, John, Kathryn Tanner, and Ian Torrance, 176–196. London: Oxford University Press, 2007.

"Something Will Come of Nothing: On A Theology of the Dark Side." In *Challenging to Change: Dialogues with a Radical Baptist Theologian: Essays Presented to Dr. Nigel G. Wright on His Sixtieth Birthday*, edited by Peter J. Lalleman. London: Spurgeon's College, 2009.

"Spirituality as Attentiveness: Stillness and Journey." In *Under the Rule of Christ: Dimensions of Baptist Spirituality*, edited by Paul Fiddes, 25–58. Regent's Study Guides 14. Macon, GA: Smyth & Helwys, 2008.

"The Status of Women in the Thought of Karl Barth." In *After Eve*, edited by Janet Martin Soskice, 138–155. London: Marshall Pickering, 1990.

"Story and Possibility: Reflections on the Last Scenes of the Fourth Gospel and Shakespeare's The Tempest." In *Revelation and Story: Narrative theology and the Centrality of Story*, edited by Gerhard Sauter, Gerhard and John Barton, 29–52. Aldershot: Ashgate, 2000.

"The Story and the Stories: Revelation and the Challenge of Postmodern Culture." In *Faith in the Centre: Christianity and Culture*, edited by Paul Fiddes, 75–96. Oxford: Regent's Park College, 2001. Also published by Smyth & Helwys, 2001.

"Suffering, Divine." In *The Blackwell Encyclopaedia of Modern Christian Thought*, edited by A. E. McGrath, 633–636. Oxford: Blackwell, 1993.

"The Theology of the Charismatic Movement." In *Strange Gifts? A Guide to Charismatic Renewal*, edited by David Martin and Peter Mullen, 19–40. Oxford: Blackwell, 1984.

"The Understanding of Salvation in the Baptist Tradition." In *For Us and for Our Salvation: Seven Perspectives on Christian Soteriology*, edited by Walter J. Hollenweger, 15–37. Utrecht: Interuniversitair Instituut voor Missiologie en Oecumenica, 1994.

"'Where Shall Wisdom be Found?' Job 28 as a Riddle for Ancient and Modern Readers." In *After the Exile, Essays in Honour of Rex Mason*, edited by John Barton and David Reimer. Macon, GA: Mercer University Press, 1996.

"When Text Becomes Voice: 'You've Got Mail.'" In *Flickering Images: Theology and Film in Dialogue*, edited by Paul Fiddes, 97–112. Oxford: Regent's Park College, 2006. Also published by Smyth & Helwys, 2006.

"'Woman's Head Is Man': A Doctrinal Reflection Upon a Pauline Text." *Baptist Quarterly* 31, no. 8 (1986): 370–383.

APPENDIX B

Select Works of Dumitru Stăniloae

*Catolicismul de după războ*i [Catholicism after the war]. Sibiu: Editura Arhidiecezană, 1933.

"Curente noi în teologia protestantă germană" [New currents in German Protestant theology]. *Revista Teologică* 19, no. 7–8 (1929): 234–238.

"Doctrina luterană despre justificare și Cuvânt și câteva reflexii ortodoxe" [The Lutheran doctrine of justification and word and some Orthodox reflections]. *Ortodoxia* 35, no. 4 (1983): 495–509.

"Dumnezeiasca Euharistie în cele trei confesiuni" [The divine Eucharist in the three confessions]. *Ortodoxia* 5, no. 1 (1953): 46–115.

"Ființa Tainelor în cele trei confesiuni" [The being of sacraments in the three confessions]. *Ortodoxia* 8, no. 1 (1956): 3–28.

"Filosofia existențială și credința în Iisus Hristos." *Gândirea* 18, no. 10 (1939): 565–572.

"Metafizica lui Lucian Blaga" [Lucian Blaga's metaphysics]. *Revista Teologică* 24, nos. 11–12 (1934): 393–401.

"Organizarea sinodală a Bisericii Ortodoxe în paralel cu cezaro-papismul catolic" [Sinodal organisation of the Orthodox church in parallel with Catholic cesar-papism]. *Studii Teologice* 2, no. 9–10 (1950): 541–555.

"Pentru Pacea confesională" [For the confessional peace]. *Telegraful Român* 79, no. 33–34 (1931): 1–2.

"Posibilitatea reconcilierii dogmatice între Biserica Ortodoxă și Vechile Biserici Orientale" [The possibility of dogmatic reconciliation between the Orthodox Church and the Old Oriental Churches]. *Ortodoxia* 17, no. 1 (1965): 5–27.

"Reîntoarcerea filosofiei" [The return of philosophy]. *Telegraful Român* 85, no. 43 (1937): 1.

"Romanian Orthodox Anglican Talks: A Dogmatic Assesement." In *Romanian Orthodox Church and the Church of England*, 129–148. Bucharest: Biblical and Orthodox Missionary Institute, 1976.

"Starea primordială a omului în cele trei confesiuni" [The primordial estate of man in the three confessions]. *Ortodoxia* 8, no. 3 (1956): 323–357.

"Tendinţa Vaticanului după comuniunea euharistică cu ortodocşii" [The tendency of the Vatican after the eucharistic communion with the Orthodox]. *Ortodoxia* 34, no. 3 (1972): 492–494.

Bibliography

Andronovienė, Lina and Parush Parushev. "Church, State, and Culture: On the Complexities of Post-Soviet Evangelical Social Involvement." *Theological Reflections: Euro-Asian Journal of Theology* 3 (2004): 194–212.

Aquinas, Thomas. *The Summa Theologica*. Chicago: Encyclopedia Britannica, 1952.

———. *Summa Theologiae*. 12:9. London: Eyre & Spottiswoode, 1964.

Atanasie. *Scrieri 2*. Translated by Dumitru Stăniloae. Bucuresti: EIBMBOR, 1988.

Athanasius. "Defense against the Arians." In *Nicene and Post-Nicene Fathers*. Series 2, Vol. 4, edited by Philip Schaff, 277–349. Peabody, MA: Hendrickson, 1999.

———. "Defense of the Nicene Definition." In *Nicene and Post-Nicene Fathers*. Series 2, Vol. 4, edited by Philip Schaff, 150–172. Peabody, MA: Hendrickson, 1999.

———. "On The Incarnation of the Word." In *Nicene and Post-Nicene Fathers*. Series 2, Vol. 4, edited by Philip Schaff, 183–237. Peabody, MA: Hendrickson, 1999.

Augsburger, Myron. *The Peace Maker*. Nashville, TN: Abington, 1987.

———. *The Robe of God: Reconciliation, the Believers Church Essential*. Scottsdale, PA: Herald Press, 2000.

Augustine. "Treatise on the Merits and Forgiveness of Sins and on the Baptism of Infants." In *A Select Library of the Nicene and Post-Nicene Fathers*. Series 1, Vol. 5, edited by Philip Schaff, 15–78. Peabody, MA: Hendrickson, 1995.

Baban, Octavian. "The Bible in the Life of the Orthodox Church." In *Baptists and the Orthodox Church: On the Way to Understanding*, edited by Ian Randall, 15–29. Prague: International Baptist Seminary, 2005.

Baird, J. S. "Preaching." In *Evangelical Dictionary of Theology*, edited by Walter A. Elwell, 868–869. Grand Rapids, MI: Baker Books, 1984.

Balz, Horst. "προσευχη." In *Exegetical Dictionary of the New Testament*. Vol. 3, edited by Horst Balz and Gerhard Schneider, 164. Grand Rapids, MI: Eerdmans, 1993.

Baptism and Confirmation: A Report Submitted by the Church of England Liturgical Commission to the Archbishop of Canterbury and York in November 1958. London: SPCK, 1959.

Baptism, Eucharist and Ministry 1982-1990: Report on the Process and Responses. Faith and Order, Paper 149. Geneva: WCC Publications, 1992.

Barnett, C. K. *A Commentary of the First Epistle to the Corinthians.* London: Black, 1968.

Barth, Karl. *Against the Stream: Shorter Post-War Writings, 1946-52.* London: SCM, 1954.

———. *Christ and Adam: Man and Humanity in Romans 5.* New York: Harper & Brothers, 1956.

———. *Church Dogmatics: A Selection.* New York: Harper & Row, 1962.

———. *The Doctrine of the Word of God.* Vol. 1.1 of *Church Dogmatics.* Edited by G. W. Bromiley and T. F. Torrance. Translated by G. W. Bromiley. Edinburgh: T & T Clark, 1936.

———. *The Doctrine of the Word of God.* Vol. 1.1 of *Church Dogmatics.* Peabody, MA: Hendrickson, 2004.

———. *The Doctrine of the Word of God.* Vol. 1.1. 2nd ed. *Church Dogmatics.* Peabody, MA: Hendrickson, 2010.

———. *The Doctrine of the Word of God.* Vol. 1.2 of *Church Dogmatics.* Edinburgh: T & T Clark, 1956.

———. *The Doctrine of God.* Vol. 2.1 of *Church Dogmatics.* Edinburgh: T & T Clark, 1936.

———. *The Doctrine of Creation.* Vol. 3 of *Church Dogmatics.* Edinburgh: T & T Clark, 1960.

———. *The Doctrine of Creation.* Vol. 3.3 of *Church Dogmatics.* Edinburgh: T & T Clark, 1966.

———. *The Doctrine of Reconciliation.* Vol. 4.1 of *Church Dogmatics.* 2nd ed. Peabody, MA: Hendrickson, 2010.

———. *The Doctrine of Reconciliation.* Vol. 4.4 of *Church Dogmatics.* Edinburgh: T & T Clark, 1969.

———. *The Epistle to the Romans.* London: Oxford University Press, 1933.

———. *God Here and Now: Religious Perspectives.* New York: Harper & Row, 1964.

———. *The Teaching of the Church Regarding Baptism.* Eugene, OR: Wipf & Stock, 2005.

———. *The Word of God and the Word of Man.* New York: Harper & Row, 1928.

Barth, Markus. *Ephesians: Introduction, Translation, and Commentary on Chapters 1-3.* New York: Doubleday, 1974.

———. *Ephesians: Translation and Commentary on Chapters 4–6.* New York: Doubleday, 1974.

Bibliography

Barth, Markus, and Helmut Blanke. *Colossians: A New Translation with Introduction and Commentary.* New York: Doubleday, 1994.

Bartoş, Emil. *Conceptul de îndumnezeire în Teologia lui Dumitru Stăniloae* [The concept of deification in Dumitru Stăniloae's theology]. Oradea: Cartea Creştină, 2002.

———. *Deification in Eastern Orthodox Theology: An Evaluation and Critique of the Theology of Dumitru Stăniloae.* Carlisle, Cumbria: Paternoster, 1999.

———. "Salvation in the Orthodox Church." In *Baptists and the Orthodox Church: On the Way to Understanding*, edited by Ian Randall, 46–63. Prague: International Baptist Seminary, 2005.

Basil of Caesarea. "The Hexameron." In *Nicene and Post-Nicene Fathers*, Series 2, Vol. 8, edited by Philip Schaff and Henry Wace, 51–107. Peabody, MA: Hendrickson, 1995.

———. "On the Spirit." In *Nicene and Post-Nicene Fathers*, Series 2, Vol. 8, edited by Philip Schaff and Henry Wace, 1–50. Peabody, MA: Hendrickson, 1995.

Beasley-Murray, G. R. *Baptism in the New Testament.* Carlisle, Cumbria: Paternoster, 1962.

Beker, J. C. "Second Letter of Peter." In *The Interpreter's Dictionary of the Bible*, edited by George Arthur Buttrick, 767–771. Nashville, TN: Abingdon, 1962.

Berdiaev, Nikolai. *Sensul Creaţiei: Încercare de îndreptăţire a omului.* Bucuresti: Humanitas, 1992.

Berkhof, Louis. *Systematic Theology.* New edition. Grand Rapids, MI: Eerdmans, 1996.

———. *Systematic Theology.* London: Banner of Truth, 1958.

Beyer. "διακονεω, διακονια, διακονος." In *Theological Dictionary of the New Testament.* Vol. 2, edited by Gerhard Kittel and Gerhard Friedrich, translated by Geoffrey W. Bromiley, 81–93. Grand Rapids, MI: Eerdmans, 1964.

Bianchi, Eugene C. *Reconciliation the Function of the Church.* New York: Sheed and Ward, 1969.

Bloesch, D. G. "Prayer." In *Evangelical Dictionary of Theology*, edited by Walter A. Elwell. Grand Rapids, MI: Baker Books, 1984.

Blum, Edwin A. "2 Peter." In *The Expositor's Bible Commentary: New Testament.* Abridged edition, edited by Kenneth L. N. Barker and John R. Kohlenberger, III, 255–289. Grand Rapids, MI: Zondervan, 1994.

Blumenfeld, Bruno. *The Political Paul: Justice, Democracy and Kingship in a Hellenistic Framework.* Sheffield: Academic Press, 2001.

Bobrinskoy, Boris. *The Mystery of the Trinity: Trinitarian Experience and Vision in the Biblical and Patristic Tradition.* Crestwood, NY: St. Vladimir's Seminary Press, 1999.

Bonhoeffer, Dietrich. *The Cost of Discipleship*. 6th edition. London: SCM, 1959.
———. *Ethics*. New York: Macmillan, 1962.
Bordeianu, Radu. *Dumitru Stăniloae: An Ecumenical Ecclesiology*. London: T & T Clark, 2011.
Breck, John. *Scripture in Tradition: The Bible and Its Interpretation in the Orthodox Church*. Crestwood, NY: St. Vladimir's Seminary Press, 2001.
Bria, Ion. *Romania: Orthodox Identity at a Crossroad of Europe*. Geneva: WCC Publications, 1995.
———. *Spațiul nemuririi sau eternizarea umanului în Dumnezeu* [The space of immortality or the eternization of humaness in God]. Iași: Trinitas, 1994.
Briggs, John. "Evangelicals and Orthodox." *Journal of European Baptist Studies* 12, no. 1 (September 2011): 5–19.
Brown, C. "Proclamation, Preach, Kerygma." In *Dictionary of New Testament Theology*. Vol. 3, edited by Collin Brown, 44–68. Grand Rapids, MI: Zondervan, 1978.
Brown, Raymond. *The Message of Hebrews: Christ Above All*. Leicester: Inter-Varsity Press, 1982.
Bruce, F. F. *The Epistle to the Galatians*. New International Greek Testament Commentary. Grand Rapids, MI: Eerdmans, 1982.
———. *The Gospel of John*. Grand Rapids, MI: Eerdmans, 1983.
Brueggemann, Walter. *A Social Reading of the Old Testament: Prophetic Approaches to Israel's Communal Life*, edited by Patrick D. Miller. Minneapolis, MI: Fortress, 1994.
Bulgakov, Sergius. *The Orthodox Church*. Crestwood, NY: St. Vladimir's Seminary Press, 1988.
Bunaciu, Otniel Ioan. "The Meaning of Tradition." In *Baptists and the Orthodox Church: On the Way to Understanding*, edited by Ian Randall, 30–45. Prague: International Baptist Seminary, 2005.
Calvin, John. *Institutes of Christian Religion*. Edited by John T. McNeil. Translated by Ford Lewis Battles. Philadelphia, PA: Westminster, 1960.
Carroll, Lesley. "Forgiveness and the Church." In *Forgiveness: Embodying Forgiveness*, 2–11. Belfast: Centre for Contemporary Christianity in Ireland, 2002.
Chan, Simon. *Liturgical Theology: The Church as Worshiping Community*. Downers Grove, IL: InterVarsity Press, 2006.
Clement of Alexandria. "The Instructor." In *Ante–Nicene Fathers*. Vol. 2, *Fathers of the Second Century*, edited by Alexander Roberts and James Donaldson, 207–296. Peabody, MA: Hendrickson, 2004.
Climacus, John. *The Ladder of Divine Ascent*. New York: Paulist Press, 1982.
Clowney, Edmund. *The Message of 1 Peter: The Way of the Cross*. Leicester: Inter-Varsity Press, 1988.

Cole, R. Alan. *The Gospel According to Mark: An Introduction and Commentary.* Leicester: Inter-Varsity Press, 1989.
Collins, Paul M. *Trinitarian Theology, West and East: Karl Barth, the Cappadocian Fathers and John Zizioulas.* Oxford: Oxford University Press, 2001.
Constantineanu, Corneliu. *The Social Significance of Reconciliation in Paul's Theology: Narrative Readings in Romans.* London: T & T Clark, 2010.
Constantinescu, Emil. "Pr. Prof. Dr. Dumitru Stăniloae: profil de teolog și filosof creștin ortodox." In *Persoană și Comuniune: Prinos de cinstire Părintelui Profesor Academician Dumitru Stăniloae la înplinirea vârstei de 90 de ani,* edited by Antonie Plămădeală, 90–93. Sibiu: Editura Arhiepiscopiei ortodoxe, 1993.
Conzelmann, Hans. "ευχαριστεω, ευχαριστια." In *Theological Dictionary of the New Testament.* Vol. 9, edited by Gerhard Kittel and Gerhard Friedrich. Translated by Geoffrey W. Bromiley, 359–376. Grand Rapids, MI: Eerdmans, 1974.
———. *A Commentary of the First Epistle to the Corinthians.* Philadelphia, PA: Fortress, 1975.
Cullmann, Oscar. *Christ and Time.* London: SCM, 1951.
———. *The Christology of the New Testament.* Philadelphia, PA: Westminster, 1963.
Cyril of Alexandria. *The Commentary on the Gospel of Saint John.* Peabody, MA: InterVarsity Press, 2013.
Cyril of Jerusalem. "Lectures 22:3, 9." In *Nicene and Post-Nicene Fathers,* Series 2, Vol. 7, *Cyril of Jerusalem, Gregory Nazianzen,* edited by Philip Schaff. Buffalo, NY: Christian Literature Publishing Co, 1894.
Davids, Peter H. *The First Epistle of Peter.* Grand Rapids, MI: Eerdmans, 1990.
Dionysius. *The Divine Names and Mystical Theology.* London: SPCK, 1975.
Dockery, D. S. "Fruit of the Spirit." In *Dictionary of Paul and His Letters,* edited by Gerald F. Hawthorne and Ralph P. Martin, 316–319. Downers Grove, IL: InterVarsity Press, 1993.
Dodd, C. H. *The Epistle of Paul to the Romans.* London: Hodder & Stoughton, 1932.
Donaldson, Terence L. "The Origin of Paul's Gentile Mission." In *The Road from Damascus: The Impact of Paul's Conversion on His Life, Thought, and Ministry,* edited by Richard Norman Longenecker, 62–84. Grand Rapids, MI: Eerdmans, 1997.
Dumitrescu, Sorin. *7 dimineți cu părintele Stăniloae.* București: Anastasia, 1992.
Dunn, James D. C. *The Epistles to the Colossians and to Philemon: A Commentary on the Greek Text.* Grand Rapids, MI: Eerdmans, 1996.
Dyrness, William. *Themes in Old Testament Theology.* London: Paternoster, 1998.
Ebeling, Gerhard. *Theology and Proclamation.* London: Collins, 1966.

Eichrodt, Walther. *Theology of the Old Testament*. Vol 1. Philadelphia, PA: Westminster, 1961.
Elliott, Neil. "The Anti-Imperial Message of the Cross." In *Paul and Empire: Religion and Power in Roman Imperial Society*, edited by Richard A. Horsley, 167–183. Harrisburg, PA: Trinity Press, 1997.
———. *Liberating Paul: The Justice of God and the Politics of the Apostle*. Sheffield: Academic, 1995.
Ellis, E. Earle. *Pauline Theology: Ministry and Society*. Exeter: Paternoster, 1989.
English, Donald. *The Message of Mark: The Mystery of Faith*. Downers Grove, IL: InterVarsity Press, 1992.
Evdokimov, Paul. *L'Esprit Saint dans la tradition orthodoxe*. Paris: Éditions du Cerf, 1969.
———. *L'Orthodoxie*. Neuchâtel: Delachaux et Niestlé, 1959.
———. *Vârstele vieții spirituale*. Bucuresti: Christiana, 1993.
Fee, Gordon D. *The First Epistle to the Corinthians*. Grand Rapids, MI: Eerdmans, 1987.
———. *God's Empowering Presence: The Holy Spirit in the Letters of Paul*. Peabody, MA: Hendrickson, 1994.
———. *Paul, The Spirit and the People of God*. Peabody, MA: Hendrickson, 1996.
Felici, Pericle. "Lumen Gentium 1: 9 and 48." In *The Documents of Vatican II*, edited by Walter M. Abbott, 14–101. Baltimore, MD: America Press, 1966.
Fiddes, Paul, S. "Baptism and Creation." In *Reflections on the Water: Understanding God and the World through the Baptism of Believers*, edited by Paul Fiddes, 46–67. Macon, GA: Smyth & Helwys, 1996.
———. "Baptism and the Process of Christian Initiation." *The Ecumenical Review* 54, no. 1 (Jan–Apr 2002): 48–65.
———. "Baptism and the Process of Christian Initiation. " In *Dimensions of Baptism: Biblical and Theological Studies*, edited by Stanley E. Porter and Anthony R. Cross, 280–303. London: Sheffield Academic Press, 2002.
———. "Concept, Image and Story in Systematic Theology." *International Journal of Systematic Theology* 11, no. 1 (January 2009): 3–23.
———. "Contributors." *Eclessiology* 7, no. 2 (2011): 137–139.
———. "Covenant: Old and New." In *Bound to Love: The Covenant Basis of Baptist Life and Mission*, edited by Paul Fiddes, R. Hayden, R. Kidd, K. Clements, and B. Haymes, 9–23. London: Baptist Union, 1985.
———. *The Creative Suffering of God*. Oxford: Clarendon, 1988.
———. "Introduction: The Novel and the Spiritual Journey Today." In *The Novel, Spirituality and Modern Culture: Eight Novelists Write about their Craft and their Context*, edited by Paul S. Fiddes, 1–21. Cardiff: University of Wales Press, 2000.

———. "A Journey of Discovery: Christian Initiation, Archbishop Rowan Williams and Ecumenism." *Ecclesiology* 8, no. 2 (2012): 153–161.

———. "Old Testament Principles of Wholeness." In *Iosif Ton: Orizonturi noi in Spiritualitate și slujire*, edited by Sorin Sabou and Dorothy Ghitea, 15–48. Oradea: Cartea Creștină, 2004.

———. *Participation in God: A Pastoral Doctrine of the Trinity*. London: Darton, Longman and Todd, 2000.

———. "Participation in the Trinity." *Perspectives in Religious Studies* 33, no. 3 (2006): 375–391.

———. *Past Event and Present Salvation: The Christian Idea of Atonement*. London: Darton, Longman & Todd, 1989.

———. "The Root of Religious Freedom: Interpreting Some Muslim and Christian Sacred Texts." *Oxford Journal of Law and Religion* 1, no. 1 (2012): 169–184.

———. "The Signs of Hope." In *A Call to Mind: Baptist Essays Towards a Theology of Commitment*, Paul S. Fiddes, Keith Clements, Roger Hayden, Brian Haymes, and Richard Kidd, 33–45. London: Baptist Union, 1987.

———. "Spirituality as Attentiveness: Stillness and Journey." In *Under the Rule of Christ: Dimensions of Baptist Spirituality*, edited by Paul S. Fiddes, 25–57. Oxford: Regent's Park College; Macon, GA: Smyth & Helwys, 2008.

———. "Story and Possibility: Reflections on the Last Scenes of The Fourth Gospel and Shakespeare's *The Tempest*." In *Revelation and Story: Narrative Theology and the Centrality of the Story*, edited by Santer Gerhart and Barton John, 29–51. Aldershot: Ashgate, 2000.

———. "The Story and the Stories: Revelation and the Challenge of Postmodern Culture." In *Faith in the Centre: Christianity and Culture*, edited by Paul S. Fiddes, 75–96. Oxford: Regent's Park College; Macon, GA: Smyth & Helwys, 2001.

———. "Theology and a Baptist Way of Community." In *Doing Theology in a Baptist Way*, edited by Paul S. Fiddes, 19–38. Oxford: Whitley, 2000.

———. "The Theology of the Charismatic Movement." In *Strange Gifts? A Guide to Charismatic Renewal*, edited by David Martin and Peter Mullen, 19–40. Oxford: Blackwell, 1984.

———. *Tracks and Traces: Baptist Identity in Church and Theology*. Carlisle, Cumbria: Paternoster, 2003.

———. "When Text Becomes Voice: You've Got Mail." In *Flickering Images: Theology and Film in Dialogue*, Paul S. Fiddes and Anthony J. Clarke, 97–111. Oxford: Regent's Park College; Macon, GA: Smyth & Helwys, 2005.

———. "Woman's Head Is Man." *Baptist Quarterly* 31, no. 8 (1986): 370–383

Forsyth, P. T. *The Work of Christ: Lectures to Young Ministers*. London: Independent Press, 1938.

Frame, John M. *No Other God: A Response to Open-Theism*. New Jersey: P & R, 2001.
France, R. T. *The Gospel According to Matthew*. Grand Rapids, MI: Eerdmans, 1985.
Franke, John R. "God is Love: The Social Trinity and the Mission of God." In *Trinitarian Theology for the Church: Scripture, Community, Worship*, edited by Daniel J. Treier and David Lauber, 105–119. Downers Grove, IL: InterVarsity Press, 2009.
Freeman, Curtis W., James William McClendon, Jr, and Rosalee Velloso de Silva, eds. *Baptist Roots: A Reader in the Theology of a Christian People*. Valley Forge: Judson Press, 1999.
Gaebelein, Arno C. *The Gospel of Matthew: An Exposition*. Neptune, NJ: Loizeaux Brothers, 1961.
Galeriu, Constantin. *Jertfă și răscumpărare*. Bucuresti: Harisma, 1991.
Geldenhuys, Norval. *The Gospel of Luke*. Grand Rapids, MI: Eerdmans, 1977.
Gorman, Michael J. *Cruciformity: Paul's Narrative Spirituality of the Cross*. Grand Rapids, MI: Eerdmans, 2001.
Govier, Trudy. *Forgiveness and Revenge*. London: Routledge, 2002.
Grass, Tim. "Orthodoxy and the Doctrine of the Church." In *Baptists and the Orthodox Church: On the Way to Understanding*, edited by Ian Randall, 5–14. Prague: International Baptist Seminary, 2005.
Green, Joel B. *1 Peter*. Grand Rapids, MI: Eerdmans, 2007.
Greeven. "προσευχομαι, προσευχη." In *Theological Dictionary of the New Testament*. Vol. 2, edited by Gerhard Kittel and Gerhard Friedrich. Translated by Geoffrey W. Bromiley, 775–784. Grand Rapids: Eerdmans, 1964.
Gregory of Nyssa. "The Great Catechism." In *Nicene and Post-Nicene Fathers*, Series 2, Vol. 5, *Gregory of Nyssa, Dogmatic Treatises*, edited by Philip Schaff, 471–509. Peabody, MA: Hendrickson, 2007.
———. "Catechetical Oration." In *Nicene and Post-Nicene Fathers*, Series 2, Vol. 5, *Gregory of Nyssa, Dogmatic Treatises*, edited by Philip Schaff, 513–524. Peabody, MA: Hendrickson, 2007.
Grudem, Wayne. *Systematic Theology: An Introduction to Biblical Doctrine*. Leicester: Inter-Varsity Press, 1994.
Gundry, Robert H. *Mark: A Commentary on His Apology for the Cross*. Grand Rapids, MI: Eerdmans, 1993.
Gunton, Colin E. "The Church on Earth: The Roots of Community." In *On Being the Church: Essays on the Christian Community*, edited by Colin E. Gunton and Daniel W. Hardy, 48–80. Edinburgh: T & T Clark, 1989.
———. *The One, the Three and the Many: God, Creation and the Culture of Modernity*. Cambridge: Cambridge University Press, 1993.

Gushee, David P. *Only Human: Christian Reflections on the Journey Towards Wholeness*. San Francisco, CA: Jossey-Bass, 2005.
Hammond, T. C. *In Understanding be Men: A Handbook of Christian Doctrine*. Leicester: Inter-Varsity Press, 1968.
Hauerwas, Stanley. *Matthew*. Ada, MI: Brazos Press, 2006.
Hays, Richard B. *First Corinthians*. Louisville, KY: Westminster John Knox, 1997.
Hendriksen, William. *Ephesians: New Testament Commentary*. London: Banner of Truth, 1967.
Herrick, Vanessa, and Ivan Mann. *Jesus Wept: Reflections on Vulnerability in Leadership*. London: Darton, Longman, and Todd, 1998.
Hess, K. "Serve, Deacon, Worship." In *Dictionary of New Testament Theology*. Vol. 3, edited by Colin Brown, 544–553. Exeter: Paternoster, 1971.
Hildebrand, Dietrich Von. *Transformation in Christ: On the Christian Attitude*. San Francisco, CA: Ignatius Press, 2001.
Hodge, Charles. *A Commentary on the Epistle to the Ephesians*. London: Banner of Truth, 1964.
———. *1 Corinthians*. Wheaton, IL: Crossway Books, 1995.
Holeton, David R., ed. *Christian Initiation in the Anglican Communion. The Toronto Statement "Walk in Newness of Life": The Findings of the Fourth International Anglican Liturgical Consultation, Toronto 1991*. Grove Worship Series no. 118. Bramcote, UK: Grove Books, 1991.
Holmes, Stephen R. *The Holy Trinity: Understanding God's Life*. London: Paternoster, 2012.
Hooker, Morna D. *From Adam to Christ: Essays on Paul*. Cambridge: Cambridge University Press, 1990.
Ică, Ioan I., Jr. "Împărtășirea continuă pro și contra – o dispută perenă și lecțiile ei." In *Împărtășirea continuă cu Sfintele Taine*, 5–88. Sibiu: Deisis, 2006.
Ierunca, Virgil. "Teologia Dogmatică Ortodoxă' a Părintelui Dumitru Stăniloae." In *Persoană și Comuniune: Prinos de cinstire Părintelui Profesor Academician Dumitru Stăniloae la înplinirea vârstei de 90 de ani*, edited by Antonie Plămădeală, 103–107. Sibiu: Editura Arhiepiscopiei Ortodoxe, 1993.
Jenson, Robert W. *Systematic Theology: The Works of God*. Vol. 2. Oxford: Oxford University Press, 1999.
Jervis, L. Ann. "Becoming like God through Christ: Discipleship in Romans." In *Patterns of Discipleship in the New Testament*, edited by Richard N. Longenecker, 143–162. Grand Rapids, MI: Eerdmans, 1996.
Joantă, Serafim. "Din istoria isihasmului până în secolul al XV-lea." In *Persoană și Comuniune: Prinos de cinstire Părintelui Profesor Academician Dumitru Stăniloae la înplinirea vârstei de 90 de ani*, edited by Antonie Plămădeală. Sibiu: Editura Arhiepiscopiei ortodoxe, 1993.

Jobes, Karen H. *1 Peter*. Grand Rapids, MI: Baker Academic, 2005.

Jones, Christopher. "Losing and Binding: The Liturgical Mediation of Forgiveness." In *Forgiveness and Truth: Explorations in Contemporary Theology*, edited by Alister McFayden, Marcel Sarot, and Anthony Thiselton, 31–52. Edinburgh: T & T Clark, 2001.

Jones, Tony. *The Sacred Way: Spiritual Practices for Everyday Life*. Grand Rapids, MI: Zondervan, 2005.

Kaiser, Walter C., Jr. "Israel as the People of God." In *The People of God: Essays on the Believers' Church*, edited by Paul Basden and David S. Dockery, 99–108. Nashville, TN: Broadman Press, 1991.

Kärkkäinen, Veli-Matti. *Christology: A Global Introduction*. Ada, MI: Baker Academic, 2003.

———. *An Introduction to Ecclesiology: Ecumenical, Historical and Global Perspectives*. Downers Grove, IL: InterVarsity Press, 2002.

Karmiris, John N. *The Status and Ministry of the Laity in the Orthodox Church*. Brookline, MA: Holy Cross, 1994.

———. "Concerning the Sacraments." In *Eastern Orthodox Theology: A Contemporary Reader*, edited by Daniel B. Clendenin, 21–32. Grand Rapids, MI: Baker Academic, 2003.

Kasemann, Ernst. *Essays on New Testament Themes*. Philadelphia, PA: Fortress, 1982.

Kasper, Walter. *Theology & Church*. London: SCM, 1989.

Keener, Craig S., ed. *The IVP Bible Background Commentary: New Testament*. Downers Grove, IL: InterVarsity Press, 1993.

Keown, Gerald L., Pamela J. Scalise, and Thomas G. Smothers. *Jeremiah 26–52*. Word Biblical Commentary. Vol. 27, edited by David A. Hubbard and Glenn W Barker. Dallas, TX: Word Books, 1995.

Kim, Seyoon. *Paul and the New Perspective: Second Thoughts on the Origin of Paul's Gospel*. Grand Rapids, MI: Eerdmans, 2002.

Klappert, B. "Lord's Supper." In *Dictionary of New Testament Theology*. Vol. 2, edited by Colin Brown, 520–538. Grand Rapids, MI: Zondervan, 1971.

Knowles, Michael P. "Christ in You the Hope of Glory: Discipleship in Colossians." In *Patterns of Discipleship in the New Testament*, edited by Richard N. Longenecker, 180–202. Grand Rapids, MI: Eerdmans, 1996.

Koester, Craig R. *Hebrews: A New Translation with Introduction and Commentary*. New York: Doubleday, 2001.

Kreider, Eleanor. *Given for You: A Fresh Look at Communion*. Leicester: InterVarsity Press, 1998.

Kreitzer, L. Joseph. *The Gospel According to John*. Oxford: Regent's Park College, 1990.

Kummel, W. G. *The Theology of the New Testament: According to Its Major Witnesses Jesus–Paul–John*. London: SCM, 1974.

LaCugna, Catherine Mowry. *God for Us: The Trinity and Christian Life*. San Francisco, CA: HarperSanFrancisco, 1993

Ladd, George Eldon. *The Presence of the Future: The Eschatology of Biblical Realism*. Grand Rapids, MI: Eerdmans, 1974.

Lamb, Jonathan. *Integrity: Leading with God Watching*. Nottingham: InterVarsity Press, 2006.

Lampe, G. W. H. "The Eucharist in the Thought of the Early Church." In *Eucharistic Theology Then and Now*, edited by R. E. Clements, 34–58. London: SPCK, 1968.

Leonard, Bill J. *Baptist Ways: A History*. Valley Forge, PA: Judson Press, 2003.

Lewis, Scott M. *The Gospel According to John and the Johannine Letters*. Collegeville, MI: Liturgical Press, 2005.

Lightfoot, J. B. *St Paul's Epistles to the Colossians and to Philemon*. London: Macmillan, 1875.

Lincoln, Andrew T. *Ephesians*. Word Biblical Commentary 42, edited by David Hubbard, Glenn W. Barker. Dallas, TX: Word Books, 1990.

Lindvall, Michael L. *The Christian Life: A Geography of God*. Louisville, KY: Geneva Press, 2001.

Lloyd-Jones, D. M. *Darkness and Light: An Exposition of Ephesians 4:17-5:17*. Edinburgh: Banner of Truth, 1982

———. *Life in the Spirit, In Marriage, Home and Work: An Exposition of Ephesians 5:18 to 6:9*. Carlisle, PA: Banner of Truth, 1973.

Lossky, Vladimir. *The Mystical Theology of the Eastern Church*. Cambridge: James Clarke, 1973.

———. *The Vision of God*. Crestwood, NY: St. Vladimir's Seminary Press, 1983.

Louth, Andrew. "Review Essay: The Orthodox Dogmatic Theology of Dumitru Stăniloae." *Modern Theology* 13, no. 2 (1997): 253–267.

Mariş, Marius Daniel. "Biblical Theology of Creation as Basis for the Christian Dialogue between Evangelicals and the Orthodox Church in Post-Communist Romania." Unpublished PhD diss., Bucharest University, 2006.

Marshall, I. Howard. *1 Peter*. Leicester: Inter-Varsity Press, 1991.

———. "A New Understanding of the Present and the Future: Paul and Eschatology." In *The Road from Damascus: The Impact of Paul's Conversion on His Life, Thought, and Ministry*, edited by Richard N. Longenecker, 43–61. Grand Rapids, MI: Eerdmans, 1997.

Martin, Ralph P. *Colossians: The Church's Lord and the Christian Liberty*. Exeter: Paternoster, 1972.

Matei, Eugen. "The Practice of Community in Social Trinitarianism: A Theological Evaluation with Reference to Dumitru Stăniloae and Jürgen Moltmann." Unpublished PhD diss., Fuller Theological Seminary, 2004.

Mănăstireanu, Dănuţ. "Dumitru Stăniloae's Theology of Ministry." In *Dumitru Stăniloae, Tradition and Modernity in Theology*, edited by Lucian Turcescu, 126–144. Iasi: Center for Romanian Studies, 2002.

———. *Locul Scripturii în tradiţia ortodoxă*. Cluj-Napoca: Alma Mater, 2006.

———. "A Perichoretical Model of the Church: The Trinitarian Ecclesiology of Dumitru Stăniloae." Unpublished PhD diss., Brunel University, 2005.

———. *A Perichoretic Model of the Church: The Trinitarian Ecclesiology of Dumitru Stăniloae*. Saarbrucken: Lambert Academic, 2012.

McClendon, James W., Jr. "The Believers Church in Theological Perspective." In *The Wisdom of the Cross: Essays in Honor of John Howard Yoder*, edited by Stanley Hauerwas, Chris K. Huebner, Harry J. Huebner, and Mark Thiessen Nation, 309–326. Grand Rapids: Eerdmans, 1999.

———. *Systematic Theology*. Vol. 2, *Doctrine*. Nashville, TN: Abingdon, 1994.

———. *Systematic Theology*. Vol. 1, *Ethics*. Nashville, TN: Abingdon, 1986.

———. *Systematic Theology*. Vol. 1, *Ethics*. Revised edition. Nashville, TN: Abingdon, 2002.

McFague, Sallie. *Models of God: Theology for an Ecological, Nuclear Age*. Philadelphia, PA: Fortress, 1987.

Meeks, Wayne A. *The First Urban Christians: The Social World of the Apostle Paul*. New Haven, CT: Yale University Press, 1983.

———. *The Origins of Christian Morality: The First Two Centuries*. New Haven: Yale University Press, 1993.

Meye, R. P. "Spirituality." In *Dictionary of Paul and his Letters*, edited by G. F. Hawthorne, R. P. Martin, and D. G. Reid, 906–916. Downers Grove, IL: InterVarsity Press, 1993.

Meyendorff, John. *St. Gregory Palamas and Orthodox Spirituality*. New York: St. Vladimir's Seminary Press, 1974.

———. *A Study of Gregory Palamas*. New York: St. Vladimir's Seminary Press, 1998.

Mikoski, Gordon S. "Baptism, Trinity, and Ecclesial Pedagogy in the Thought of Gregory of Nyssa." *Scottish Journal of Theology* 59, no. 2 (2006): 175–182.

Miller, Charles. *The Gift of the World: An Introduction to the Theology of Dumitru Stăniloae*. Edinburgh: T & T Clark, 2000.

Milne, Bruce. *The Message of John: Here is Your King*. Leicester: Inter-Varsity Press, 1993.

Moltmann, Jürgen. *The Church in the Power of the Spirit: A Contribution to Messianic Ecclesiology*. London: SCM, 1992.

———. *The Crucified God: The Cross of Christ as the Foundation and Criticism of Christian Theology*. London: SCM, 1974.

———. *God in Creation: An Ecological Doctrine of Creation*. London: SCM, 1985.

———. "God in the World – The World in God: Perichoresis in Trinity and Eschatology." In *The Gospel of John and Christian Theology*, edited by Richard Bauckham and Carl Mosser, 369–381. Grand Rapids, MI: Eerdmans, 2008.

———. *The Source of Life: The Holy Spirit and the Theology of Life*. Minneapolis, MN: Fortress, 1997.

———. *The Spirit of Life: A Universal Affirmation*. Minneapolis, MN: Fortress, 2001.

———. *The Trinity and the Kingdom of God: The Doctrine of God*. London: SCM, 1981.

Moo, Douglas. *Romans 1-8*. The Wycliffe Exegetical Commentary. Chicago, IL: Moody, 1991.

Morden, Peter. "The Spirituality of C.H. Spurgeon: II Maintaining Communion: The Lord's Supper." *Baptistic Theologies* 4, no. 1 (Spring 2012): 27–50.

Muller-Fahrenholz, Geiko. *The Art of Forgiveness: Theological Reflections on Healing and Reconciliation*. Geneva: WWC Publications, 1996.

Murphy, Francesca Ann. *God is Not a Story: Realism Revisited*. Oxford: Oxford University Press, 2007.

Myers, Allen C., ed. *The Eerdmans Bible Dictionary*. Grand Rapids, MI: Eerdmans, 1987.

Negruţ, Paul. "The Development of the Concept of Authority within the Romanian Orthodox Church during the twentieth Century." Unpublished PhD diss., Brunel University, 1995.

Newbigin, Lesslie. *The Gospel in a Pluralistic Society*. London: SPCK, 1992.

———. *The Household of God: Lectures on the Nature of the Church*. London: SCM, 1964.

———. *The Light Has Come: An Exposition of the Fourth Gospel*. Grand Rapids, MI: Eerdmans, 1982.

Noble, Ivana. "Conversion and Postmodernism." In *Bekehrung und Identität: Ökumene als Spannung zwischen Fremdem und Vertrautem*, edited by Dagmar Heller, 45–68. Frankfurt am Main: Lembeck, 2003.

———. "Doctrine of Creation within the Theological Project of Dumitru Stăniloae." *Communio Viatorum* 49, no. 2 (2007): 185–209.

———. "Memory and Remembering in the Post-Communist Context." *Political Theology* 9, no. 4 (2008): 455–475.

———. *Tracking God: An Ecumenical Fundamental Theology*. Eugene, OR: Wipf & Stock, 2010.

———. *Theological Interpretation of Culture in Post-Communist Context: Central and East European Search for Roots.* Burlington, VT: Ashgate, 2010.

———. "How to Avoid Grand Narratives in Christology: A Challenge of Postmodern Hermeneutics." *Milltown Studies* 65 (2010): 42–58.

Nouwen, Henri J. M. *Reaching Out: The Three Movements of the Spiritual Life.* New York: Doubleday, 1986.

O'Brien, Peter T. *The Letter to the Hebrews.* Pillar New Testament Commentary. Grand Rapids, MI: Eerdmans, 2010.

Okholm, Dennis L. "Prayer." In *Baker Theological Dictionary of the Bible*, edited by Walter A. Elwell, 621–626. Grand Rapids, MI: Baker Books, 1996.

Oprean, Daniel G. *Comuniune și participare: Reflecții teologice cu privire la dimensiunea spirituală a existenței.* Timişoara: Excelsior Art, 2011.

———. "Reconciliation in Church and Society: Church's Ministry as God's Reconciliation Agency." In *Reconciliation: The Way of Healing and Growth*, edited by Janez Juhant, Bojan Zalec, 179–187. Zürich: Lit Verlag, 2012.

———. "When Salt Loses its Saltiness: Causes of Spiritual Abuse within the Church." Unpublished paper, Osijek, 2003.

Osterhaven, M. E. "Views of Lord's Supper." In *Evangelical Dictionary of Theology*, edited by Walter A. Elwell, 654–656. Grand Rapids, MI: Baker Books, 1984.

Păcurariu, Mircea. "Pr. Prof. Acad. Dumitru Stăniloae. Câteva coordonate biografice." In *Persoană și Comuniune: Prinos de cinstire Părintelui Profesor Academician Dumitru Stăniloae la înplinirea vârstei de 90 de ani*, edited by Antonie Plămădeală. Sibiu: Editura Arhiepiscopiei ortodoxe, 1993.

Pannenberg, Wolfhart. *Christian Spirituality.* Philadelphia, PA: Westminster, 1983.

Parushev, Parush R. "Doing Theology in a Baptist Way." In *Doing Theology in a Baptist Way: The Plenary Papers Collection of the Symposium*, edited by Teun van der Leer, 1–33. Amsterdam: Vrije Universiteit, 2009. Re-published as, "Doing Theology in a Baptist Way (Theologie op een baptistenmanier)." In *Zo zijn onze manieren! In Gesprek over gemeente theologie*, edited by Teun van der Leer, 7–22. Baptistica Reeks, vol. 1. Amsterdam: Vrije Universiteit, 2009.

Patsch, H. "ευχαριστεω." In *Exegetical Dictionary of the New Testament.* Vol. 2, edited by Horst Balz and Gerhard Schneider, 87–88. Grand Rapids, MI: Eerdmans, 1991.

Paul VI. "Constitution of the Sacred Liturgy (*Sacrosantum Concilium*)." In *The Documents of Vatican II*, edited by Walter M. Abbott, 137–178. Baltimore, MD: America Press, 1966.

Bibliography

Pelikan, Jaroslav. *The Christian Tradition: A History of the Development of Doctrine*. Vol. 1, *The Emergence of the Catholic Tradition (100-600)*. Chicago, IL: University of Chicago Press, 1971.

———. *Tradiția creștină: O istorie a dezvoltării doctrinei, 1: Nașterea tradiției universale (100-600)*. Iași: Polirom, 2004.

———. *Tradiția Creștină, O istorie a dezvoltării doctrinei, 2: Spiritul creștinătății răsăritene (600-1700)*. Iași: Polirom, 2005.

———. *The Vindication of Tradition*. New Haven, CT: Yale University Press, 1984.

Peterson, David. *Possessed by God: A New Testament Theology of Sanctification and Holiness*. Grand Rapids, MI: Eerdmans, 1995.

Pickard, William M. *Rather Die Than Live – Jonah*. New York: Education and Cultivation Division Board of Global Ministry, 1974.

Pinnock, Clark. "Systematic Theology." In *The Openness of God: A Biblical Challenge to the Traditional Understanding of God*, edited by Clark Pinnock, Richard Rice, John Sanders, William Hasker, and David Basinger, 101–125. Carlisle, Cumbria: Paternoster, 1994.

Piper, John. *Desiring God: Meditations of a Christian Hedonist*. Portland, OR: Multnomah Press, 1986.

Plămădeală, Fr. Antonie. "Generația Stăniloae." In *Persoană și Comuniune: Prinos de cinstire Părintelui Profesor Academician Dumitru Stăniloae la împlinirea vârstei de 90 de ani*, edited by Antoine Plămădeală, xi–xx. Sibiu: Editura Arhiepiscopiei ortodoxe, 1993.

Popescu, Alexandru. *Petre Țuțea: Between Sacrifice and Suicide*. Aldershot: Ashgate, 2004.

Popovici, Alexa. *Istoria Baptiștilor din România, 1856-1989*. Oradea: Ed. Faclia, 2006.

Pratt, Richard L., Jr. "Baptism as a Sacrament of the Covenant." In *Understanding Four Views on Baptism*, edited by John H. Armstrong, 59–72. Grand Rapids, MI: Zondervan, 2007.

Prestige, G. L. *God in Patristic Thought*. London: SPCK, 1952.

Prior, David. *The Message of 1 Corinthians: Life in the Local Church*. Leicester: Inter-Varsity Press, 1985.

von Rad, Gerhard. *Old Testament Theology*. Vol. 1, *The Theology of Israel's Historical Traditions*. London: SCM Press Ltd, 1975.

Rahner, Karl. *Foundations of Christian Faith: An Introduction to the Idea of Christianity*. New York: Crossroad, 1978.

———. *Theological Investigations*. Vol. 4. London: Darton, Longman & Todd, 1966.

———. *The Trinity*. New York: Crossroad, 1997.

Ratzinger, Joseph Cardinal. *Called to Communion: Understanding the Church Today*. San Francisco, CA: Ignatius Press, 1996.

Ridderbos, Herman. *Paul: An Outline of His Theology*. Grand Rapids, MI: Eerdmans, 1975.

Riddell, Michael. *Threshold of the Future: Reforming the Church in the Post-Christian West*. London: SPCK, 1998.

Rogobete, Silviu Eugen. *O ontologie a iubirii: Subiect și Realitate Personală în gândirea părintelui Dumitru Stăniloae*. Iasi: Polirom, 2001.

———. "Subject and Supreme Personal Reality in the Theological Thought of Fr. Dumitru Stăniloae. An Ontology of Love." Unpublished PhD diss., London, Brunel University, 1997.

Schattenmann, J. "κοινονια." In *New International Dictionary of New Testament Theology*. Vol. 1, edited by Collin Brown. Exeter: Paternoster, 1975.

Schillebeeckx, Edward. *Church: The Human Story of God*. New York: Crossroad, 1990.

Schleiermacher, Friedrich. *Christian Faith*. Edinburgh: T & T Clark, 1968.

Schmemann, Alexander. *Din Apă și din Duh: Studiu Liturgic al Botezului*. București: Symbol, 1992.

———. *The Eucharist: Sacrament of the Kingdom*. New York: St Vladimir's Seminary Press, 1988.

———. *For the Life of the World: Sacraments and Orthodoxy*. Crestwood, NY: St Vladimir's Seminary Press, 1973.

Schreiner, Thomas R. *Romans*. Grand Rapids, MI: Baker Books, 1998.

Schweitzer, Albert. *The Mysticism of Paul the Apostle*. New York: Holt, 1931.

Gura de Aur, Ioan. *Cateheze baptismale*. Sibiu: Editura Oastea Domnului, 2003.

Sheriffs, Deryck. *The Friendship of the Lord: An Old Testament Spirituality*. Carlisle, Cumbria: Paternoster, 1996.

Sider, Ronald J. *Rich Christians in an Age of Hunger: A Biblical Study*. Downers Grove, IL: InterVarsity Press, 1977.

Sobrino, Jon. *Christology at the Crossroads: A Latin American Approach*. London: SCM, 1978.

Sölle, Dorothee. *Christ the Representative: An Essay in Theology after the "Death of God."* London: SCM, 1967.

———. *Suffering*. Philadelphia, PA: Fortress, 1975.

Spurgeon, Charles Haddon. "The Double Forget-Me-Not." In *Metropolitan Tabernacle Pulpit* 54 (1908): sermon no. 3099. London: Passmore & Alabaster, 1908.

Stamoolis, James J. *Eastern Orthodox Mission Theology Today*. Maryknoll, NY: Orbis Books, 1986.

Stăniloae, Dumitru. *Ascetica și Mistica Ortodoxă*. Alba Iulia: Deisis, 1993.

———. *Catolicismul de după război*. Sibiu: Editura Arhidiecezană, 1933.

———. *Chipul evanghelic al lui Iisus Hristos.* Sibiu: Editura Centrului Mitropoilitan, 1991.

———. "Curente noi în teologia protestantă germană." In *Revista Teologică* 19, no. 7–8 (1929): 234–238.

———. "Desăvârşirea noastră în Hristos după învăţătura bisericii Ortodoxe." Part 1. *Mitropolia Olteniei* 32, nos. 1–2 (1980): 76–111.

———. "Desăvârşirea noastră în Hristos după învăţătura bisericii Ortodoxe." Part 2. *Mitropolia Olteniei* 32, nos. 3–6 (1980): 403–426.

———. "Doctrina luterană despre justificare şi Cuvânt şi câteva reflexii ortodoxe." *Ortodoxia* 35, no. 4 (1983): 495–509.

———. "Drumul cu Hristos prin tainele si sarbatorile ortodoxe" [The way with Christ through the sacraments and Orthodox celebrations]. *Ortodoxia*, no. 2 (April-June 1976): 402–416.

———. "Dumnezeiasca Euharistie în cele trei confesiuni." *Ortodoxia* 5, no. 1 (1953): 46–115.

———. *The Experience of God.* Brookline: MA, Holy Cross Orthodox Press, 1994.

———. *The Experience of God: Orthodox Dogmatic Theology 1: Revelation and Knowledge of the Triune God.* Brookline, MA: Holy Cross Orthodox Press, 1998.

———. *The Experience of God, Orthodox Dogmatic Theology 2: The World: Creation and Deification.* Brookline, MA: Holy Cross Orthodox Press, 2005.

———. *The Experience of God, Orthodox Dogmatic Theology 3: The Person of Jesus Christ as God and Savior.* Brookline, MA: Holy Cross Orthodox Press, 2011.

———. *The Experience of God, Orthodox Dogmatic Theology 5: The Sanctifying Mysteries.* Brookline, MA: Holy Cross Orthodox Press, 2012.

———. "The Faces of Our Fellow Human Being." *International Review of Mission* 71, no. 281 (1982): 29–35.

———. *Filocalia sfintelor nevoinţi ale desăvârşirii*, 1. Bucureşti: Harisma, 1993.

———. "Filosofia existenţială şi credinţa în Iisus Hristos." *Gândirea* 18, no. 10 (1939): 565–572.

———. "Fiinţa Tainelor în cele trei confesiuni." *Ortodoxia* 8, no. 1 (1956): 3–28.

———. *The Holy Trinity: In the Beginning There was Love.* Brookline, MA: Holy Cross Orthodox Press, 2012.

———. "Image, Likeness, and deification in the human person." *Communio* 13 (1986): 64–83.

———. *Iisus Hristos sau Restaurarean Omului.* Craiova: Omniscop, 1993.

———. "Metafizica lui Lucian Blaga." *RevistaTeologică* 24, no. 11–12 (1934): 393–401.

———. "Organizarea sinodală a Bisericii Ortodoxe în paralel cu cezaro-papismul catolic." *Studii Teologice* 2, no. 9–10 (1950): 541–555.

———. "Pentru Pacea confesională." *Telegraful Român* 79, no. 33–34 (1931): 1–2.

———. "Posibilitatea reconcilierii dogmatice între Biserica Ortodoxă și Vechile Biserici Orientale." *Ortodoxia* 17, no. 1 (1965): 5–27.

———. *Priere de Jesus et experience du Saint-Esprit*. Paris: Desclee dr Brouwer, 1981.

———. *Reflexii despre spiritualitatea poporului român*. Craiova: Scrisul Românesc, 1992.

———. "Reîntoarcerea filosofiei." *Telegraful Român* 85, no. 43 (1937): 1.

———. "Romanian Orthodox Anglican Talks: A Dogmatic Assesement." In *Romanian Orthodox Church and the Church of England*, 129–148. Bucharest: Biblical and Orthodox Missionary Institute, 1976.

———. *Rugăciunea lui Iisus și experiența Duhului Sfânt*. Sibiu: Deisis, 2003.

———. *Sfânta Treime sau La Început a fost Iubirea*. București: IBMBOR, 1993.

———. *Spiritualitatea Ortodoxă: Ascetica și Mistica*. București: IBMBOR, 1992.

———. "Starea primordială a omului în cele trei confesiuni." *Ortodoxia* 8, no. 3 (1956): 323–357.

———. "Tendința Vaticanului după comuniunea euharistică cu ortodocșii." *Ortodoxia* 34, no. 3 (1972): 492–494.

———. *Teologie Dogmatică Ortodoxă*, 1. București: EIBMBOR, 1996.

———. *Teologie Dogmatică Ortodoxă*, 2. București: EIBMBOR, 1997.

———. *Teologie Dogmatică Ortodoxă*, 3. București: EIBMBOR, 1997.

———. *Theology and the Church*. Crestwood, NY: St Vladimir's Seminary Press, 1981.

———. *Viața și învățătura Sfântului Grigorie Palama*. București: Scripta, 1993.

———. *The Victory of the Cross*. Oxford: SLG Press, 2001.

Steinhardt, Nicolae. *Prin alții spre sine*. București: Eminescu, 1988.

Stott, John R. W. *God's New Society: The Message of Ephesians*. Leicester: InterVarsity Press, 1979.

———. *The Message of Acts: To the Ends of the Earth*. Leicester: Inter-Varsity Press, 1990.

Strom, Mark. *Reframing Paul: Conversations in Grace and Community*. Downers Grove, IL: InterVarsity Press, 2000.

Sunday School Chronicle, 17 February 1882. "Spurgeon's Scrapbooks, Numbered Volumes." Vol. 6, page 8.

Tenney, Merril C. "John." In *The Expositor's Bible Commentary, New Testament*, edited by Kenneth L. N. Barker and John R. Kohlenberger, III, 1–203. Grand Rapids, MI: Zondervan, 1994.

Thiselton, Anthony C. *First Corinthians: A Shorter Exegetical and Pastoral Commentary*. Grand Rapids, MI: Eerdmans, 2006.

Thomas, Robert L. *Understanding Spiritual Gifts*. Grand Rapids, MI: Kregel, 1999.

Thomson, J. G. S. S., and Walter A. Elwell. "Spiritual Gifts." In *Evangelical Dictionary of Theology*, edited by Walter A. Elwell, 1135. Grand Rapids, MI: Baker Books, 1984.

Thurian, Max. "The Eucharistic Memorial, Sacrifice of Praise, and Supplication." In *Ecumenical Perspectives on Baptism, Eucharist and Ministry*, edited by Max Thurian, 90–103. Faith and Order Papers. Geneva: World Council of Churches, 1983.

Tidball, Derek. *The Social Context of the New Testament*. Grand Rapids, MI: Zondervan, 1983.

Tillard, J. M. R. "The Eucharist, Gift of God." In *Ecumenical Perspectives on Baptism, Eucharist and Ministry*, edited by Max Thurian, 104–118. Faith and Order Papers. Geneva: World Council of Churches, 1983.

Tillich, Paul. *Love, Power, and Justice*. London: Oxford University Press, 1954.

Titus, Eric J. "The Perfections of God in the Theology of Karl Barth: A Consideration of the Formal Structure." *Kairos Evangelical Journal of Theology* 4, no. 2 (November 2010): 203–222.

Toon, Peter. "Lord's Supper." In *Baker Theological Dictionary of the Bible*, edited by Walter A. Elwell. Grand Rapids, MI: Baker Books, 1996.

Torrance, Alan J. *Persons in Communion: Trinitarian Description and Human Participation*. Edinburgh: T & T Clark, 1996.

———. "The Trinity." In *The Cambridge Companion to Karl Barth*, edited by John Webster, 72–91. Cambridge: Cambridge University Press, 2000.

Torrance, T. F. "Spiritus Creator." *Verbum Caro* 23, no. 89 (1969): 63–85.

Tracy, David. *The Analogical Imagination: Christian Theology and the Culture of Pluralism*. London: SCM Press, 1981.

Turcescu, Lucian. "Eucharistic Ecclesiology or Open Sobornicity?" In *Dumitru Stăniloae, Tradition and Modernity in Theology*, edited by Lucian Turcescu, 38–103. Iasi: The Center for Romanian Studies, 2002.

Turner, Daniel. *Charity the Bond of Perfection: A Sermon, The Substance of which was Preached at Oxford, November 16, 1780, On Occasion of the Re-establishment of a Christian Church of Protestant Dissenters in that City*. London: T. Evans, 1780.

———. *A Compendium of Social Religion*. London: John Ward, 1758.

Turner, Denys. *The Darkness of God: Negativity in Christian Mysticism*. Cambridge: Cambridge University Press, 1995.

Turner, Max. *Power from on High: The Spirit in Israel's Restoration and Witness in Luke–Acts*. Sheffield: Sheffield Academic Press, 1996.

Vanhoozer, Kevin J. *Is There a Meaning in This Text?* Grand Rapids, MI: Zondervan, 1998.

Vassady, Bela. "Gleanings." In *How Karl Barth Changed My Mind*, edited by Donald K. McKim, 27–36. Grand Rapids, MI: Eerdmans, 1986.

Volf, Miroslav. *After Our Likeness: The Church as the Image of the Trinity*. Grand Rapids, MI: Eerdmans, 1998.

———. "Being as God Is: Trinity and Generosity." In *God's Life in Trinity*, edited by Miroslav Volf and Michael Welker, 3–12. Minneapolis, MN: Fortress, 2006.

———. *Captive to the Word of God: Engaging the Scriptures for Contemporary Theological Reflection*. Grand Rapids, MI: Eerdmans, 2010.

———. *Exclusion and Embrace: A Theological Exploration of Identity, Otherness, and Reconciliation*. Nashville, TN: Abingdon, 1996.

Wallace, R. S. "Lord's Supper." In *Evangelical Dictionary of Theology*, edited by Walter A. Elwell, 652. Grand Rapids, MI: Baker Books, 1984.

Ware, Bruce. A. *God's Lesser Glory: The Diminished God of Open Theism*. Wheaton, IL: Crossway, 2000.

Ware, Kallistos. "Communion and Intercommunion." In *Primary Readings on the Eucharist*, edited by Thomas J. Fisch, 185–208. Collegeville, MN: Liturgical Press, 2004.

Ware, Timothy. *The Orthodox Church*. London: Penguin Books, 1993.

Weinandy, Thomas G. *Does God Suffer?* Edinburgh: T & T Clark, 2000.

———. *The Father's Spirit of Sonship: Reconceiving the Trinity*. Edinburgh: T & T Clark, 1995.

———. *In the Likeness of Sinful Flesh: An Essay on the Humanity of Christ*. Edinburgh: T & T Clark, 1993.

Weiser, A. "διακονεω, διακονια, διακονος." In *Exegetical Dictionary of the New Testament*. Vol. 1, edited by Horst Balz and Gerhard Schneider, 302. Grand Rapids, MI: Eerdmans, 1990.

Wenham, David. "How Jesus Understood the Last Supper: A Parable in Action." *Churchman* 105, no. 3 (1991): 246–260.

———. *Paul: Follower of Jesus or Founder of Christianity?* Grand Rapids, MI: Eerdmans, 1995.

Wijngaards, John. *The Spirit in John*. Wilmington, DE: Michael Glazier, 1988.

Wilcock, Michael. *The Message of Luke: The Saviour of the World*. Downers Grove, IL: InterVarsity Press, 1979.

Willmer, Haddon. "Jesus Christ the Forgiven, Christology, Atonement and Forgiveness." In *Forgiveness and Truth: Explorations in Contemporary Theology*, edited by Alister McFayden, Marcel Sarot, and Anthony Thiselton, 15–30. Edinburgh: T & T Clark, 2001.

Wink, Walter. *Naming the Powers: The Language of Power in the New Testament.* Philadelphia, PA: Fortress, 1984.

Witherington, Ben, III. "Contemporary Perspectives on Paul." In *The Cambridge Companion to St. Paul*, edited by James D. G. Dunn, 256–269. Cambridge: Cambridge University Press, 2003.

———. *Paul's Narrative Thought World: The Tapestry of Tragedy and Triumph.* Louisville, KY: Westminster John Knox, 1994.

Witherington, Ben, III, and Laura M. Ice. *The Shadow of the Almighty: Father, Son, and Spirit in Biblical Perspective.* Grand Rapids, MI: Eerdmans, 2002.

Wright, Christopher J. H. *Salvation Belongs to God: Celebrating the Bible's Central Story.* Nottingham: Inter-Varsity Press, 2008.

Wright, N. T. *The Climax of the Covenant: Christ and Law in Pauline Theology.* Minneapolis, MN: Fortress, 1992.

———. *Colossians and Philemon.* Leicester: Inter-Varsity Press, 1986.

———. *Jesus and the Victory of God.* London: SPCK, 1996.

———. *John for Everyone.* Part 2, *Chapters 11–21.* London: SPCK, 2002.

———. *The New Testament and the People of God.* London: SPCK, 1992.

———. "Paul's Gospel and Caesar's Empire." In *Paul and Politics: Ekklesia, Israel, Imperium, Interpretation*, edited by Richard A. Horsely, 160–183. Harrisburg, PA: Trinity Press International, 2000.

———. *Surprised by Hope.* London: SPCK, 2007.

Wright, Nigel G. *Free Church, Free State: The Positive Baptist Vision.* Milton Keynes: Paternoster, 2005.

———. *New Baptists, New Agenda.* London: Paternoster, 2002.

———. "Spirituality as Discipleship: the Anabaptist Heritage." In *Under the Rule of Christ: Dimensions of Baptist Spirituality*, edited by Paul S. Fiddes, 97–101. Oxford: Regent's Park College; Macon, GA: Smyth & Helwys, 2008.

Wyatt, John. *Matters of Life and Death: Today's Healthcare Dilemmas in the Light of Christian Faith.* Leicester: Inter-Varsity Press, 1998.

Yannaras, Christos. *Elements of Faith: An Introduction to Orthodox Theology.* Translated by Keith Schram. Edinburgh: T & T Clark, 1991.

Ziesler, John. *Paul's Letter to Romans.* London: SCM Press, 1989.

———. *Pauline Christianity.* Oxford: Oxford University Press, 1990.

Zizioulas, Ioannis. *Creația ca Euharistie.* București: Editura Bizantină, 1999.

Zizioulas, John. *Being as Communion: Studies in Personhood and the Church.* Crestwood, NY: St. Vladimir's Seminary Press, 1993.

Langham Literature, with its publishing work, is a ministry of Langham Partnership.

Langham Partnership is a global fellowship working in pursuit of the vision God entrusted to its founder John Stott –

> *to facilitate the growth of the church in maturity and Christ-likeness through raising the standards of biblical preaching and teaching.*

Our vision is to see churches in the majority world equipped for mission and growing to maturity in Christ through the ministry of pastors and leaders who believe, teach and live by the Word of God.

Our mission is to strengthen the ministry of the Word of God through:
- nurturing national movements for biblical preaching
- fostering the creation and distribution of evangelical literature
- enhancing evangelical theological education

especially in countries where churches are under-resourced.

Our ministry

Langham Preaching partners with national leaders to nurture indigenous biblical preaching movements for pastors and lay preachers all around the world. With the support of a team of trainers from many countries, a multi-level programme of seminars provides practical training, and is followed by a programme for training local facilitators. Local preachers' groups and national and regional networks ensure continuity and ongoing development, seeking to build vigorous movements committed to Bible exposition.

Langham Literature provides majority world preachers, scholars and seminary libraries with evangelical books and electronic resources through publishing and distribution, grants and discounts. The programme also fosters the creation of indigenous evangelical books in many languages, through writer's grants, strengthening local evangelical publishing houses, and investment in major regional literature projects, such as one volume Bible commentaries like the *Africa Bible Commentary* and the *South Asia Bible Commentary*.

Langham Scholars provides financial support for evangelical doctoral students from the majority world so that, when they return home, they may train pastors and other Christian leaders with sound, biblical and theological teaching. This programme equips those who equip others. Langham Scholars also works in partnership with majority world seminaries in strengthening evangelical theological education. A growing number of Langham Scholars study in high quality doctoral programmes in the majority world itself. As well as teaching the next generation of pastors, graduated Langham Scholars exercise significant influence through their writing and leadership.

To learn more about Langham Partnership and the work we do visit **langham.org**

www.ingramcontent.com/pod-product-compliance
Lightning Source LLC
Chambersburg PA
CBHW051537230426
43669CB00015B/2633

This book is a welcome and important contribution to the field of religious dialogue between the Orthodox and the Baptist communities. Dr Oprean works on the basis that dialogical theology enriches Christian understanding, and he develops his themes by means of an interdisciplinary conversation between the Romanian Orthodox theologian Dumitru Stăniloae, and the Baptist theologian Paul Fiddes. Areas of common agreement between the two are explored, as well as significant differences. The author affirms the uniting centrality of Trinitarian theology. This is a book that will serve to enhance the conversation between Orthodox and Baptist communities in Romania, and deepen the mutual understanding of each other's religious traditions.

Ian J. Shaw, PhD
Provost, Union School of Theology,
Bridgend, South Wales, UK

In his book, *Theology of Participation: A Conversation of Traditions*, Daniel Oprean explores the way in which the theological perspectives of two important theologians can contribute to a deeper understanding of the respective traditions through a theological dialogue. The author engages with the writings of Paul Fiddes, a British Baptist theologian, and of Dumitru Stăniloae, a Romanian Orthodox theologian, introducing the readers to some of the positions they share in common, while at the same time acknowledging their differences. Oprean contributes in this way in a significant manner to the effort to bring the two theologians in conversation. He recognizes that Fiddes and Stăniloae ground their language and concepts in an understanding of the Trinity which opens up the possibility of man's participation. The book is a welcome and important step towards more engagement between the two Christian traditions. This can lead to a discovery of new and surprising avenues of theological discussion which can lead to a more adequate understanding of each other.

Otniel Ioan Bunaciu, PhD
Dean, Faculty of Baptist Theology,
University of Bucharest, Romania

Daniel Oprean's proposal for meaningful dialogue between Christian communities that have been, many a time, on opposite sides of the fence makes *Theology of Participation: A Conversation of Traditions*, a book that is both contextually relevant and globally necessary. Contextually relevant because the author, himself a Baptist addressing a majority Eastern-Orthodox environment, provides an excellent example of theological engagement with one's religious milieu from a minority position. And globally necessary because Oprean's method of "conversation" is easily transposable and therefore may provide for engaging alternative theological traditions in other multi-faith environments.

Marcel V Măcelaru, PhD
Faculty of Humanities and Social Sciences,
Aurel Vlaicu University, Arad, Romania